Zed Books Titles on International Relations

Nassau Adams, *Worlds Apart: The North–South Divide and the International System*

Jon Barnett, *The Meaning of Environmental Security: Environmental Politics and Policy in the New Security Era*

Robert Biel, *The New Imperialism: Crisis and Contradictions in North/South Relations*

Nicholas Guyatt, *Another American Century? The United States and the World after 2000*

Bjorn Hettne et al., *International Political Economy: Understanding Global Disorder*

Terence Hopkins and Immanuel Wallerstein et al., *The Age of Transition: Trajectory of the World-System, 1945–2025*

Federico Mayor in collaboration with Jerome Binde, *The World Ahead: Our Future in the Making*

Linda Melvern, *A People Betrayed: The Role of the West in Rwanda's Genocide*

Hans-Peter Martin and Harald Schumann, *The Global Trap: Globalization and the Assault on Prosperity and Democracy*

Michael Schulz, Fredrik Soderbaum and Joakim Ojendal (eds), *Regionalization in a Globalizing World: A Comparative Perspective on Forms, Actors and Processes*

For full details of this list and Zed's other subject, area studies and general catalogues, please write to: The Marketing Department, Zed Books, 7 Cynthia Street, London N1 9JF, UK

or e-mail: sales@zedbooks.demon.co.uk

Visit our website at: http://www.zedbooks.demon.co.uk

a1_813629_common

Common Ground or Mutual Exclusion? Women's Movements and International Relations

Edited by
Marianne Braig and Sonja Wölte

Zed Books
LONDON · NEW YORK

Common Ground or Mutual Exclusion? Women's Movements and International Relations was first published by Zed Books Ltd, 7 Cynthia Street, London N1 9JF, UK and Room 400, 175 Fifth Avenue, New York, NY 10010, USA in 2002.

www.zedbooks.demon.co.uk

Cover designed by Andrew Corbett
Set in Monotype Dante by Ewan Smith, London
Printed and bound in the United Kingdom by Bookcraft, Midsomer Norton

Distributed in the USA exclusively by Palgrave, a division of St Martin's Press, LLC, 175 Fifth Avenue, New York, NY 10010.

A catalogue record for this book is available from the British Library

ISBN 1 84277 158 2 cased
ISBN 1 84277 159 0 limp

Contents

Acknowledgements

This book would never have been published without the tremendous response to the international symposium 'Common Ground or Mutual Exclusion? Women's Movements and International Relations', held at the University of Frankfurt am Main, Germany, from 30 June to 2 July 2000. The conference offered a forum for very stimulating and lively debates between students, scholars and activists from around the globe. In the aftermath, people encouraged us to capture the outcome in a publication. The symposium and this book are part of the activities of the Cornelia Goethe Centre for Women's and Gender Studies at the Johann Wolfgang Goethe University, Frankfurt am Main, Germany. We want to thank our colleagues and students at the Cornelia Goethe Centre who offered their support and advice throughout the symposium. In particular, we owe very special thanks to Gülay Caglar, Martina Blank and Frank Herwig for their enthusiasm and tireless assistance in the preparation of the conference and in helping to create a welcoming atmosphere for everyone during it.

This book also benefited from the help and support of a number of people. Most importantly, we thank Heike Brabandt for her thorough work on the first draft of the manuscripts. We are very grateful to Gerard Holden for his careful reading of the second draft and helpful suggestions and to Jessica Gevers for assisting us in finishing the last details of the book. Finally, for financial support at the various stages of the project we gratefully acknowledge the funds provided by the Cornelia Goethe Centre and by the Ministry of Science and Education of the State of Hesse.

About the Contributors

Fatima Ahmed Ibrahim is a human rights activist from Sudan and a senior researcher at the African Studies Center at the University of California in Los Angeles, USA. Her research focuses on the Sudanese women's movement. Ibrahim is active in several women's organizations: she is president of the banned Sudanese Women's Union (SWU) and a member of the executive committee of the Arab Women's Union as well as of the Pan African Women's Federation. In 1965, she was the first elected woman member of parliament in Sudan. The previous Sudanese military government imprisoned her many times and Amnesty International campaigned for her release. Ibrahim now lives in exile in London. She has published three books in Arabic on women's issues. Currently, she is working on two books, *Islam and Women's Rights* and *To My Son Ahmed and His Generation*.

Marianne Braig is professor of development studies, with particular focus on gender issues and Latin America, in the Institute for Comparative Politics and International Relations at the Goethe University, Frankfurt am Main. She is on the board of directors at the Cornelia Goethe Centre for Women's and Gender Studies at the Goethe University in Frankfurt/M., Germany. Braig has worked and published for many years on development policies, political culture in Latin America, and gender and international relations. Her latest publications include several articles on women's human rights and the co-editing of a book on women's human rights with Ute Gerhard, *Frauenrechte als Menschenrechte* (Frankfurt/M., 1999). She has also written on women's civil society organizations, for instance: 'Espacios femeninos y politica o la politica como un espacio para mujeres', in Hengstenberg, P. et al., *Sociedad Civil en America Latina: representacion de intereses y gobernabilidad* (Caracas, Ed. Nueva Sociedad, 1999; and 'Continuity and Change in Mexcian Political Culture. The Case of PRONASOL (Programa Nacional de Solidaridad)', in Panster, W. G. (ed.), *Citizens of the Pyramid. Essays on Mexican Political Culture* (Amsterdam: Thela Publishers, 1997).

Claudia von Braunmühl is honorary professor of political science at the

Free University, Berlin in Germany. Her research focuses on the development debate, development co-operation, and women/gender in development. She also works as a consultant for binational and multilateral organizations and NGOs. In addition, she serves in different functions in academic associations and national and international NGOs. Her recent work includes articles on gender and development published in German books, for example 'Women's Inquiries into Development' (Frauenanfragen an Entwicklungspolitik) in a book edited by Uta Ruppert in 1998 (see below), and on the development debate, such as 'Situational Analysis of Development Policy and Development Cooperation' (Zur Ortsbestimmung von Entwicklungspolitik and Entwicklungszusammenarbeit), in Kreibich, R. and U. E. Simonis (eds), *Global Change – Globaler Wandel. Ursachenkomplexe und Lösungsansätze. Causal Structures and Indicative Solutions* (Berlin: Berlin Verlag, 2000).

Lothar Brock is professor of political science with special reference to IR in the Institute for Comparative Politics and International Relations at the Goethe University, Frankfurt am Main. He is director of the research unit on democracy and development at the Peace Research Institute, Frankfurt. He also serves as chamber president on development and environment in the Protestant Church of Germany. His main areas of research are North–South relations; conflict constellations and the economy of organized violence in the context of globalization; peace theory and theory building on world society. Among his recent publications is a co-authored book on the new global economy, *Die neue Weltwirtschaft.* (Frankfurt: Suhrkamp, 1999) and the co-edited English book, *Civilizing World Politics. Society and Community Beyond the State* (Lanham, MD: Rowman & Littlefield, 2000). In 1999 he wrote the introduction to the special issue on territorialities, identities and movement of the journal *Millennium*, 'Observing Change, "Rewriting" History: A Critical Overview' (*Millennium 3*).

Nighat Said Khan is dean of the Institute for Women's Studies in Lahore, Pakistan, which has developed out of the women's movement and runs academic programmes for women. Nighat Said Khan teaches and focuses on a range of issues: the women's movement, feminist theory and political economy. She is active in several social movements including the women's movement and the struggles against the military, for democracy, human rights and workers' rights. Khan is a founder of the Women's Action Forum and executive president of the ASR Resource Centre for Women in Pakistan. Her most recent publications include several works published by the ASR Resource Centre, Lahore, Pakistan, such as *Up Against the State. Essays on Islamisation and Women in Pakistan.*

She has also co-edited *Against All Odds. Essays on Women, Religion and Development in India and Pakistan* (New Delhi: Kali for Women, 1994), and recently written 'The Women's Movement Revisited: Areas of Concern for the Future', in Suki, A. et al., *Global Feminist Politics. Identities in a Changing World* (London, New York: Routledge, 2000).

Gert Krell is professor of IR in the Institute for Comparative Politics and International Relations at the Goethe University, Frankfurt am Main. Previously he was a senior researcher and executive director of the Peace Research Institute, Frankfurt. His research interests include international relations, peace research and US foreign policy. From 1987 to 1994 he co-edited and contributed regularly to the 'Friedensgutachten', a yearbook on the state of peace and conflict in the world, published by three peace research institutes in Germany. His most recent book is a German introduction to the theory of International Relations, *Weltbilder und Weltordnung. Einführung in die Theorie der Internationalen Beziehungen* (Baden-Baden: Nomos Verlag, 2000).

Akua Kuenyehia is dean of the Faculty of Law, University of Ghana, Legon. Her research mainly focuses on family law. She explores legal issues of interest to women, such as property rights. Currently she is directing a research project on 'Women and Law in West Africa'. She was a member of the UN Expert Groups on Legal Literacy for Women in 1992 and on Economic and Social Rights of Women in 1997. Recently she has served on a number of boards at the local, regional, and international levels. She is a founding member of Women in Law and Development in Africa (WiLDAf). She has edited a book on *A Situational Analysis of Some Key Issues of Concern to Women* (Accra: WalWa, 1998) and is currently working on a second book, *Gender Relations in the Family in West Africa*.

Carolyn Medel-Añonuevo is a sociologist and senior research specialist on women's education at the UNESCO Institute for Education (UIE) in Hamburg, Germany. She designed the women's programme of the institute and has developed four projects: women's education and empowerment; women and literacy; women's education and economy; monitoring and evaluation from a gender perspective. She is also responsible for mainstreaming gender issues in programmes and projects at UIE and she actively networks with women's organizations and UN agencies. Carolyn Medel-Añonuevo has edited four publications on women's education.

Harald Müller is professor of IR in the Institute for Comparative Politics and International Relations at the Goethe University, Frankfurt am

Main. Since 1976 he has been working in different capacities at the Peace Research Institute, Frankfurt, since 1996 as its executive director. Harald Müller is a member of the Advisory Committee for Disarmament to the UN Secretary-General and was a member of the expert committee to the German government on the reform of the military structure. His latest books include a reply to Samuel Huntington's *Clash of Civilizations* (*Das Zusammenleben der Kulturen. Ein Gegenentwurf zu Huntington*, Frankfurt am Main: Fischer-Tachenbuch-Verlag, 1998).

Donna Pankhurst is senior lecturer in the Department for Peace Studies and associate dean in the School of Social and International Studies at the University of Bradford, UK. Her research background is in land and gender issues in Africa, along with work on democracy and civil society. Her current research focuses on post-conflict settlement and peace-building in Africa. In her work as a consultant she has produced the following publications: *Conflict Impact Monitoring and Assessment: Does it Exist? Can it Work?* (Bradford: Department of Peace Studies at the University of Bradford, 1998) for Oxfam UK, and *Gender and Peace-building: The Way Ahead* (Bradford: Department of Peace Studies at the University of Bradford, 1999), for International Alert. Her most recent articles include 'Unravelling Reconciliation and Justice? Land and the Potential for Conflict in Namibia', *Peace and Change*, Vol. 25, No. 2, 2000, and 'Women and Politics in Africa: The Case of Uganda', *Parliamentary Affairs*, special issue on women in politics, 2001.

Cordula Reimann holds a BA (Hons) in politics and IR and a German diploma in political science. She is a postgraduate researcher and doctoral candidate in the Department of Peace Studies at the University of Bradford, UK. Her research focuses on the gender dimension of conflict and conflict management, both in theory and practice. She has worked in various peace research institutions, has been active in local and national groups of Amnesty International and worked in their international office in London. Recently, she conducted field work and research on the gender discourses prevalent in conflict management/conflict resolution in Sri Lanka. She has published *Directory zivile Konfliktbearbeitung – Ein Wegweiser deutscher NROs und Einrichtungen* (Berlin: Berghof Stiftung, 1998), and *The Field of Conflict Management: Why Does Gender Matter?*Information Unit Peace Research (Bonn: Information Unit Peace Research, 1999), and more recently, 'Towards Conflict Transformation – Assessing the State-of-Art in Conflict Management – Reflections from a Theoretical Perspective', in Berghof Research Centre for Constructive Conflict Management (ed.), *Berghof Handbook for Conflict Transformation* (2000/2001); and in her consultancy work for German development co-operation, GTZ, *Towards Gender Mainstreaming in Crisis Prevention and Conflict Management* (Eschborn, 2001).

Renate Rott, a sociologist, is professor in the Institute for Latin American Studies at the Free University in Berlin, Germany. In the past her research has focused on women's work in the formal sector as well as under unprotected informal circumstances in Latin America (particularly Brazil); urban development; social movements; population and development policy. She works as a consultant for German and international development agencies on different topics, for example, social funds; poverty reduction; urban reconstruction; human rights work; development work of political foundations and churches. She has edited a book on development and gender, *Entwicklungsprozesse und Geschlechterverhältnisse* (Saarbrücken: Breitenbach, 1992) and has recently written on gender constructions in Latin America.

Uta Ruppert is assistant professor in the Department of Political Science at Giessen University. Her areas of research include international women's politics; feminist theory in IR; globalization and global governance; and transition processes in West Africa. Among her recent publications are two co-edited books which cover most of these subjects: in 1998, she edited an introductory book on gender in International Relations in German, *Lokal bewegen – global verhandeln* (Frankfurt am Main: Campus), and in 2000 she co-edited a book on the implications of global political processes for women's politics, *Frauenpolitische Chancen globaler Politik* (Opladen: Leske und Budrich). In 1999 Uta Ruppert co-organized and moderated the web-conference, 'Women Politics from a Global Perspective – International Policy Processes and Women's Activism', hosted by the Heinrich Böll Foundation. In 2000 she also taught a class on women's global politics at the International Women's University in Hanover, Germany.

Christa Wichterich is a sociologist and 'patchwork-economist in the informal sector'. She earns her living as a freelance journalist, author, guest lecturer at universities and consultant on development co-operation projects, mainly in South and South-east Asia and Africa. As a researcher, journalist and author, her main topics include women's movements and organizations; economy, women's work and ecology; and the impact of globalization on gender. In addition, she is active in German NGOs and European women's networks, and she has been involved in the Bejing + 5 process. Most recently she has published *The Globalized Woman: Reports from a Future of Inequality* (London: Zed Books, 2000); French: *La femme mondialisée* (Solin: Actes Sud, 1999);

orig. German: *Die globalisierte Frau, Berichte aus der Zukunft der Ungleich-heit* (Reinbek bei Hamburg: Rowohlt, 1998).

Sonja Wölte is a junior lecturer and research associate for feminism and IR in the Institute for Comparative Politics and International Relations at the Goethe University, Frankfurt am Main. She is an associate member of the Cornelia Goethe Centre for Women's and Gender Studies at Goethe University. Sonja Wölte works and publishes on women's human rights, violence against women and international/UN women's politics. Among her recent work in German is an article on the relationship between international and national women's human rights discourses, 'Von lokal nach international und zurück: Gewalt gegen Frauen und Frauenmenschenrechtspolitik', in Dackweiler, R. and R. Schäfer, *Gewalt-Verhältnisse* (Frankfurt: Campus, 2002) as well as a contribution on 'Women and the UN', in Volger, H. (ed.), *A Concise Encyclopedia of the United Nations* (The Hague: Kluwer Law International, 2002). Her current research focuses on the impact of the international women's human rights discourse in East Africa.

Marysia Zalewski teaches at the Centre for Women's Studies at Queen's University in Belfast, Northern Ireland. Her research centres on feminist theories as well as gender and International Relations. In addition, she is convenor of the British International Studies Association (BISA) gender working group and a regular attendee and participant at the annual conferences of BISA and ISA (International Studies Association). Her recent publications include two edited collections: *The 'Man' Question in International Relations* (with Jane Parpart, Boulder, CO: Westview Press, 1998) and *International Theory: Positivism and Beyond* (with Steve Smith and Ken Booth, 1996). Her latest book is *Feminism After Postmodernism: Theorizing Through Practice* (New York: Routledge, 2000). She is currently working on a book on feminism in Northern Ireland.

CHAPTER ONE

Introduction: Common Ground or Mutual Exclusion? Women's Movements in International Relations

Marianne Braig and Sonja Wölte

At the beginning of the twenty-first century, women and women's movements are no longer invisible as actors in international relations. Women look back at a long history of international organizing dating from the end of the nineteenth century. The history of women's international activism prior to the First World War has been hidden in traditional scholarship and has only recently begun to be rediscovered and explored by feminist scholars.[1] By contrast, the more recent politics and activities of women's movements since the Second World War and in particular since the international women's decade (1976–85) have received broad and steadily growing attention within feminist scholarship over the last 15 years. Although we are aware of the fact that international women's activism did not start with the UN International Year of Women 1975 and the first World Women's Conference in Mexico in the same year, we take these institutionalized forms of women's politics as the framework for the themes of this book. On one hand, the sequence of UN conferences on women, which for the time being came to an end with the Beijing + 5 Review Conference in June 2000,[2] gave rise to a large body of programmes for legislative, policy and institutional changes on the international and national levels around the globe. On the other hand, parallel to the UN world conferences, existing women's non-governmental organizations (NGOs) were strengthened and numerous new international NGOs and transnational networks of women's NGOs emerged, linking women's organizations and movements worldwide. The rapid economic and political globalization process of the past decade has resulted in the political agendas of women's movements and organizations becoming increasingly international. Today, women's organizations consider themselves not only as forces for social and political change in their own local and national spheres, but also as global political actors aiming to influence core issues in international politics. As an answer to the increasing global interlinkages and interdependencies, women's movements explicitly combine the local, national and international levels of political activism, well aware that changes guaranteeing greater social and political justice need to involve politics at all of these levels. What is more, women's movements and organizations around the globe today do not confine their activities at all these levels to areas considered to be typical women's issues. They claim and occupy spaces for influence and resistance in almost every policy field, be it the economy, peace and security issues, human rights, etc.

In looking back at the historical development of international institutionalized women's politics and of the politics of the international women's movement during the past 25 years and more, we felt prompted to raise some questions which amount to an attempt to initiate a process of taking stock of international women's politics. How and to what extent have women and women's movements been included into international politics, and where are they still excluded today? What opportunities, in which fields, have international women's movements been able to shape and influence the international political agenda? What are the risks and challenges? Where is the common ground between the politics of women's movements and international politics, and where are there patterns of exclusion?

Fully conscious of the broad scope and ambitious character of this set of questions, we do not wish to claim that we can provide ready or clear-cut answers. In the chapters here, we wish to contribute to the growing body of literature about the relationship between women's movements and international politics.[3] We chose three international policy fields in which we think the influence of women's movements has become particularly visible: development policy/studies, women's human rights, and peace and conflict resolution. We asked the authors to discuss the above questions in relation to these three fields from their specific perspectives. Although distinctions between feminist activism and scholarship are often hard to make (feminist scholars may also be engaged in political activism and feminist activists may do feminist research), these chapters very broadly include perspectives by feminist activists and feminist scholars in general (Part I) and in each of the three policy fields in particular (Parts II, III and IV). This is supplemented by perspectives from mainstream male scholars of international relations who, by way of comments, offer their views on our central questions with regard to our three policy areas (Part V). The book, therefore, aims to combine different approaches and dimensions which rarely come together in one publication, but which we consider to be important when addressing the role of women's movements and feminism in international relations in general, and in relation to the particular questions we wish to address. In this Introduction, we attempt to show more concretely how these different dimensions can come together, first by outlining the approaches we have chosen and then presenting an overview of the book. Despite their diverse points of departure, many contributors raise similar problems and arrive at similar conclusions when reflecting on the questions we raise.

One approach, the movement approach, looks at women's movements as social and political actors or forces which aim to make visible and change the subordination, discrimination and inequalities suffered by women at the local, national and international levels. However, as several authors point out, postcolonial and post-modern feminist critiques[4] have shown that we cannot think of the women's movement as a homogeneous actor, either on the national level or from an international perspective. Rather, we have to conceptualize it as a plurality of social movements of women – and partially men – consisting of and encompassing diversity and differences between class, ethnicity and other distinctions that manifest themselves as hierarchical relationships. It is women's movements understood in that sense which try to articulate injustices and effect change within their specific cultural and social settings, and come together to engage in international politics. This results in the well-known challenge to feminists of how to deal in a productive manner with the various problems that arise from the inclusion of diversity and power relationships between women into a common international feminist political agenda. These problems relate to the differences in perspectives and political positions between women from the North/West and the South. But they also relate to the political changes that have taken place within the international women's movement(s) over time, leading to controversies over the aims, contents and positions of feminist international politics. Hence, some contributions argue that women's movements and the international women's movement understood as a transformative force which aims to bring about fundamental changes has ceased to exist. Instead, it has given way to a political approach that is satisfied with being integrated into and added on to mainstream politics and institutions. These differences are not confined to political feminist practice, but extend into and intersect with the relationship between women's politics and feminist theory in the global context.

A second approach, then, is feminist theorizing on women's politics from an international point of view. The nexus between feminist politics pursued by women's movements, and feminist theorizing and scholarship, has always been of great importance to feminism. It runs as a central thread through the book. At issue is the specific character of this relationship, posing the question of whether feminist scholarship today takes place removed from women's movements and politics, and whether it pursues a 'sanitized' version of women's politics which is adapted to mainstream academic logic and discourses. The dialogue between feminist scholarship and women's movements seems to be all the more pertinent in the light of the controversies about political aims and strategies within the international women's movement. When focusing on their common experiences rather than on their differences, feminist scholars and women's activists may discover structural parallels in each of their relationships with their respective *malestream* 'counterparts' – mainstream politics and mainstream academia. Hence, within the feminist academic communities we come across debates about the aims of feminist scholarship and its potential to transform male-dominated scholarship that are similar to those that take place within the women's movements. A constructive exchange between reflecting activists and active theorists can produce insights on these issues which are useful for feminist politics and theory as a whole, and may at the same time be able to narrow the gap between them. We hope to stimulate such an exchange by combining contributions from representatives of women's movements and feminist academia, as well as gender consultants who critically reflect upon their profession.

The third approach relates these controversies to specific issues by situating them within three policy fields – development, peace and conflict resolution, and human rights. In bringing together the theoretical and practical/activist perspectives, this approach discusses the opportunities, chances, risks and challenges of women's influence on mainstream politics. Again, the central controversy revolves around the issue of whether the radical potential of social movements and feminist critiques is lost when entry points in national or international politics open up and are seized. Do efforts to lobby, exert influence and seek inclusion into the mainstream amount to the instrumentalization of social movements and a loss of their transformative potential? Are women's movements today too integrated into mainstream discourses, institutions and policies to sustain their critical perspectives? What exactly has changed through the inclusion of women into these policy fields – and are these changes perhaps purely rhetorical, while women remain excluded from core political and economic decision-making processes in these very same fields? And what are the benefits for women, women's movements and feminism of being integrated into mainstream politics and scholarship?

The fourth and last approach introduces a change in perspective that is intended to open up the internal feminist debate on these questions to an exchange with mainstream views. With regard to the three policy fields, it aims to bring together two discussion contexts – feminism and the mainstream – that usually run parallel to each other and rarely meet. We invited male mainstream scholars to reflect upon their views on entry points and common ground between feminism and mainstream debates, in particular with regard to the impact of feminist discussions on mainstream scholarship and research in each policy field. With these three contributions, which are presented as comments, we neither intend to give a comprehensive picture of the mainstream debates on feminism, nor claim to have overcome the distance between the two discussion contexts. This book points to many concrete opportunities for future debates beyond the current situation. Whether and how these may bear fruit depends not only on the openness of individual scholars. More importantly, it requires changes in the institutional framework within which such discussions take place, and which is still characterized by a hierarchical relationship between the mainstream and feminism, making dialogue between equal partners difficult. But whatever one's view on this issue, we hope that this book will encourage people to enter into such a dialogue and will stimulate thinking and discussion about ways to close the gaps between the different parties involved in these conversations.

Feminist political and theoretical practice: between subversive transformation and appendix to patriarchal structures

While seeing positive developments through the integration of gender perspectives in the three policy areas of development, human rights, and peace and conflict resolution, many contributors remain sceptical about the impact of women's movements on international relations, both from the political and the theoretical perspectives. Scepticism arises when these successes are evaluated in the light of feminism's original claim – in politics as well as in academia – to transform social inequalities and create autonomous practices and spaces. In pointing to feminism's intention to be a critical, subversive force and activity, the two introductory contributors – Nighat Said Khan from a women's movement perspective and Marysia Zalewski from the perspective of a feminist scholar – open up the central line of controversy. Has the inclusion of women in global politics, and in academic thinking about the subject, become an expression of women's integration into hegemonic patriarchal institutions where they are reduced to a lobbying group, an appendix without influence? Have women's movements and feminism, with their fundamental criticism of global inequalities, particularly in North/West–South relations, ceased to exist, as Khan argues? Are only sanitized feminist practices, as Zalewski argues, able to enter patriarchal political and academic institutions and discourses? Or are there spaces where feminist politics can insert itself without compromising feminism's own goals? If the women's movement(s), with the aim of abolishing structures and mechanisms of inequality and exclusion, continue(s) to exist – as several contributors to this book argue – these questions compel the rethinking of feminist practices, politics and concepts. They also call for renewed discussions about feminism's contribution to shaping the relationship between the 'real world of actions' and the academic thought and theorizing about it.

Using a post-modernist approach, Zalewski tackles the question of feminism's influence on the discipline of International Relations (IR)[5] by turning it around to look at the contribution of IR to the development of feminist theories. She wants to escape the one-way street in which 'feminism is seen as an "add on", a "contributor" rather than a "creator" and as such mirrors a gendered hierarchical practice that feminists have so consistently worked to get rid of for many years now'. What counts for her are not so much the particular questions feminists raise, such as the feminization of poverty, but rather whether these questions manage to undermine the epistemology, ontology, subjectivity and objectivity of theories, policies and politics. By way of thinking about what we do instead of thinking about what we want to tell others that they should do, we may be able to understand the relationship between theory and practice differently. And we may also be able to think differently about the role of theory and scholarship: 'Thinking about theory as everyday practices and everyday behaviours – in other words what people think and do – has potentially more transformative possibilities than expecting theory to be something which provides a blueprint for changing the world.'

In this perspective, feminist movements and thinking are important in that they turn against and undermine hegemonic practices and ideologies, or as Zalewski puts it, they are 'absolutely vital for exposing and disturbing the practices of hegemonic ideologies but also for exposing how fragile hegemonies often are'. Hence she invites women's movement(s) and feminists to look at their 'work, locally and internationally', as 'vital in its own right' and not reduce themselves to the status of 'add-ons' to the mainstream.

A product of the women's movement of the 1960s and 1970s, Nighat Said Khan employs an approach inspired by critical theory. In exploring the impact of the international women's movement on international relations, understood as relations between nations, Khan sees women's claims to act and speak in their own right endangered. The need to speak up about silenced inequalities and subordination lies at the root of the emergence of national women's movements worldwide, and it also stood at the beginning of the international women's decade. Now, after 25 years of international women's politics, one might think that the women's movement has succeeded in making its voices heard and in changing the international political agenda. Khan is sceptical about this claimed success. In her view, the women's movement has been 'permitted entrance, albeit selectively, in the corridors of governments and the United Nations, yet one continuously hears the refrain that the women's movement doesn't exist any more'. She considers the women's movement to have become weak since the Nairobi Conference in 1985, because it has been 'co-opted and diluted' through its focus on 'mainstreaming', lobbying and its desire to be included into patriarchal institutions that once were identified by women as part of a system that produces global inequalities. For her, the question is whether the women's movement has 'this critique any longer – of patriarchy, the state or the UN'. According to Khan, instead of having changed the international political agenda, the *engendering* of international documents and policies has been a cosmetic exercise. Moreover, women's NGOs have been instrumentalized by governments and international institutions as key actors, for example in the new poverty reduction programmes which serve to stabilize the global economic structures characterized by asymmetrical relations. In the same vein, women's issues have been used to legitimize a new ideological world order in the name of democracy and human rights defined by the West, in which, for instance, Islam and the Muslim world are constructed as being the new enemies of the West.

In her comment on the two previous contributions, Christa Wichterich takes a closer look at the UN Beijing + 5 Conference. She points out that the women's movement has succeeded in adding new topics to the international agenda, but at the same time has lost its critical and radical approaches. To escape the dilemma between transformation and seeking change through integration, thereby risking adaptation, Wichterich reminds us of the concept of achieving transformation through participation suggested by the Southern women's network, Development Alternatives of Women for a New Era (DAWN), at the Beijing Conference in 1995. Like her two predecessors, Wichterich notices that so far there has been no genuine dialogue between the mainstream and feminism that is characterized by acknowledging feminism as an equal partner.

In taking these questions and positions as starting points, the subsequent contributors discuss their validity and consequences for feminist theory and practice, looking at the three policy areas of development, peace and conflict, and human rights. The focus is on a critical review of the entry points of feminist concepts – such as empowerment, the critique of the private–public dichotomy, or women's human rights – into the mainstream. When comparing these three issue areas, it is the field of development studies and policies that has seemingly been 'most successful' in integrating gender and women's issues, as mainstream scholars in particular often note. Therefore, the question emerges of whether development policy/studies can be considered a model for studying the common ground between feminism and/or women's issues and international politics, and even as a gateway for the entry of feminism into international politics and studies. However, as the overall scepticism in the contributions to this topic shows, there is a considerable gap between engendered institutional rhetoric and women's issues as an add-on in mainstream policies (in Zalewsky's sense) on the one hand, and marginalized feminist approaches and concepts on the other. Looked at another way, then, the field of development studies and policies may also serve as a case study for feminists on how mainstream mechanisms of co-optation, dilution and selective exclusion may operate. Moreover, it suggests the conclusion that a feminist transformation of the international political agenda, or the discipline and study of International Relations, by way of 'engendering' development, is unlikely to happen. This may also be due to the fact that development policies and studies as 'soft' or 'low' issues do not belong to the core of IR, leading to a double marginalization – as feminists and as development experts. In order to probe these questions further, we have therefore included the somewhat 'harder' and 'higher' issue areas in international relations: peace and conflict resolution and human rights.

Developing the mainstream or mainstreaming women into development?

In her introductory contribution to the section on development, Claudia von Braunmühl traces the evolution of institutional women's and gender policies and takes a critical look at the concept of *gender mainstreaming*. She demonstrates the risks and precarious effects of gender mainstreaming by showing the changes the empowerment concept (see also Carolyn Medel Añonuevo) has gone through during its institutionalization. Introduced into the international debate by the feminist network DAWN, the concept was originally based on a comprehensive feminist critique of power relationships. It looks at gender hierarchies in the context of other global hierarchies, such as the hierarchies between the global North/West and the South. With this approach, it has become the key reference point for a feminist vision of development. Integrated into mainstream development policies, the empowerment concept has, as von Braunmühl argues, been reduced to the legitimization of institutional *gender and development* policies and deprived of its original political impetus and critical edge. Furthermore, in her view, the increasingly technical debates on gender mainstreaming among gender experts tend to ignore social movements, with their interests and demands as actors and bearers of social transformation, including the transformation of gender relationships. Donor agencies and international development bureaucracies, on the other hand, are quite inadequate as actors if what is sought is a change in power relationships. Similarly, women's NGOs cannot replace a women's movement as a force for change. In fact, the NGO-ization of the women's movement, as von Braunmühl points out with reference to Latin America, may produce new risks for the movement(s). Detached from the movement's basis, women's NGOs often run the risk of silencing other women who wish to speak and act in their own right, and of reducing them to 'target groups' of their own internationally funded development projects. Hence, for von Braunmühl, gender policies and concepts which are void of the goal and ambition of a comprehensive transformation in gender hierarchies cannot successfully tackle the issues raised by women's movements.

Building on von Braunmühl's critique, Carolyn Medel-Añonuevo considers the popularization and institutionalization of the empowerment concept to be both a loss and a gain for the women's movement(s). Aware of its instrumentalization by the mainstream, she sees empowerment as 'a site of contestation and resistance', and urges women not to give it up but rather 'to reappropriate the empowerment discourse by resharpening it so that it continues to be relevant for our work and our life'. In order to do so, Medel-Añonuevo takes a closer look at the concept of power and its practices and understandings by women in diverse settings and locations. In her view, feminist practices and notions of power tend to be the *power to do* something together *with* others rather than to have *power over* somebody or something. Drawing on the example of education, she demonstrates how empowerment based on this understanding can be practised in a whole range of different spaces within and outside institutions, transforming them into sites and 'practices of power'. This approach empowers people by putting everyone, wherever they are, in a position of agency and power. Such a practice of empowerment may also have the potential to create the preconditions for genuine dialogues between women and men, feminists and the mainstream, as equals.

Taking a look at the relationship between women and international social policy, Renate Rott shows how women feature only rhetorically in the social policy programmes of international and national agencies. She examines internationally financed social investment funds, which were designed as a safety net to cushion the worst consequences of the neoliberal economic structural adjustment programmes, looking at the examples of Nicaragua and Guatemala. While the international rhetoric code, as Rott calls it, on the empowerment and integration of women into poverty reduction is reflected in the discourse around social funds, the programmes themselves have had hardly any material impact on women. Furthermore, as she shows, despite the discourse of inclusion women are actually excluded from programme planning, design and implementation. Rott also criticizes the donor-induced and donor-controlled social policy approach, which ignores the importance of societal democratization, in the sense that domestic societal actors and institutions are included in the decision-making, controlling and planning of social policy. In a political setting characterized by clientelistic relationships, as is the case in Central America, this may not only lead to the instrumentalization of social policies for individual political interests, but is also unlikely to strengthen civil society or to transform the relationship between civil society and the government.

Instrumental silence? Women and gender in conflict management theory and practice

Issues of security, war and peace belong to the core of international relations in practice and as an academic field. In the real and the academic worlds, these were and still are male-dominated spheres – women feature mostly as victims of war, or, more recently, as peacemakers. The expanding field of conflict resolution and management (it covers all areas of conflict prevention, conflict settlement and post-conflict peacebuilding) is situated at the low end of 'high' international politics, and its practical activities are 'interventions into the social fabric' (Müller), often taking place at community levels. Of late, women's movements, especially in Africa, have continually demanded the inclusion of women as actors in peace and conflict issues, and international policy documents have reproduced this in emphasizing the role of women in peacebuilding. For these reasons, when turning to conflict management concepts, one would expect women to appear as actors and gender to be an analytical category. Even more so, from a critical feminist perspective and based on experiences with development policies, one might fear a certain degree of instrumentalization of women. However, as the contributions in this section show, 'women as actors and gender issues are consistently marginalized' (Pankhurst) in the theory and practice of conflict resolution.

Asking why gender 'does not (appear) to matter', Cordula Reimann examines gender blindness in conflict management theories. In reviewing the most important body of mainstream literature, she attributes the absence of gender to its generally weak theoretical foundations, which lead to the unquestioned adoption of masculinist assumptions from the underlying disciplines such as International Relations theory. On the other hand, she notices a feminist silence in the field of conflict resolution. According to Reimann, this may be due to feminism's overall normative closeness to peace and its implicit assumption that conflict management corresponds to feminist – or feminine – values such as peacefulness and empathy. This prevents critical feminist scrutiny of approaches in conflict management, and ignores the fact that many peace agreements are either oblivious to questions of gender equality or are even explicitly brokered on the basis of gender injustice. Furthermore, this attitude feeds into the patriarchal dichotomy of 'peaceful woman/male warrior', which leads to the reinforcement of women's roles as mediators and thus delegates the responsibility for peace – at least at the lower political levels – to them.

Reimann concludes that the inclusion of gender analysis and the deconstruction and reconstruction of 'gendered imagery, categories and institutions' would be beneficial for the field of conflict management, in that it would provide an 'important entry point for understanding ... the complex, internal power dynamics of conflict management activities and promoting social justice in peacebuilding activities'. This would be achieved by a better understanding of questions of identity, social symbolisms and exclusionary social structures along gender constructions. Aware of the danger of feminism becoming a marginalized add-on, she nevertheless recommends a strengthened dialogue between the two strands, and the integration of feminist approaches into the mainstream, under the condition that feminist approaches are systematically institutionalized and thus treated as equal partners.

But would a more gender-sensitive analysis also result in conflict management concepts and practices aimed at transforming gender inequalities? With this question in mind, Donna Pankhurst examines institutional conflict resolution and peacebuilding practices. Arguing that gender came comparatively late to the field of conflict resolution because, unlike the field of development, there was no 'efficiency imperative to take gender issues seriously', she notes that up until now women have been effectively marginalized in its institutional practices. However, she observes a shift in the discourse, in that the inclusion of women is increasingly considered to positively affect the efficacy of peace arrangements at the micro-level. Even so, Pankhurst notes that women continue to be excluded from negotiating peace settlements at the macro-level. Making and building peace is added to women's work, especially in post-conflict developing countries, while local structures of inequality are not challenged. Strengthening this trend, a second, recently evolving, development in institutional conflict management approaches aims at strengthening – or reinventing – 'traditional' conflict resolution mechanisms, which often explicitly exclude women or build on gender inequalities.

Here, parallels to the development field emerge. On the one hand, there is an increasing tendency to include gender analysis and women rhetorically, while in practice the inclusion is selective, as it is designed to fit into the overall programme rationale. So, once again, women as actors in their own right and with their own interests are excluded. Pankhurst notes the challenges involved in listening to women's voices. She points out that women-oriented peacebuilding activities, for instance in African countries, which are based on feminist ideologies questioning the structures and practices of inequality, tend to be informed by international feminist approaches. Local women often consider these values to be imported and not acceptable in local contexts. Hence, a feminist transformative agenda may not correspond to the articulated desires of local women. On the other hand, locally accepted approaches, fostered by international agencies, may offer no space for systematically addressing women's inequalities. Pankhurst observes a clash of discourses, resulting in the silencing of women as actors for change in gender relations. She believes that more systematic thinking and a review of feminist experiences with development studies and practice could offer new perspectives, not only for ways of facing these challenges but also for conflict management and peacebuilding as a whole.

An example of a case in which women's voices are loud, yet not adequately heard, is given by Fatima Ahmed Ibrahim, president of the Sudanese Women's Union. Formerly persecuted in Sudan and then exiled in London, Ibrahim gives an account of the war and the situation of women in Sudan since independence in 1957. Linking the quest for peace and democracy to the women's human rights situation, Ibrahim describes the role of the Sudanese Women's Union as resister against war and all forms of violence and especially against women's oppression. She particularly criticizes the silence of the international community and media about the regime and the war in Sudan, which she calls 'a war in empty rooms'. Embodying feminist practice, Ibrahim speaks about the real yet silenced human rights violations committed against women, men and children in her country, and she thus reminds women of the political importance of combining theory with practice if change is to be achieved in the world. She also challenges the international women's movement(s) to take action, asking for support for a petition.[6] Thus Ibrahim demonstrates the necessity for the existence and activities of a global women's movement against oppression and violence, built on solidarity and conversations between women from all continents and backgrounds.

Women's human rights – new spaces for women's activism?

It can be said that since the beginning of the 1990s, the international women's movement has succeeded in transforming the international human rights agenda and discourse to include 'women's rights as human rights'. In the course of this process it has challenged core assumptions, such as the private–public divide, that had led to the exclusion of women's rights violations from the international human rights agenda. Hence it may not come as a surprise that the contributions on the topic of women's human rights have a more positive tone, although they do not ignore the obstacles to the realization of women's human rights. By comparison with the long experience in institutional development policies and studies, women's rights activists and academics are only now beginning to evaluate the impact of the ongoing feminist appropriation and revision of the human rights concept, first on the international political discourse and practices of women's human rights protection, and second on the reality of women's lives.

Uta Ruppert's contribution focuses on the implications of the women's human rights discourse for the international women's movement. She notices a mutually constitutive relationship between the evolution of a global women's movement and the international women's rights discourse. For Ruppert, today's international women's movement is *global* because it reflects women's global differences and targets the personal, local, national and international levels as intersecting political arenas of women's political activity. Ruppert ascribes to the women's movement an underlying strategic aim of achieving 'globality', in the sense of striving for global norms and values and establishing global responsibilities for governments as the only viable solution for women's – and humanity's – problems.

In Ruppert's view, the women's human rights discourse was instrumental in the 'globalizing' of the women's movement, for which the empowerment concept had laid the conceptual foundation and women's organizations' networking the practical foundation. From this perspective, Ruppert redescribes the process by which the women's movement drew up an inclusive and indivisible concept of human rights, treating all human rights dimensions as interdependent. This 'universal' understanding of human rights was the foundation of the feminist reinterpretations of 'human rights as women's rights' and 'women's rights as human rights'. Using these premises, the new concepts were able to integrate the variety and differences in perspectives within the international women's movement under one umbrella, and thus 'globalize' its values and practices. Because of its unifying function and normative goals, Ruppert argues for the 'globalizing of women's human rights' as a strategic base from which the international women's rights movement can exert influence in political spaces from which it has so far been excluded, such as international trade and financial policies.

Akua Kuenyehia takes us from the global to the national level, by showing how the West African women's movements base their struggle for economic and social rights on international human rights language and documents. Relating international discourse to the activities of national women's movements, she argues that the international human rights standards, including the women-specific documents, serve as an analytic and normative framework for the fight against discrimination by reframing socio-economic injustices against women as human rights violations. Citing the examples of education, violence against women and health, Kuenyehia shows how international human rights norms legitimize women's demands for the improvements of their status and how they empower women's organizations to put pressure on governments. On the other hand, Kuenyehia recognizes the shortcomings of the human rights approach, which lie mainly in its narrow focus on the nation state as the central target for human rights protection, and as such may not capture the roots of the violation of both economic and social rights. Particularly in Africa, the struggle for the realization of women's rights needs to be placed within the context of an 'international system of allocation of resources that is neither just nor equitable', and which sets the parameters for the violation of women's and men's rights. However, while pointing out these limitations emanating from globally unequal economic structures, she does not make excuses for poor government performances. Finally, Kuenyehia underlines the need for national and international strategic alliances between women to promote women's human rights and to protect what has already been achieved against continual attempts on the national and international levels to dilute existing norms and agreements.

But what happens to feminism when feminists adopt the concept of human rights as the core claim of global feminist politics? Are they giving up the differentiation won in post-modern and postcolonial theories? Feminists are very familiar with the polarities within human rights debates between universalism and particularism and cultural relativism. On one side, the critics of women's rights as human rights even identify the specific rights of women as the essence to 'cultural shocks'. On the other side, many feminist intellectuals and activists have become aware of the complexities of women's politics of difference. The polarization between universalism and relativism can be transcended by looking in a new way at the spaces opened by the *Déclaration des droits de l'homme et du citoyen* in the French Revolution of 1789. Following Cornelia Visman's[7] arguments, the *Déclaration* opens two different readings because it entails two texts, one protecting the rights of the human being, and the other the rights of the French citizen. While the latter authorizes (at that time only male) French citizens to speak about their rights, the former, as a text of universal and supra-historical validity, builds the bases of self-authorization for any human being to speak about injustice in the language of right. Since Olympe de Gouges' 'Declaration of the Rights of Woman and Citizen' in 1791, innumerable individuals and social groups all over the world have attempted to rewrite the Declaration, using it as a reference point to validate their own experiences of injustice and prevent them from falling into oblivion. In this sense, the concept of human rights allows us to speak about very different experiences of injustice.

In many countries, where neither the laws of the modern state nor 'customary law' are instruments of justice, speaking about human rights can be an act of self-authorization. Sonja Wölte explains in her contribution that it is possible to have contextualization of human rights or, as she says, 'domestication' without relativization. Her example of Kenya shows that the international women's human rights discourse may open up new, albeit contested, spaces for women's political rights and activism in the domestic setting, and that it provides women and their movements with a framework for the renegotiation of the relationship between women and culture/tradition as well as of that between women and the state. But the impact of this discourse as an instrument of local and national political change depends on its legitimacy in the different socio-political contexts. As she demonstrates, the legitimacy from 'above' needs to be complemented by a legitimacy which stems from women and their organizations at the local level, that is, a legitimacy from 'below'.

Feminist intrusions into the discipline of international relations? Perspectives from the mainstream

Picking up on the question of dialogue between feminism and mainstream scholarship in International Relations, the last section introduces views of male mainstream scholars on entry points and common ground between feminism and mainstream debates. Here, the central question to address was not feminism's contribution to the mainstream, but rather how this may have had an impact on mainstream scholarship, which could be an indicator for dialogue spaces.

In looking for reasons for the lack of an 'inter-paradigm' debate, as he calls it, with respect to development studies, Lothar Brock criticizes the self-referentiality of feminist writings. After a short review of his perception of the gender discourse in development studies, he then picks up the concept of social embeddedness and the feminist critique, and revision of the universal notion of human rights, as reference points which might help to close the conceptual gap between feminism and the mainstream. In Brock's view, the idea of cultural embeddedness of poverty, for example, offers new insights into the implications and meaning of poverty and consequently carries new opportunities and challenges for institutional approaches to fighting poverty. On a more abstract conceptual level, Brock points to the potential of feminism 'as a universalistic concept which, however, has learned to face the specificity of problems which it deals with. It thus has a lot to offer to the task of unfolding a reflexive universalism which lives up to its own claims without using these claims as yet another device for fostering particularistic needs'.

In his assessment of the compatibility of academic feminism with different theoretical mainstream strands of IR, Harald Müller concludes that the largest common ground is to be found between feminism and post-modern and constructivist approaches. With regard to conflict resolution and conflict management, he agrees with Reimann and Pankhurst that they are 'both largely atheoretical and largely ungendered' because they are 'praxeologies, built on successful and failed attempts to stop, contain, and resolve conflicts'. Müller considers the lack of theory to be an opportunity to engender conflict management, drawing on the conceptual and practical experiences of applying gender perspectives in development studies/policies. When engendering conflict management, and when trying to dialogue with the mainstream, he warns, however, of a theoretical gender bias that may lead feminists to overlook other inequalities apart from gender inequalities. In order to counter the 'risk of engendering non-gendered social relationships', he advises feminists to engage in 'regular self-deconstruction, and dense dialogue with other theories ... to avoid flawed analysis and prescription out of theoretical bias'.

In his comment, Gert Krell looks in an exemplary manner at the entry points of feminist human rights notions into mainstream politics and the International Relations discipline, as well as at the influence of the women's movement on mainstream IR overall. After presenting his view of the relationship between men and feminism, he reminds us of the long history of women's human rights struggles and their successes, and of the challenges they face in improving women's lives. Krell argues that the political and conceptual underpinnings of this struggle have presented a number of challenges and 'been very influential in enlarging or revising traditional concepts in international relations'. The feminist critique of the dichotomization of the private and the public spheres and the borders between the local, national and international, for instance, 'helped to weaken ... the division between different levels of analysis, in particular states versus societies on the one hand and the international system on the other'. According to Krell, feminists have further opened up the debate on universalism versus cultural relativism, and subjective versus objective rights, and they have challenged the androcentric concept of civilization. However, the significance or impact of these interfaces and entry points for dialogue empirically manifest themselves in a limited manner, as Krell's cursory survey of standard IR textbooks shows. This seems to apply even more strongly to the German academic context than to the Anglo-American world, where feminist scholarship in International Relations now looks back on a tradition lasting more than twelve years. Nevertheless, from his – albeit not representative – assessment we can conclude that the rift between the mainstream and feminist discourses has not greatly narrowed even in the Anglo-American context, a view that the British contributions to this volume confirm.

Conclusion

The assessments of the introductory questions – where and how have women's movements influenced international relations in theory and practice? – leave us with a diverse set of answers based on the different approaches and perspectives chosen and the policy fields involved. While generalized conclusions cannot and should not be drawn, as to do so would blur the specific analytical strengths and the concrete potentials for change in each policy field, some similarities can be detected. The contributions show that, as a result of the political activities of the international women's movement(s) during the past 25 years, the international and institutional discourses in the three fields have been 'engendered' to varying degrees. However, this has generally not resulted in the application of programmes and policies which manage to overcome, or even challenge, structural gender or other inequalities. Hence, gender and women's issues have often been integrated into a dominant institutional or academic logic. They have either met with some resistance or been added to existing mainstream paradigms. Furthermore, in certain instances – particularly with reference to development policies – it even seems that the gap between women's movements' agendas and international agendas has widened in the course of the integration of women's issues and gender perspectives into the institutional, conceptual or political mainstream. In other instances, such as with the human rights discourse, it still remains to be seen how far the international engendering efforts have empowering effects on women's movements in the international as well as in the national and local contexts. On the one hand, the 'engendering' of international politics has ambiguous and often precarious results for women's movements and feminism. On the other, there are still larger areas of core fields in international politics that this volume does not even touch upon, such as international security, trade and finance policies, from which women are still excluded.

The majority of the contributions in this volume do show, however, that feminism in its practical and theoretical strands has not entirely lost its critical analytic approach or its normative goals, which aim at transforming social and political inequalities and at being a subversive force for change. On this basis, it can perhaps be said that, in the face of a rather sobering assessment of its successes, feminist practice and theory has arrived at a point where it recalls its own original intentions, agendas and goals. There is a sense of a need to pause, to reassess and think about new directions in feminist theory and practice based on the old goals. This may offer the opportunity for and be the beginning of a process in which feminists search for new ways to think about new practices, concepts and strategies based on their original intentions, practices and concepts and in the light of political, institutional and academic contexts that have integrated feminist concepts and – to varying extents – adapted them to their own logic. It may also be an opportunity to reassess feminism's relationship to the mainstream, be it in political discourses, institutional practices or scholarship, based on this search for new concepts and strategies.

While some contributions indicate that the rift between feminist theorizing and women's movements has widened, the discovery of commonalities in each of their situations may offer an opportunity and trigger for new dialogues, thus narrowing this gap. In fact, the basis of and the key to finding new concepts and strategies for feminist theory and practice lies in building a renewed strong relationship between feminist theory and practice, leading to fruitful dialogues and debates. Furthermore, this relationship and the conversations between feminists of all strands, we believe, offer the basis and backbone for those feminists who wish to enter into renewed dialogue with the mainstream and to seek inclusion in conversations with them as equal partners.

Notes

1. See, for example, Rupp, L. (1997) *Worlds of Women. The Making of an International Women's Movement*, Princeton: Princeton University Press; Stienstra, D. (1994) *Women's Movements and International Organizations*, Basingstoke: Macmillan.

2. By the time of publication, it was commonly seen as unlikely that another world conference would be held. Most states within the UN have opted for a Beijing review process, with the next review conference (Beijing + 10) to be held in 2005.

3. For a selection of works, see the Appendix, *Selected Further Readings*.

4. See, for example, Spivak, G. (1985) 'Can the Subaltern Speak? Speculation on Widow Sacrifice', *Wedge*, Vol. 7, No. 8 (Winter/Spring), pp. 120–30; Mohanty, C. T., A. Russo and L. Torres (eds) (1991) *Third World Women and the Politics of Feminism*, Bloomington: Indiana University Press.

5. When referring to the academic discipline of International Relations, the term is capitalized and abbreviated as IR.

6. Fatima Ibrahim can be contacted via the editors or at the African Studies Centre, University of California, Los Angeles.

7. Visman, C. (1998) 'Menschenrechte: Instanz des Sprechens – Instrumente der Politik', in Brunkhorst, H. (ed.), *Demokratischer Experimentalismus. Politik in der komplexen Gesellschaft*, Frankfurt/M.: Suhrkamp, pp. 279–304.

PART I

*Feminist Political and Theoretical Practice:
Between Subversive Transformation
and Appendix to Patriarchal Structures*

CHAPTER 2

Feminists in International Relations: What Impact on the Discipline?

Marysia Zalewski

Since the formal introduction of feminist work into the discipline of International Relations (IR) over ten years ago, feminist scholarship and teaching have arguably become part and parcel of IR.[1] Why is this so? Why would such a paradigmatically masculinized and exclusionary discipline like International Relations permit the infiltration of a body of ideas and practices, namely feminism, which so clearly has subversive and disruptive intentions? One answer to this question is that it did not have a choice. It was impelled to undergo changes in reaction to changes in the 'real world' of international politics, the break-up of the Soviet Bloc along with the fall of the Berlin Wall being one example. The old ways of theorizing about IR seem to have been proved faulty, and the discipline as such has had to go through a process of transformation, which has been marked by the proliferation of new theories including feminist theories, post-modernism, post-structuralism, critical theory and, of late, constructivism.[2] The arrival of these new approaches, with their overall intention of opening up how we can think about and analyse how human beings behave towards one another, has arguably ushered in a sense of hope that International Relations would begin to deserve its own description – that is, it would be truly 'International' and be about 'Relations'.

In this chapter I am most concerned with the question of the impact of feminist approaches on IR. How have feminists been involved in the overall challenge to this most traditional of disciplines? What effect have they had? A classic way to answer this question is to examine the current state of the discipline in order to ascertain its feminist credentials. This might be done by describing the positive impact of feminist work on IR. For example, the explicit inclusion of women in the IR academic agenda, and particularly women in traditional roles (such as diplomatic wives and mothers), surely lends more credibility to the label 'International' than does the traditional concern with only one sex and, of course, in reality, with only a small portion of that community. Additionally, the classic feminist emphasis on the effects of discrimination and injustice has surely helped the discipline to begin understanding relationships between people and ideas, and to facilitate social interaction at international levels much more than when it largely relied upon realist or idealist methods.

However, I want to start approaching the impact of feminist work on the discipline of IR somewhat differently. Rather than concentrating on the question, What have feminists contributed to International Relations?, I will instead focus on What has International Relations contributed to feminism?

What has International Relations contributed to feminism?

This might seem to be a counter-intuitive question. Thus, before I address it, I want to explain why I have turned the question round in this way. At first glance, investigating the contributions of feminism seems an obvious and rational approach. There is clearly something called 'the discipline of International Relations' which many of us work within or around; feminist analyses reveal the gendered or even sexist character of the discipline, and as feminists we try and make others see this in order to achieve some changes for the better. However, asking the question about what feminism has contributed to 'something', in this case IR, immediately places feminist work in a secondary and subordinate position. From this perspective feminism is seen as an add-on, a 'contributor' rather than a 'creator', and as such mirrors a gendered hierarchical practice that feminists have worked so consistently to eradicate for many years now.[3]

In my view, this 'contributor' approach is not very successful. Indeed, I would go further and argue that thinking about feminism in this way facilitates a tendency of the discipline of International Relations to tolerate only an apparently sanitized kind of feminism, that is, a feminism that does not seriously challenge the status quo and is therefore a kind of feminism which, to all intents and purposes, has lost its radical and subversive edge. I suggest that this is the case, *not* because feminists are not doing their work adequately, but rather because the discipline itself, as it is currently constituted, can only *resist* feminist intrusions. I argue that this is so because, in my view, IR and feminist theories are working towards different ends and using radically different epistemologies, ontologies and politics.[4] For example, feminists have traditionally worked towards dislodging the status quo and upsetting traditional orders (such as patriarchal ones), whereas IR is classically concerned with maintaining traditional orders (notably by resisting anarchy) and working within traditional theoretical and arguably masculinist frameworks (such as positivism).

The argument that International Relations and feminist theories are working towards different ends and by different means, is not a position shared by all feminist scholars currently active within IR. For example, J. Ann Tickner has recently claimed that IR scholars, including feminists, are all working towards a common end, that is, trying to understand the roots of war in order to prevent future wars.[5] The concern with war has certainly been a persistent feature of traditional IR and I am not suggesting that feminist scholars are not interested in understanding and/or ending wars. Best feminist and non-feminist IR scholars clearly do share some empirical areas of concern, such as war and violence. However, feminists' concern with prioritizing marginalized subjects and with radically questioning traditional methodologies and theories, necessarily implies that the ontological and epistemological frameworks of feminist scholarship are essentially antagonistic to mainstream theoretical practices of International Relations.[6]

As such, one answer to the question, What has International Relations contributed to feminism? is a persistent series of challenges and resistances. But as far as feminism is concerned, I do not think that these challenges are necessarily negative. I will come back to this point later on. What I want to do now is to elaborate my arguments. In order to do this, I will first give a brief and necessarily selective view of the trajectory of feminist work within International Relations over the last decade or so, then I will say a few words about the current state of the discipline generally. Finally, I will return to my point about the resistances to feminism having positive possibilities.

A decade (and more) of feminism and/in International Relations

There was a great sense of excitement generated in the early days of 'feminism and IR'. At the feminist and gender panels I attended or participated in during the late 1980s and early 1990s – at events such as the British International Studies Association's annual conferences and the International Studies Association Conventions – there appeared to be a genuine interest in and desire to hear what feminists 'had to say'. Of course, this genuine interest did not apply to *all* IR scholars, and nor did feminists expect it to. But the time certainly seemed 'right' for the discipline to be exposed to feminist theories and ideas. Many feminist scholars working in IR at that time were passionately keen to ask the traditional 'woman question'. That is, we were interested in advancing the traditional agenda of Western feminist politics, for example, by asking questions about the absence of women in both the academic world of IR and the public arena of world politics, with the ultimate aim of transforming socially constructed gender inequalities. We also wanted to know why it appeared so easy for the discipline to ignore women and issues and practices traditionally associated with women. This placing of woman and women at the centre, in classic Cynthia Enloe style, appeared to be very welcome at the time.[7]

Since the 1980s, work on women in International Relations has continued and much valuable scholarship has emerged at all levels, from undergraduate essays to PhD dissertations, to a whole range of published work.[8] However, the general sense of interest in and excitement about this work in IR began to wane rather swiftly. This became particularly apparent in the explicitly theoretical literature and accompanying debates alongside the continual marginalization of feminist work within the discipline.[9] As the 1990s progressed and the fortunes and visibility of critical theorists, post-modernists, post-structuralists and constructivists increased in the context of fashionable theory within IR, the interest in feminist analyses of woman and women tended to dissipate. This became particularly obvious with feminist work which emphasized women or woman in the context of structural disadvantage. One result was that this type of work began, in the main, to attract a retrograde aura – one frequently associated with essentialist, and therefore suspect and anachronistic, forms of feminist theorizing.[10] In addition, traditional and neo-traditional IR scholars seemed to be becoming more and more dissatisfied with the answers feminist scholars came up with to the ubiquitous question, 'What is the feminist perspective on X?' (X being something from the traditional or neo-traditional IR agenda), further entrenching the idea that feminist work in IR could only ever be an 'add-on' to the traditional (and thereby tautologically central) agenda.[11] All in all, asking the 'woman question', and thereby placing woman at the centre of analysis, began to be seen by many in the mainstream – and indeed by many from the so-called margins of the discipline – as a problematic strategy to probe the gendered character of the subject of IR.

Of course, asking the 'woman question' *can* be problematic in that it can reinforce the framework that 'all things masculine' are the norm and 'all things feminine' are a problem to be sorted out – which is yet another manifestation of gender hierarchy that feminists have consistently worked to eradicate. One way in which some feminists in IR have tried to avoid this reification of woman as a 'problem to be solved' is by moving their focus towards masculinity and gender. I am not saying that this is the wrong thing to do. Indeed, as the co-editor of a book called *The 'Man' Question in International Relations*,[12] written specifically to investigate the hegemony of masculinity in IR, I believe it is an important thing to do. However, the argument can certainly be made that moving too quickly away from a focus on women and woman too easily allows the discipline to *return* to its traditional focus on men, but this time with a new twist in that men can begin to be represented as the new and invisible victims of gender.[13]

However, none of this implies that feminist work which places women and woman at the centre has declined. Far from it. What I am saying is that this work began to be represented in the discipline of International Relations as not having the same theoretical calibre or intellectual purchase as other critically inspired approaches. In the late 1990s and early 2000s this has been clearly manifested in the idea that feminist theory is seen as something of an *adjunct* to theories such as critical theory or post-modernism, and arguably of late, constructivism. Or as I have phrased it elsewhere, feminists are portrayed as the 'lodgers' or 'tenants' in the houses of critical theory or post-modernism.[14]

The result of all this is that IR is still overwhelmingly male-dominated and increasingly uninterested in and seemingly unaffected by most feminist work. A brief survey of recent issues of some of the main journals in the field lends credence to this – although my view is based on a wider understanding of and engagement with the discipline generally. However, the journals I looked at specifically are *International Studies Quarterly*, *Review of International Studies* and the *European Journal of International Relations*. Both *Review of International Studies* and the *European Journal of International Relations* published articles on the contemporary state of IR. Michael Nicholson considers the question, 'What's the use of International Relations?'[15] and Knud Erik Jørgensen examines the claim, 'Continental IR Theory: The Best Kept Secret'.[16]

The goal of these two articles is to provide an overall view of the state of IR in the context of theoretical approaches, and the appropriateness or utility of the various theories currently being used. What is striking about the articles is the avid attention they pay to a rather small group of Anglo-American IR scholars (though Jørgensen himself criticizes this dominance) alongside a total avoidance of any feminist scholarship at all. What might be regarded as surprising, however, is the inclusion of an article on gender in the very traditionalist pages of *International Studies Quarterly*. This article, by Mark Tessler, Jodi Nachtwey and Audra Grant, is entitled, 'Further Tests of the Women and

Peace Hypothesis: Evidence from Cross-National Survey Research in the Middle East'.[17] As the title suggests, the authors want to investigate the traditional idea that women are inherently more peaceful than men. Their conclusion is that they are not, since 'none of the nine Middle Eastern data sets yields a statistically significant relationship between sex and attitudes toward international conflict'.[18]

Clearly it has been the case that more men than women have been involved in violent conflict – but this does not necessarily imply that women are not involved in violence. Additionally, women's relationship to violence may have little to do with their biological sex and more with their ascribed gender. However, the most significant point in the context of this discussion is that using this positivist format to question whether women are more peaceful than men is extremely unlikely to disturb the boundaries or foundations of the discipline of International Relations in any way, whatever the outcome of the analysis. One reason I claim that this is so, is because this kind of analysis paradigmatically presents gender as a *variable*, which, in my view, seriously inhibits the capacity of feminism to be anything other than sanitized and tamed.[19] As such, this approach is not especially provocative precisely because it seems to disturb very little in International Relations.

Does this provide us with another answer to the question I raised at the beginning of this chapter: Why would the discipline of International Relations permit the infiltration of such a subversive body of ideas and practices as feminism? Is it because it only allows the inclusion of a certain kind of feminism – one which does *not* threaten the status quo of the discipline? To explain what I mean, I will briefly summarize my arguments and then return to the question of the impact of feminist work on the discipline of International Relations in the context of the issues I have raised.

Summary

By way of a summary I would like to highlight four points:

- It is a mistake to spend too much time considering the *contributions* of feminism to the discipline of IR.
- The discipline of IR is not *capable* of taking feminist work seriously.
- After a decade and more of feminist work, the discipline is as masculinized and as exclusionary as ever.
- Feminist work in and on International Relations is as powerful and as subversive as ever *despite*, or indeed *because* of, the discipline's resistances to this work.

In my view, this leads us to one pressing question: How does the traditional disciplinary resistance to feminist work empower feminisms?

International Relations empowering feminisms?

The discipline of International Relations consistently and persistently resists feminist inroads into the field. It is impelled to do this in order to protect its own sovereign boundaries and its own agendas. How could this practice be of help to feminisms? One answer is that much of the discipline's resistance to feminism is based on some profound misperceptions about its potential.

Feminists ask questions about women for a wide variety of reasons. These questions might be about material inequities suffered by some women, or questions intended to destabilize the ideas about gender and sex on which the category of woman itself is constructed. Whatever the questions or the intentions behind them, they necessarily open up and challenge ideas about epistemology, ontology, subjectivity, objectivity, theory and politics. I would suggest that the vast majority of mainstream and neo-mainstream IR scholars do not recognize this. Or if they do, they are not prepared fully to examine the implications.[20] However, many IR scholars believe that feminists are concerned only with so-called women's issues. The mistake here is not that it isn't the case that some feminists concentrate on these so-called women's issues, but that these concerns are then reduced to something which is regarded as atheoretical, often trivial and irrelevant, and as such of little real interest or threat to the discipline.

This reduction of feminist work is yet another manifestation of gender hierarchy, which reinforces my earlier suggestion that the only reason that the discipline of IR permits feminist work, is because it screens what it lets in. But the crucial point is that asking questions, in whatever form, about, for and by women deeply disturbs the discipline of IR, which is why its practitioners work so hard to contain these questions, even if they are aware that they are containing the subversions of feminism by incorporating what appears to be its 'milder' forms. In this sense the persistent series of challenges to feminism illustrates IR's weaknesses and feminism's strengths.

Turning the traditional question on its head and asking what International Relations has contributed to feminism, encourages us to look at the intriguing relationship between feminism and IR in fresh ways. For one thing, it helps to remind us how traditional gendered hierarchies tautologically appear to represent normality. Once this is exposed (which it consistently needs to be) it can open up a few windows of conceptual opportunity to reconsider this vexed relationship between feminism and IR. The results of this reconsideration lead to some paradoxical conclusions.

Paradoxical conclusions?

I have argued that the discipline of International Relations can tolerate only a sanitized version of feminism, as this is believed to be relatively unthreatening. But in truth, it is very difficult for feminism to be fully sanitized. To be sure, the kinds of feminist analyses that are generally tolerated by mainstream International Relations are often those that understand gender as a variable or perceive 'women's issues' as something separable from 'International Relations issues'. But, as V. Spike Peterson argued almost a decade ago,

> 'adding women' (an empirical gesture) turns out to be more complicated. To the extent that 'adding women' means adding 'that which constitutes femininity' to categories constituted by their masculinity ... a contradiction is exposed.[21]

The contradiction she alludes to concerns the mutually constitutive character of the concepts of masculinity and femininity. If femininity (the usually excluded half of the binary) is to be explicitly included into the discourses and practices of IR, then this necessarily 'reconfigures the gendered meaning of the original category – including the construction of masculinity it presupposed'.[22] In other words, if femininity – in all its guises – is *really* to be recognized as a serious and relevant part of IR theory, then IR theory is likely to metamorphose into something quite unrecognizable. And to be frank, this is not what most traditional and neotraditional International Relations theorists desire.

A second concluding point is that by refusing to think of feminist work as a 'contributor' we can logically claim that feminists may not actually need the discipline of International Relations *at all* in order to pursue their questions about the International. This idea that women are 'inadequate', or indeed 'not fully formed' *on their own* is another classic patriarchal representation.[23] However, it seems to me that women are already very much *doing* International Relations. As such, women and/or feminists do not so much *contribute* to either the discipline of IR or the 'real world' of international politics; rather, they fully participate in creating, knowing and understanding it.

But what do we do with this? What many of the contributors to this book seem to want is an IR theory which is more useful in the pursuit of their goals. This might include looking for a promise, even a guarantee, of *effective* agency out there in the 'real world'. In the context of the concerns of the conference from which this book emanated, this implies that IR should provide us with a set of plausible and legitimate arguments, not only to *demand*, but to *ameliorate*, the inequitable impact of development practices and policies, and to find a concrete way to use the puzzle of the relationship between gender identity and violence in order ultimately to obtain the elusive goal of peace.

However, just as we turned around the question of who is influencing whom in the relationship between feminism and IR, perhaps we need to look for a different way to think about the equation between theory and practice. To continually think of theory, or to ask of theory to be an effective tool in the world of policy and practice, does not always make the best use of theory and, additionally, places *ownership* of it in the hands of the (masculinist) academic institutions. Theory is so much more than a tool, and exists in a far wider setting than academic institutions. Thinking about theory as everyday practices, conversations and behaviours – in other words, what people do and think – has potentially more transformative possibilities than expecting theory to be something which is manufactured by academics in order to provide a blueprint for understanding and changing the world.[24]

Perhaps it is less important to try and tell others what to do and better to think instead about *what* we do. Of course those who work within the confines of IR might think this suggestion is inadequate as it seems to have little to do with the 'big picture' of the world of international politics that the discipline of IR is attempting to grapple with. Here I would return to the work of Cynthia Enloe and her unflagging insistence on the politics of feminism. More often than not, this commitment appears in the form of refusing to accept what we are told 'the bigger picture is'. In her words, 'the bigger picture is always one in which gender is not important'.[25] It is always very tempting to be seduced by mainstream demands and agendas, as their very centrality is tautologically attractive. Mainstream (and neo-mainstream) International Relations, however, is not seriously interested in gender or feminism: the consequences of a serious engagement are too high. But this does not have to be a cause of lament for feminists working with international politics. We are, after all, already doing it ourselves.

Notes

My thanks go to Helen Brocklehurst, Bernie Hayes, Spike Peterson and Cynthia Weber.

1. This introduction is commonly dated back to two specific conferences

and two specific books, namely, the 'Women and International Relations' conference held at the London School of Economics in 1988 and the 'Women and War' conference held at the University of Southern California in 1989. The books are Elshtain, J. B. (1987) *Women and War*, Brighton: Harvester Press and Enloe, C. (1989) *Bananas, Beaches and Bases: Making Feminist Sense of International Politics*, London: Pandora Press.

2. Selected texts include (feminism), Peterson, V. S. and A. Sisson Runyan (1993) *Global Gender Issues*, Oxford: Westview Press; Pettman, J. J. (1996) *Worlding Women: A Feminist International Politics*, London: Routledge; Tickner, J. A. (1992) *Gender in International Relations*, Oxford: Columbia University Press; Steans, J. (1997) *Gender and International Relations*, Cambridge: Polity Press; Sylvester, C. (2002) *Feminist International Relations: An Unfinished Journey*, Cambridge: Cambridge University Press. (Post-modernism/post-structuralism), Derian, J. and M. Shapiro (1989) *International/Intertextual Relations: Postmodern Readings of World Politics*, Lexington, MA: Lexington; Walker, R. B. J. (1993) *Inside/Outside: International Relations as Political Theory*, Cambridge: Cambridge University Press. (Critical theory), Cox, R. W. (1986) 'Social Forces, States, and World Orders: Beyond International Relations Theory', in Keohane, R. O. (ed.), *Neorealism and its Critics*, New York: Columbia University Press; Linklater, A. (1990) *Beyond Realism and Marxism: Critical Theory and International Relations*, London: Macmillan; Neufeld, M. (1995) *The Restructuring of International Relations Theory*, Cambridge: Cambridge University Press. (Constructivism), Onuf, N. (1997) 'A Constructivist Manifesto', in Burch, K. and R. Denmark (eds), *Constituting International Political Economy*, International Political Economy Yearbook, Vol. 10, Boulder, CO: Lynne Rienner, pp. 7–17.

3. See Susan Bordo's discussion on this in her book, *Twilight Zones*, Berkeley: University of California Press, 1997, especially the chapter on 'The Feminist as Other', pp. 192–213.

4. See discussion in Zalewski, M. (1999) 'Playing "Like a Girl": A Response to Molly Cochran', *Cambridge Review of International Affairs*, Vol. XII, No. 2, pp. 57–61 and Whitworth, S. (1994) *Feminism and International Relations*, London: Macmillan, p. ix.

5. Tickner, J. A. (1999) 'Why Women Can't Run the World: International Politics According to Francis Fukuyama', *International Studies Review*, Vol. 1, No. 3, pp. 3–11.

6. See discussions with regard to the destabilizing character of feminist work in Hekman, S. (1992) *Gender and Knowledge: Elements of a Postmodern Feminism*, Boston, MD: Northeastern University Press; Weeks, K. (1998) *Constituting Feminist Subjects*, Ithaca, NY: Cornell University Press; Zalewski, M. (2000) *Feminism After Postmodernism: Theorizing Through Practice*, London: Routledge.

7. Enloe, C. (1989) *Bananas, Beaches and Bases: Making Feminist Sense of International Politics*, Berkeley: University of California Press.

8. See notes one and two.

9. Tickner, J. A. (1999) 'Why Women Can't Run the World', p. 3.

10. This view was also echoed in (and/or derived from) feminist theoretical work. See Barrett, M. and A. Phillips (eds) (1992) *Destabilizing Theory: Contemporary Feminist Debates*, Oxford: Polity Press; Butler J. and J. W. Scott (eds) (1992) *Feminists Theorize the Political*, London: Routledge.

11. For a recent example of this, see the interview with Ken Waltz by Fred Halliday and Justin Rosenberg (1998), *Review of International Studies*, Vol. 24, No. 3, pp. 371–86. The editors of the journal put two additional questions to Professor Waltz, one of which was, 'What is the feminist contribution to IR theory?' Waltz's reply: 'Feminists offer not a new or revised theory of international politics but a sometimes interesting interpretation of what goes on internationally', p. 388.

12. Zalewski, M. and J. Parpart, *The 'Man' Question in International Relations*, Boulder, CO: Westview Press. See also Hooper, C. (2001) *Manly States: Masculinities, International Relations and Gender Politics*, New York: Columbia University Press.

13. See Carver, T., M. Cochran and J. Squires (1998) 'Gendering Jones: Feminisms, International Relations, Masculinities', *Review of International Studies*, Vol. 24, No. 2, pp. 283–98; Zalewski, M. (1999) 'Where is Woman in International Relations? "To Return as a Woman and be Heard"', *Millennium*, Vol. 27, No. 4, pp. 847–67.

14. Zalewski, M. (1999) 'Where is Woman in International Relations?'

15. Nicholson, M. (2000) 'What's the use of International Relations?', *Review of International Studies*, Vol. 26, No. 2, pp. 183–98.

16. Jørgensen, K. E., 'Continental IR Theory: The Best Kept Secret', *European Journal of International Relations*, Vol. 6, No. 1, pp. 9–42.

17. To be sure, there have been a few more articles on gender in *International Studies Quarterly (ISQ)*. These include the dialogue between Keohane, Robert O. and Marianne H. Marchand and J. Ann Tickner (1998), Vol. 42, No. 1, pp. 193–210; and Locher, Birgit and Elisabeth Prügl (2001) 'Feminism and Constructivism: Worlds Apart or Sharing the Middle Ground?', Vol. 45, No. 1, pp. 111–29. However, I would have to point out that the 'dialogue' between Keohane, Marchand and Tickner is headed up by Keohane, thereby placing him in his usual – if bizarre – position of senior and most legitimate voice on the subject of feminism and gender, and the whole dialogue is heavily influenced by non-feminist authors. Locher and Prügl's article is rather different to this – though I would venture a guess that *ISQ* would not have considered it without its connection to the latest masculinist theoretical pursuit in IR – namely, constructivism. There have also been several other surveys of the field, including Walt, S. (1998) 'International Relations: One World, Many Theories', *Foreign Policy*, Vol. 110, Spring, pp. 29–46; Katzenstein, P., R. Keohane and S. Krasner (1998) 'International Organization and the Study of World Politics', *International Organization*, Vol. 52, No. 4, Autumn, pp. 645–85; Waever, O. (1998) 'The Sociology of a Not So International Discipline: American and European Developments in International Relations', *International Organization*, Vol. 52, No. 4, Autumn, pp. 687–727.

34 · *Feminist political and theoretical practice*

18. Tessler, M., J. Nachtwey and A. Grant (1999) 'Further Tests of the Women and Peace Hypothesis: Evidence from Cross-National Survey Research in the Middle East', *International Studies Quarterly*, Vol. 43, No. 3, pp. 519–31.

19. See the dialogue about the problem with perceiving gender as a variable, between Jones, Adam and Carver, Cochran and Squires (1998) in *Review of International Studies*, Vol. 24, No. 2, pp. 283–98.

20. See Fred Halliday's early comment about 'unacceptable conclusions' [of feminist work in IR]: Halliday, F. (1988) 'Hidden from International Relations: Women and the International Relations Arena', *Millennium*, Vol. 17, No. 3, p. 423. Also Steve Smith's recent comments on the (unacceptable?) implications of feminist work: Smith, S. (2000) 'The Discipline of International Relations: Still an American Social Science?', *British Journal of Politics and International Relations*, Vol. 2, No. 3, pp. 374–402.

21. Peterson, V. S. (1992) 'Introduction', in Peterson, V. S. (ed.) *Gendered States: Feminist (Re)Visions of International Relations Theory*, Boulder, CO: Lynne Rienner, pp. 1–29, see p. 17.

22. Ibid.

23. Zalewski, M. (1999) 'Where is Woman in International Relations?'

24. See discussion in Zalewski, M. (1996), '"All These Theories Yet the Bodies Keep Piling Up": Theory, Theorists, Theorizing', in S. Smith, K. Booth and M. Zalewski (eds), *International Theory: Positivism and Beyond*, Cambridge: Cambridge University Press, pp. 340–53.

25. Enloe, C. (1999) 'What if They Gave a War ... A Conversation About Militarism, Women and the Superfluity of War', *Ms*, Vol. 9, No. 5, August/September, pp. 14–22, see p. 16.

CHAPTER 3

The Impact of the Global Women's Movement on International Relations: Has it Happened? What has Happened?

Nighat Said Khan

The editors of this book asked me to think about the impact of women's activism on international relations and politics. First of all, I was honoured to be considered an 'expert' (as the invitation described me) on feminist theory and politics. This honour was also intimidating. I have been involved in feminist activism and academic work almost all my life, but I have been propelled by both a passionate commitment that stems from a very subjective anger and an instinctive resistance to forms of oppression. I was also intimidated because, although I have been active on both fronts nationally and globally, I had not really stepped back to consider whether all that we, as feminists and women's rights activists and academics, have done has had an impact on international relations, by which I understand a 'relationship between nations'. Had there been such an impact, it would imply for me a more just and equitable world, and this has not happened yet! Nevertheless, I have enjoyed being forced to think about this issue and to relive or recall moments in my own life when there was a dynamism, an energy, as well as the excitement of social and political movements opening up new territories and spaces; of expanding people's choices; of dreaming of a new world and believing that one was close enough to touch it.

I am a product of the 1960s – a period, a struggle, a time, that was so energetic, so dynamic, so political and so consuming, that some of us have still not been able to move outside those frames – and nor do we think we should, for that energy pushed the next three decades forward, and much of what we may have achieved today is the result of it. Yet, three decades on, there is a urgent need to restate what was, to build on that statement, and to enrich the present for a more dynamic and political future. While this would be valid for all movements that sought to articulate the interests of the oppressed and the exploited, I am concerned here with the women's movement and specifically with feminism. That such a restatement is needed, is exemplified by the fact that although the women's movement is consciously celebrating itself and its achievements, as it did at the UN Beijing + 5 Conference in New York in June 2000, there is an enormous void in the movement, an emptiness, a frustration and even a despair – often articulated as exhaustion or burnout (or even boredom) by those of my generation – and of having 'arrived' or having nothing more to fight for (or the view that the struggle is not worth it) by generations younger than mine.

At the Beijing + 5 Conference, I could not help but notice the many contradictions that we grapple with on a daily basis, and which I hear articulated no matter where I go and by whomever I ask. On the one hand, the women's movement has 'made it', as it were, by being permitted entrance – albeit selectively – to the corridors of governments and the United Nations, yet I continually hear the refrain that the women's movement doesn't exist any more. At the same time, while there is supposedly a consensus document to which, in some form, women in all our countries agreed, and that we worked together to create, the North–South divide has intensified and there seems to be less understanding and sensitivity, especially on the part of white women from the North. What was also extremely tangible at the Beijing + 5 Conference was that a unipolar world as defined by the United States and Europe, and the construction and positioning of Islam as the new 'other' – a 'monolithic', 'barbaric' and 'sinister' force replacing communism as the new 'enemy' – has been internalized by the global women's movement. This has happened without questioning the fact that not only is there enormous diversity in what is called the Muslim world, but that Islamic fundamentalism, in its present form, was created by the United States and Europe for its own geopolitical imperatives – specifically, to fight the Soviet Union in Afghanistan. What was also extremely clear in New York is that the women's movement, or women's groups and networks, if we take the position that the movement does not exist any more, have accepted the more conservative position of 'reform within the system', and increasingly they are not challenging the system itself. Perhaps it is in order now to go over the past few decades and see why this may have happened, and, if we are unhappy about it, where we might go from here.

It was the women's movement in the 1960s and the early 1970s that put pressure on the United Nations to hold the first Women's Conference in Mexico in 1975. The problem then, as indeed now, was that development was not addressing women and that the 'trickle-down effect' was not working. The next decade was then declared the Decade of Women, on the assumption that development would specifically address women. The conference held in Nairobi in 1985 was to assess how the UN and individual governments had incorporated and implemented the agreements made in 1975. For women in the movement, however, Nairobi was a coming together of the movement, across borders and across divides – a coming together in an international women's movement, seeking understanding and political alliances, and identifying common struggles among ourselves. Most of us were oblivious of the UN Conference, and in any case were critiqueing not only our own nation states and their inter-relations or lack of them, but the UN itself.

Nairobi should have been a watershed for the international women's movement, but much had changed in the intervening years between 1985 and 1995: more specifically, in the name of 'mainstreaming', the movement itself was co-opted and diluted. As women, we are responsible for some of this, since we bought into the notion of 'mainstreaming' and of being a part of the new political, economic and ideological order. We were, however, also up against forces which made it impossible for a single movement to challenge the entire system, especially one that challenges the patriarchy inherent in all other movements and directly addresses oppression and exploitation in the private sphere as well. History is made by people and peoples' movements – people propel history forward by confronting the status quo. History is never made by 'collaborating' (a derogatory term at best), or by being in 'partnership' with the oppressor, or by 'lobbying'. The term and process of lobbying, incidentally, is very disturbing. It comes out of the American political system, where people get paid by interest groups to hang out in the lobbies of power in order to further their particular group's interests. It is most unfortunate that this very base aspect of the American political system has been taken on by social activists, often to the exclusion of all other forms of political activity.

In any case, it seems ironic to me that if we identify the state, global institutions (including the UN) and patriarchal forces as the oppressors, that is, if we identify them as *the* problem, we then also expect them to be the solution. The question is whether we have this critique any longer – of patriarchy, the state, or the UN, or whether we are only interested now in being included in the system. Certainly we are part of the system, as academics, as non-governmental organizations, as paid social activists, dependent on resources from these very institutions and nation states, following agendas already decided, within spaces already determined.

To illustrate how working within the system changes not only our positions but also our strategies, I will briefly state our experience in Asia of moving from what were our positions in the women's movement, to explain how these positions were transformed by the politics of nation states, of the North and the South, and by global international relations. As women of Asia and the Pacific, we met in Manila in 1993 to work out our own positions for Beijing in 1995. Given the type of development we experienced in many Asian countries, we had a strong critique of our own nation states, of the region, of global politics and the global economy, and of a unipolar world dominated by the United States. We went with this position to the inter-governmental meeting in Jakarta in 1994. The Asia-Pacific region, as defined by the UN, is not only unique but also peculiar. We have some of the poorest countries of the South, but it also includes the North, namely Japan, Australia and New Zealand, and to make matters worse from many points of view, it includes the United States and France as well, since they are still colonial powers in the region! This apart, Britain and Holland have observer status as former colonial powers and we have the Vatican, which is always omnipresent as the representative of the Catholic world. Even though we had some problems with our own governments of the Southern countries in the region, you can imagine that positions on the global economy, on global politics, on self determination, etc., were diluted considerably by the regional inclusion of Northern states. They were further diluted in the preparatory committee meeting held in New York in 1995, where an attempt was made to bring all the regional positions into a global consensus document. To a large extent, the North succeeded in asserting its political, economic and ideological hegemony. Nevertheless, the Platform for Action (PFA) agreed to in Beijing was considered to be a consensus document by the nation states, since Southern nation states have little flexibility anyway, tied as they are to international aid and international financial institutions. In any case, they could always ignore those parts of the document that they did not like!

In the women's movement in Beijing, however, there were to my mind three tendencies. There were those convinced that working within the system and being 'recognized' was positive in and of itself. Another tendency was critical at the economic and political level, but had bought into the ideological position of non-confrontation, of the neutral concept/word 'gender' as opposed to feminism, and of a liberal notion of human rights – as exemplified by the hysteria over holding the conference in China supposedly because of its lack of human rights. To me it is ironic that the very women who played a role in the Human

Rights Conference in Vienna in 1993, and who had worked on other international agreements and protocols in which the concept of human rights was redefined to include the right to food, shelter, clothing, education, health, etc., should have reverted to the older limited definition of freedom of association, expression and speech when it came to the issue of China. A third tendency, of which I was a part, was already despairing of what the reform position had led to, and argued further that if we didn't take stock of the situation and work to reverse the trend, the women's movement would be completely co-opted and depoliticized.

This co-optation and depoliticization was achieved in several ways. The more obvious was giving a certain space for some women to enter areas in which they had never previously been, to positions of perceived power and privilege. Funding of women's activities and organizations and the professionalism that is required to run bureaucracies, forced the women's movement into competing for resources, doing an enormous amount of paperwork and being anxious about sustainability. Global capitalism and the international media also played a role, especially as women in the movement internalized the notion that the only answer lay in being a part of the 'system'. A much more sinister move was the introduction of the word 'gender' and the issue of human rights.

A large number of feminists and women activists and academics began to use the word 'gender' in place of 'women' when discussing the issue of rights, equality and patriarchy. Women's equality has given way to gender equality, women's consciousness to gender consciousness, and awareness of women's issues has become gender awareness. The language of feminism has been appropriated, diffused, diluted, depoliticized and even trivialized.

The problem with the notion of 'gender' is that it can mean *both* men and women or *either* man or woman. The specificity of women's oppression disappears. The word 'gender' implies that both men and women are equally oppressed by the strict division of labour, and that emancipation for both is necessary for the society to be free. While it is true that men are also locked into strict masculine/feminine divisions, the important fact is that they are the ones who stand to gain from this division. The impression of equality or equal oppression created by this highly neutralized term obfuscates the reality that women are oppressed and subjugated by men. Men gain from patriarchy, women lose. Patriarchy cuts across class, race, region, ethnicity and religion and is universal. The notion of 'gender' denies patriarchy and, in so doing, denies structure.

By denying the structure of power, the 'neutral' word 'gender' de-politicizes women's subservience. This notion has been derived from liberal philosophy, in which all ideas have equal validity and all groups, regardless of their social position, are accorded a morally equal status. For example, in moral terms, workers cannot be equated with capitalists, since workers are *exploited* and capitalists are *exploiters* who gain from the relationship. Patriarchy is a similar structure, but the word 'gender' implies that men and women are two equal entities facing each other in a non-confrontational position. In fact, men and women stand in a relationship of mutual conflict, since their interests are not the same. In simple terms, men are not equally oppressed. In the structure of social relations, they are positioned differently from women. The women's movement, in losing its analysis of patriarchy and being enticed or convinced into using 'gender', has focused on trying to train or sensitize the oppressor, but notions of gender training and gender sensitization, much encouraged by funding agencies, fail to take into account the vastly different positions from which men and women come. Without challenging the material basis of patriarchal relations, gender sensitization and awareness will not change power relations in society. Assuming that they will is equivalent to saying that by making capitalists and workers aware of and sensitive to the exploitation involved in their relationship, they will both realize what is happening and decide to change things!

A number of feminists have increasingly begun to argue that the question of women's rights belongs under the general rubric of human rights. For the last several years, the human rights and democracy discourse has been emerging from American geopolitical and strategic interests. A version of this was packaged as the New World Order that was enthusiastically promoted in the 1990s by the American President George Bush Senior and furthered by President Clinton. Coming from a powerful and rich country which dominates the global economy and international politics, this was uncomfortably reminiscent of the nineteenth-century European discourse of 'civilizing and Christianizing the barbaric natives'. Since attempts to Christianize the world no longer seem respectable in a world which is forcing the 'great powers' to recognize diversity and multiplicity, and the avowed ideology of secularism precludes the possibility of using religion as a colonizing force, the modern superpowers have resorted to a discourse which has its origins in religious as well as liberal humanistic ethics. The new ideological strategy for dominating the world is using the rhetoric of democracy and human rights.

The human rights discourse, as produced by powerful Western states, is also designed to redefine rights, freedoms and democracy in purely economic terms. For example, it upholds the right to private ownership and to conspicuous consumption. The creation of the autonomous consumer, who should have the right to choose between different brands of products, is part of human rights rhetoric. The drive towards privatization, lowering of tariffs, and giving people the right and freedom to operate their property and business freely, as well as the right to purchase anything they like, fall within the capitalist definition of human rights.

While the point that feminists make – that every issue is a women's issue and women are entitled to *all* human rights – has enormous validity, feminists do need to re-examine the human rights discourse, since *all* the women of the world, or indeed *all* the poor, will not get even their basic rights if the rights of some are not taken away. Human rights will have to be defined on the basis of the collective and common good, even if some lose their individual rights in the process. Historically, this has usually meant the unmitigated rights of the ruling class. Feminists will also have to be mindful that although notions of human rights may be defined by the UN via some kind of consensus, in fact it is the United States and other dominant states that determine who will be punished for human rights violations. It is interesting that while we in the women's movement were inundated with negative propaganda from feminist human rights groups, mainly white feminists in the United States who were against China in 1995, we did not receive a single protest against the bombing of Kosovo. In fact, we now have information that President Clinton asked human rights groups for support, at least by their silence. They concurred, but their silence has been negatively received. Some months ago Amnesty International finally issued a statement and a report that civilian targets were part of military strategy, in an attempt to regain some of its lost credibility as an 'independent' human rights organization.

In addition, women need to be aware that the human rights discourse has subsumed women's rights. In the same way that women and feminists have disappeared in the construction of the notion of 'gender', they have also been made invisible within the constitution of human rights as an abstracted, unlocated and apolitical discourse. Just as the idea of 'gender' makes patriarchy vanish, so the idea of human rights makes male violations of women's rights vanish. Both have a negative impact on the vibrancy of the analysis and the politics of the women's movement, and both have meant the birth of the 'femocrat', regardless of whether she is in politics, government, the UN, development agencies, academia, or women's groups and NGOs. History has never been made by the bureaucracy. It cannot be made by femocrats either!

Many of these trends were already visible by the time of the World Conference in 1995. In Beijing I was asked to speak in the plenary session about Global Conservatism. I said then that I looked back on Nairobi with wonder and nostalgia – recalling a time when one could talk and struggle for socialism without being sniggered at and dream dreams without being told to be practical; when women were called women and men were called men and the institution of patriarchy was not mystified under the concept of gender; when history and, indeed, ideology had not been declared dead by a few while the majority still yearned to make history; when post-modernism had not validated every expression, every specificity, no matter how reactionary, retrogressive, immoral or amoral; when heightened individualism did not prevent people coming together into a movement; when the women's movement itself was more a spontaneous political struggle, and not a collectivity of activities and projects and action plans.

This states my position in a nutshell and my reflections on where the women's movement is today. Some of what has happened was inevitable, as the movement sought to impact on and become part of the mainstream – but in becoming that, the movement has also lost the very essence of its being and its ability to intrinsically change the structures and systems that it struggles against, and indeed its ability to determine its own future. It has also lost its ability to press for a change in international relations. These gaps notwithstanding, the Platform for Action would have been a reasonably competent first step towards a local, national and global restructuring *if* it had been implemented in spirit and in fact. What has happened, however, is a cosmetic exercise where the wording of the document has subsumed the *problematique*. Both the UN and individual nation states have used, and in many instances twisted, the language of the document to subvert the movement, and many nation states have reneged on the promises made.

What was extremely interesting in the Beijing + 5 Conference was that although many governments reported that they had moved rapidly towards the implementation of the Platform for Action, women's groups and NGOs supported this position. Indeed the NGO report was similar in content, form and language to the official positions. To give an example of how ironic and ridiculous this is, take the Pakistan NGO report. The Institute of Women's Studies, Lahore, where I work, was charged last year with being anti-state, anti-government and anti-Islam; of leading women astray; of debauchery; and of being pro-Hindu and pro-Jewish. The government said it was the most subversive organization in Pakistan and four intelligence agencies monitored our activities. Since the military government took over in October 1999, civilian and military intelligence have continued to monitor our activities. Yet the institute is mentioned in the Pakistan report as one of the successes in Pakistan, presumably as a result of the World Conference in Beijing and the subsequent government/non-government 'partnership'. (The establishment of the institute was planned long before the conference; the work had already started in 1993 and even the land for the building had been purchased before Beijing. Several times I said as much to those handling the co-ordination and the writing of the report, but they obviously wanted to credit the partnership that had developed between themselves and the government. Neither the institute nor its parent body, the ASR Resource Centre, ever joined any of the partnership structures put in place after the Beijing Conference.)

The co-optation of the women's movement by the establishment, or by the rationale of working from within, has, in Pakistan, reached what is a logical conclusion, however abhorrent it may be. Most of the women's groups have joined an illegal military regime. In 2000, 8 March was officially celebrated in Islamabad with a conference on women, at which the keynote speaker was General Pervez Musharraf. A rally and a demonstration were also organized, led by goverment ministers. Members of the Diplomatic Corps participated in these events. This makes a mockery of the women workers' strike in Chicago, and the subsequent call by Clara Zetkin (a communist!) to declare 8 March International Women's Day! The Pakistan government delegation in New York had at least four women ministers, all from the NGO sector, and representatives of an additional number of NGOs, which are now almost mandatory as a part of official delegations. Women in the NGO 'delegation' included several who had joined the government as members of advisory committees or task forces. This meant that in practice there was no difference between the two. Indeed, rather than exerting pressure on the official delegation for more radical positions, for example, on the issue of reproductive rights and the issue of sexual orientation – both of which were much contested at the conference and on which women's groups in Pakistan have well-articulated positions – the NGO 'delegation' concurred with and supported the government position. This support extended, of course, to supporting the military coup. This may be an aberration, but it is a clear case of mainstreaming or 'working from within' carried to its logical and repugnant conclusion.

To return to the UN Conference in New York: clearly, the women's movement has had an impact on the type of documents that the UN now works on and with. Although there was considerable backtracking by many countries (including those from the North) on the issue of abortion, and acrimony between women from the North and the South on the use of the word lesbianism or even sexual orientation, Northern women were also loth to raise the issues of the global economic system, or of the media and the increasing control of information and knowledge through the spread of information technology. At the same time the North had reneged on its financial commitments, except in areas such as credit schemes (which lead to income generation and a linking of women to the market); 'gender sensitization' as opposed to feminism; liberal, bourgeois human rights as defined by the North; and women who have suffered as a result of conflict situations. It is interesting that the PFA did not have a chapter entitled 'Peace', but called it 'Women in Conflict Situations'. One can only assume that war, conflict and terror are a given, and that the UN recognizes only that once conflict does occur, or war or destruction take place, women should be assisted in trying to put their lives together again.

On the larger question of whether the women's movement has impacted international relations, which I take to be the global political, economic and ideological structure, I would have to say that there is no indication that this has happened. In fact, it has perhaps gone into reverse. The movement has moved from being a movement to becoming institutionalized and part of the establishment. The antithesis has passed through a synthesis and is increasingly becoming the thesis. Women's groups are now institutions; feminists are members of the establishment; women's studies or 'gender studies' is rapidly being incorporated into the curriculum of many universities; women's lists are carried by mainstream publishers; women's issues are addressed, albeit often rhetorically, by governments, and key women are included in decision-making in state structures. If one has a dialectical understanding of history, this thesis will undoubtedly produce a new antithesis to confront it. This is already happening in some of our countries, but it will also intensify the North–South divide. If we are at all interested in a just and equitable world in which women have the same rights and privileges as men, and in which the South has the same rights and privileges as the North; if we are interested in struggling against all oppressions from the private to the global; if we want a global restructuring, we will have to reclaim global ideologies that appear to have been discarded. I refer here to marxism, socialism and feminism – reformulated in the light of the realities and imperatives of the present – but still forming the core of an ideology and of a struggle to challenge global capitalism, the supposedly 'free' market; political, social, cultural, and racial hegemony; and of course, patriarchy.

To a large extent the onus of the global movement, including a global women's movement, lies on the North, in countries such as Germany, since even a combined struggle of the South will not and cannot be successful in bringing about global change in what is called the New World Order, since this ordering is determined by a handful of countries – mainly the United States, Europe and Japan. We in the South can do our best but until the feminist movement and academics in the North also oppose the policies of their respective states and the international order, we will not see again the global women's movement that existed (without much contact between its constituent parts) in the 1960s and 1970s. I do not mean to suggest that the global women's movement must be led by the North. On the contrary, I think the movement in the North will have to be led by the South, at least in understanding, but it will need a concerted effort; feminists in the North, like privileged feminists in the South, will have to give up many of their privileges. This is a challenge, but I still believe in dreams. I cling to mine, for as Langston Hughes, an African-American poet, said: 'hold fast to dreams, for when dreams die, life is but a broken-winged bird that cannot fly'.

CHAPTER 4

Accommodation or Transformation? Women's Movements and International Relations: Some Remarks on Marysia Zalewski's and Nighat Said Khan's Contributions

Christa Wichterich

The recent Beijing + 5 Conference in New York can be considered the latest stop on the journey of the women's movements from the UN's margins to the centre of international negotiations, which has lasted for 25 years so far. On the road from the first World Women's Conference in Mexico in 1975, to New York in 2000, international women's movements changed a lot: their relationship to institutionalized politics underwent a substantial transformation, and political institutions changed as well, opening up and becoming much more flexible.

Looking at the document that was negotiated in New York, at the 188 government delegations and at UN agencies, one could lean back with the comfortable feeling that women's non-governmental organizations (NGOs) and transnational networks had finally made it, that they had finally reached centre stage: their issues and terminology had clearly found their way into policy documents ('semantic revolution'), and various NGO representatives had arrived as members of government delegations or as employees and consultants of UN agencies.

Is the circle of exclusion therefore broken? Have women's movements accomplished what they aimed for in their political struggle? Definitely, the outstanding achievement of international women's movements over the past 25 years is that they have managed to set the international agenda and have brought their issues and experiences, their problems and envisaged solutions, into institutionalized politics. The most substantial benchmarks of women's inclusion and the recognition of their values are:

1. To have overcome the public–private dichotomy and the exclusion of the private sphere from politics;
2. The recognition of violence against women as a structural and systemic principle of gender regimes;
3. To have embedded women's needs, gender justice and gender equality in a human rights / women's rights framework.

A greater approximation and compliance between institutionalized politics and women's movements has been achieved in terms of topics and objectives. In practice, co-operation is increasing. NGOs have been turned into implementing agencies for government programmes and / or projects of UN agencies. As a result of this integration process, two developments in New York could be observed:

1. During the first 20 years of the women's movements' conference journey, from Mexico (1975) to Beijing (1995), the movements and NGOs put their issues and demands forward and pressurized governments and the UN. In New York, this role of agenda setting was taken away from them: the debates were driven more by political institutions, especially UN bodies, than by NGOs.
2. Three focal issues dominated the debates in New York. The United Nations Development Programme (UNDP) or the United Nations Development Fund for Women (UNIFEM) were the leading agencies in all main events and panel discussions on:

- political participation / access to decision-making;
- engendering macroeconomics (+ micro-credit as a poverty reduction strategy); and
- women in peacebuilding.

The debate in all these areas was based on a combination of a human rights / women's rights concept and an efficiency approach. The World Bank presented the findings of a study conducted in more than 100 countries, showing that countries that reduce gender gaps in education, employment and property rights tend to have 'cleaner' governments, less corruption and faster growth. Often, in all three debates, the discussions boiled down to the essentialist assumption that women *per se*, that is, per sex, are less corrupt, 'cleaner', more peaceful, socially more responsible, more geared towards sustainable development and more efficient in fighting poverty etc.. The main conclusion was that the female social character should be mobilized as an 'anti-corruption weapon', a 'poverty-reduction catalyst' and a last resource in peacebuilding efforts. This discursive pattern points to the ambivalence of women's integration into international politics: on the one hand there is a potential for their empowerment, on the other hand there is the risk of them being exploited because of their 'inherent characteristics'.

Nighat Khan would call this co-optation, and regard it as the price paid for women's inclusion. As much as she did, I missed the autonomous positioning of women's organizations *vis-à-vis* governments and UN positions, and subversive and visionary thinking on behalf of women's organizations, and I would agree that the transnational women's movement represented in New York is a tamed and structurally adjusted agent of civil society. However, I do not believe the crucial question is whether women are now integrated into the system or not. It is rather the question of what feminists have accomplished: accommodation or transformation? Where do they end up on a scale between affirmation and transformation? Didn't women's movements aim at more than just inclusion and participation?

Does integration render the safeguarding of autonomous positions impossible? Every integration requires adjustment to the rules of the game, to the contents, concepts and the language used to a certain extent. How much space is opened up for acknowledging and absorbing criticism, for the modernization of content and language, depends on power and political interests.

Fully aware of these threats, the Southern network Development Alternatives with Women for a New Era (DAWN) strategically linked integration and transformation in Beijing. The network labelled this approach 'transformation through participation'. For this purpose, the magic formula of a 'critical mass' is used: if women make up more than 30 per cent in an institution, a programme, etc., it appears difficult to co-opt them, and collectively they can develop their strength or counter-power to undermine existing structures and discourses.

Feminist movements have developed their dynamics through the dialectics of theory and practice. They wanted to overcome the division between the two, and link women's everyday experiences with cognition, and practical projects with political actions. This was the starting point for feminist political and academic intervention.

In the 1990s, feminists intensified their efforts to intervene in international politics, as well as in the discipline of International Relations (IR). They increasingly referred to the human rights/women's rights concept as an analytical, normative and strategic framework. This concept became both a tool and a topic. Women's needs and demands were legitimized by and embedded in, supranational and suprastatal human rights claims. The reference to women's human rights as globalized standards served to include gender issues in international politics and to bring about the recognition of women's NGOs and networks as political agents.

If we analyse the strategic steps taken for policy and academic intervention, following Jacques Derrida, three logical steps can be distinguished:

1. A criticism *vis-à-vis* the exclusion of women and a feminist approach and perspective, in macroeconomics referred to as 'conceptual silence' (Isabella Baker), on the part of the discipline with regard to women.
2. The deconstruction of power regimes and of gendered hegemonic systems, in order to unmask and expose their underlying male bias. Tracing the hidden gender governance within global governance; women's rights violations within the human rights framework; the hidden sexual contract in international contracts; gender injustice in social justice systems, gender violence in armed conflicts; women's insecurity in international security, etc. led to the demystification of politics and academia.
3. The reconstruction of knowledge and political systems through the systematic and coherent inclusion of the missing links, through redefining human rights, rendering visible a feminist perspective on sustaining and caring, justice, security, livelihood, development and peace. In this process, feminists seized the power to redefine issues in politics and academia and generated discursive power *vis-à-vis* the mainstream discourse.

This last step goes further than the liberal women's movement's approach of 'bringing women into the discipline', ridiculed by Sandra Harding as 'Just add women and stir'. The discursive reconstruction outlined above implies the transformation of politics and of the academic discipline. Women's organizations have stressed often enough that they do not want merely a bigger piece of a poisoned cake (Devaki Jain), or to be mainstreamed in a polluted stream (Bella Abzug).

Assessing the effect of feminist intrusion on politics and on the academic discipline is like comparing apples and pears. The arena of international politics includes UN policies, development policies, international macroeconomic policies, environmental policies, peace policies, human rights policies and foreign policies. That is to say, hard and soft political topics and territories. The academic discipline of International Relations, on the other hand, has a much more narrowly confined spectrum of topics, the core being peace, security and power, covering the hard and high territory of foreign policies. In the recent past, women's organizations experienced quite a difference in terms of impact and inclusion in low/

soft politics and academic disciplines (for example, in linguistics and cultural studies), as against high/hard politics and corresponding academic disciplines (for example, natural sciences, economics and IR).

The strategy of mainstreaming was designed in order to integrate gender issues and women's concerns systematically into all fields of politics and disciplines. However, it is evident that the higher/harder the policy area/academic discipline is, the greater is the risk of 'evaporation' (Sara Longwe), of marginalization or subordination of women's and gender issues, and a systemic transformation is less likely to emerge.

Inclusion of women's NGOs in negotiations at UN conferences is still not guaranteed. Their participation is not institutionalized, but decided anew for each conference and each political process. It is a power play, pointing to the question of how critical and radical NGOs are allowed to be if they want to participate. This power play has developed into a state-civic tango: sometimes closer, then more distant: the degree of NGOs' participation depends on the goodwill and benevolence of governments. Undoubtedly, democratically shared decision-making and sovereignty is not yet accepted by governments.

With regard to the discipline of IR, I would like to add a few remarks on the German situation. In Germany, a point of 'exhausted conversation' – as Marysia Zalewski called it earlier – has not yet been reached. We are still waiting for a real conversation between the mainstream and the feminist communities to take place. For reasons of political correctness, a few male scholars pay lip-service to feminist approaches and acknowledge that feminist concepts exist. The majority of scholars representing the hegemonic discourse never read more than two pages of what feminist scholars have written. I agree with Marysia Zalewski that feminist thinking has the potential to upset the discipline and it should do so. This goes hand in hand with my demand for a transformative perspective. So far, however, feminist thinking has neither upset the hegemonic discourse nor destabilized it. Unfortunately not. We remain very much at the stage of challenging the established and institutionalized mainstream from outside, rather than communicating on equal terms.

We took women's movements as a starting point of our analysis of inclusion and persisting exclusion. In the recent past, as Khan pointed out, women's movements all over the world have weakened, faded away, and fragmented to a large extent into the politics of identities and differences. Simultaneously, NGOs and individual experts have turned into 'feminist professionals', with the result that interventions in international politics and IR happen far less frequently and are no longer driven by the dynamics of a social movement. Does this make a difference? Are these interventions still based on the mission and passion of feminist agency or collective feminist identities? Has the division between theory and practice (at least partly) been restored? To provide a way of assessing this, I would like to suggest a few indicators that I use in my work as a consultant when evaluating women's empowerment.

1. To what extent have feminist approaches, interventions, and the respective NGOs and movements in international politics and International Relations gained *recognition, rights* and *resources*?
2. Have feminist concepts gained a *voice* and some *space* (in terms of some legitimized place) in institutionalized politics and in the academic discipline, and some *choice* in terms of power to make decisions, to shape alternatives and to control the discourse?
3. What has happened: just integration due to specific entry points and *accommodation*? To what extent has some *transformation* and restructuring of institutions, knowledge and power systems begun?

For the time being, I hope that the challenge that feminist agency and feminist thinking have presented to politics and academic disciplines is subversive work in progress which will lead to an upsetting and reconstruction of political as well as academic power and knowledge systems.

PART II

*Developing the Mainstream
or Mainstreaming Women into
Development?*

CHAPTER 5

Mainstreaming Gender – a Critical Revision

Claudia von Braunmühl

The following reflections are based on a consultant's experience seasoned with inspirations from academia. Much of what they convey is unlikely to be entirely new to those active in the field of development or researching in it, or, for that matter, to those familiar with issues discussed in the women's movements. The particular connection attempted here between these two contexts may, it is hoped, offer some insights of value to both.

From gender blindness to Women in Development (WID)

When in the early 1960s development policy in terms of North–South transfers and the establishment of agencies designed to dispense development funds began to make its appearance in international politics, one articulated and one unspoken assumption were at work. The articulated assumption spoke, for example, with the scholarly authority of W. W. Rostow about 'stages of development', referring to an ubiquitous technology and industry-driven model of modernization which the more developed nation states had established and which the underdeveloped nations would catch up to in time, with the benefits eventually trickling down from the privileged to the rest of the population (Rostow 1960). The unspoken assumption concerned an (idealized) Western type of household organization, with a male head of household who would manage whatever wealth reached his house equitably for the benefit of wife and children, and a housewife who, apart from attending to her homely duties, might support her husband in his income-generating activities but pursued none herself.

At the end of the first development decade, the 'Commission for International Development' (1969), which had been assigned by the World Bank to review the decade's performance, found a troubling combination of economic growth and increasing poverty. Thus, from the start, the second development decade had to face critical questions regarding the trickle-down assumption, and issues of redistribution and socio-political targeting were placed on the international agenda. Development policy saw itself as part of an international reform effort.

It was at that time that the women's movement in the North started to confront governments and bureaucracies commanding resources with demands for improved representation of women in their ranks and more gender-equitable allocation of funds. These claims encountered considerable resistance, and inevitably their justification was challenged (Rogers 1991). In all societal fields, women researchers set out to collect evidence as to the very existence of women, their relevance and the consequences of overlooking them. In the area of development, ground-breaking work was done by Ester Boserup (Boserup 1970). Gloria Scott, the first WID officer appointed by the World Bank, coined the phrase 'the invisible women' to describe those who would have to be brought on to the scene (Scott 1979). Major segments of the women's movement grew out of the leftist student movements, and much of the writing of the women's movement was part of a critique of capitalism. Correspondingly, great pains were taken to highlight the contribution of women to the reproduction of society, and their unbalanced share of the benefits.

In the ensuing debate with development agencies, the main arguments mobilized to substantiate the claims made were:

- Women do not have equitable access to the resources and benefits of development and aid (equity).
- Development projects and programmes overlook women, to the detriment of the effective impact they seek (efficiency).
- Aid agencies have to recognize and overcome the inbuilt mechanisms constituting gender blindness.

In short, women were claiming their share of a modernization cake – unquestioned as such – by seeking integration into development.

When in due course, but mostly with undue delay, development agencies institutionalized recognition of and attention to women, they did so in the form of Women in Development or WID desks. In their early days, WID desks were perceived and defined themselves as 'advocacy administration' fighting for a redistributive policy that would redress the systematic disadvantages under which women suffered (Staudt 1985). Within development agencies, equity and efficiency merged into the policy of 'Integration of Women in Development'. WID policies centred on women's labour power, whether by seeking to reduce the burden of work unquestioningly placed on them, or by increasing the productivity of women's work. Usually this would take the form of adding women's components to existing projects or projects and programmes specifically addressing women. In Germany a WID machinery and WID policies emerged with some delay, only in the early 1980s. The coincidence in time with the first phases of neoliberal structural adjustment programmes imposed on indebted countries never really allowed WID policies to operate in an emancipatory framework.

WID policies did contribute to the recognition of the scale and significance of women's work. The categorization into productive, reproductive and community work introduced by C. Moser and L. Peake was soon common currency in aid agencies (Moser and Peake 1987). Also, rather than just studying the situation of women in isolation, researchers increasingly drew attention to the division of labour between men and women. Within the United Nations system, efforts began to challenge the construction of national statistics with their systematic failure to record the role women play in the production of national wealth.

At the same time, WID policies soon came under heavy criticism from within the women's movements. While the critique is certainly valid, it is crucial not to forget that every step of the process leading to WID policies entailed an inordinate amount of struggle on the part of committed women activists and professionals, and encountered an inordinate amount of resistance and outright slander on the part of men. For instance, those questioning the superimposition of idealized Western family models on developing societies time and again found themselves faced with the accusation of 'taking Western feminism to African huts'. We should not fail to acknowledge the work of those vanguard women who undertook to open hitherto firmly closed doors, even when the shortcomings of their positions have subsequently been exposed to justified critique. The main points of the critique are:

- WID defines women in terms of deficits, using a male norm as backdrop and yardstick.
- Women in the developing world are constructed as a homogeneous mass with few, if any, relevant differences among them.
- The conceptualization of women's interest in a more balanced gender order as a women's issue systematically obscures the role of men and absolves them from any responsibility.
- The term 'Integration of Women in Development' suggests that gender imbalances are due to women remaining outside of a basically positive development process, while in fact women are already inside this process, albeit in a specifically constructed way which means that they derive all too few benefits.

- Experience with the predominant type of projects designed to improve the situation of women, income-generating projects, shows that they created little income and much work and rarely affected women's subordinated status.

In sum, the most decisive barrier to equitable and just development, which is the structural oppression and subordination of women underlying the various social articulations of disadvantage, is not addressed by the WID approach. Nor is the question of whether prevailing development strategies actually aim at social and human development. Feminist epistemological critique went on to analyse the social construction of gender. The dominant development paradigm and its strategies came under attack from different quarters, influenced by considerations of social justice and/or ecological sustainability. Over time and under the impact of the social devastation brought about by structural adjustment, these initially different schools of thought feeding into the critique of WID merged into a fundamental questioning of the model and the strategy of modernization and development.

From WID to GAD

At the closing conference of the UN Decade of Women (1976–85) in Nairobi, the network Development Alternatives with Women for a New Era (DAWN) from the South introduced the concept of empowerment into the debate. 'Empowerment' gave expression to a different perspective regarding women's relationship to power, for it focused on its creative and constructive aspects (power to) rather than its oppressive one (power over). In addition, DAWN refused to get involved in endless and painful conceptual debates as an indispensable prerequisite for movement strength. With the formula 'unity in diversity', DAWN opened up the possibility of acknowledging diversity as a source of strength, and forming coalitions on specific issues irrespective of different backgrounds and political-theoretical frameworks (Sen, Grown 1987).

Empowerment offered a vision of individual autonomy at the same time as it challenged the given set of societal gender regimes and called for their fundamental transformation. The use of the category gender expressed a radical critique of the power-structured relationship between men and women and its various socially institutionalized forms. Development policy was now challenged, not only to support women in their ascribed roles and functions, but also to design programmes and projects with the core objective of women's empowerment in mind.

Coming from a background of social movements, and with the experience of neoliberal adjustment policies already well under way, DAWN's vision fully embraced the critique of the predominant development paradigm and outlined the parameters of a more just world order.

NGOs all over the world eagerly adopted the new approach. Gradually, via their WID desks, all the major development agencies followed suit. Empowerment grew to be the central reference point of development interventions designed to improve the situation of women. Gender analysis replaced the analysis of the situation of women. While most NGOs, particularly those originating in social movements, subscribed to the underlying challenge to what soon came to be widely discussed as corporate-driven globalization, multinational and bilateral aid agencies undertook some organizational reshaping and some rhetorical exercises, at the end of which, not surprisingly, little of the liberating vision remained intact.

The integration of gender into the development debate brought about significant shifts. The term 'women's issues' was replaced by 'gender issues'. What used to be seen as women's concerns were now framed as gender disparities and gender concerns, thus opening up space for the analysis of the social construction of gender and, by implication, creating a larger arena for responsibility and accountability. Development agencies renamed their WID desks as GAD (Gender and Development) desks and moved from gender analysis, undertaken with the objective of designing interventions in support of women, to the gender approach, which was to address men as well as women. The gender approach promised a much broader grasp of social reality and – again pushed forward by committed women professionals within aid agencies – began to lay claim to the revision of departmentalized WID/GAD policies as well as to the continuation of gender-blind development interventions.

With GAD to gender mainstreaming

The renamed, though rarely upgraded, GAD desks were now mandated to initiate and monitor the integration of the gender approach into the agencies' overall policy framework and implementation mechanisms. Basic policy statements, now including gender mandates, were articulated, encouragingly ambitious guidelines formulated, sector checklists and handouts elaborated. Studies of socio-cultural gender patterns, documented best practices and contracted gender advisers were to assist staff and management with the adoption and application of the new approach. The main vehicle for the institutionalization of the gender approach was gender training, with each agency developing its own gender training manual specific to its policies and processes. Most of the resulting documents make empowerment their focal point, and in doing so rely heavily on a set of definitions and instruments developed within the context of, or influenced by, feminist debates. Most influential was Caroline Moser's attempt to provide a coherent gender planning tool that would suit the mechanisms and procedures of major aid agencies (Moser 1993).

Moser in turn built on Maxine Molyneux's groundbreaking work on women's politics in the context of the Sandinista revolution in Nicaragua (Molyneux 1985). When Molyneux, a hopeful and keen observer of Sandinista politics, was investigating the impact of the revolution on women, she found the term 'women's interest' inadequate and misleading in that it tended to reduce the subjectivity of women to biologically defined social roles, and by implication overlooked gender effects in the definition of women's interest, including definitions put forward by women themselves. Molyneux proposed the term 'gender interests'. 'Gender interests are those that women (or men, for that matter) may develop by virtue of their social positioning through gender attributes' (Molyneux 1985: 232).

Molyneux differentiates between practical and strategic gender interests. Practical gender interests are articulated in immediate response to perceived needs and wants as they present themselves in given social orders and gender regimes. The definition of strategic gender interests is derived from an analysis of women's structural subordination. While the satisfaction of practical gender needs may be rewarding, it does not question or challenge underlying social and gender disparities. They may, however, acquire a strategic dimension when the process of meeting them is successfully politicized, the factors constituting recurrent deficits are explored, and the response is given a challenging transformative orientation. Strategic interests are highly contextualized; they cannot be pre-formulated, but are rather the product of explicit political will and subsequent struggle.

Molyneux's concept has since been criticized on various grounds and it has been built upon with different outcomes. Neither aspect is of immediate interest here. What is of interest is the fact that, and the way in which, Moser took the categories provided by Molyneux and built them into her concept of gender planning.

Before we continue to follow these categories on their way into the machineries and mechanisms of aid agencies, it is important to reflect on the dual nature of the gender category. It may be used as technical differentiation of ascribed roles and functions. This is exactly what happened in most major funding agencies under the notion of 'gender disaggregation', which grew to be the core imperative of the gender approach. However, gender may retain its inherently critical connotation and challenge unbalanced gender orders and gender regimes entailing subordination and repression, which is how it was conceptualized and coined within the women's movements, against the backdrop of a transformative vision of a less unjust gender order. The two readings, of course, correspond to the twin categories of practical and strategic interests, and the debate about the relationship between these two aspects has constantly accompanied the implementation of the gender approach.

In Moser's attempt to design an instrument which could fully and more or less smoothly integrate gender issues into the planning of mainstream development interventions, the notion of interest was replaced by that of needs, a familiar term in planning methodology. Attending to 'practical gender needs' and 'strategic gender needs' has since been adopted in the standard repertoire of all GAD desks. Following Molyneux's dialectic, Moser's notion of gender planning 'utilizes practical gender needs as the basis on which to build a secure support base, and a means through which strategic needs may be reached' (Moser 1993: 77). Using the concept in this way, Moser does not lose sight of the political concern of empowerment. In fact: 'The purpose of gender planning then is to provide the means by which to operationalize this political concern, and to ensure that it becomes institutionalized practice' (Moser 1993: 87).

Moser uses a concept of planning developed in the 1970s by social movements addressing urban issues, which happens to be her professional field, namely, 'planning as debate'. To her, the essence of gender planning lies in 'a process of negotiated debate about the redistribution of power and resources within the household, civil society and the state' (Moser 1993: 190). She transfers the empowerment concept as developed by DAWN into this setting. She also refers to the rating that DAWN proposed in regard to the emancipatory potential of various types of women's organizations. However, she does not integrate a social actor of transformation into her concept of gender planning. By implication, the immediate articulation of interests in debate and direct interaction is replaced by given mechanisms of representation in programme and project planning. The definition of needs, and of the ways and means of meeting them, is placed in the hands of the political directorate, the technical management, or the expertise of development planners, with grassroots participation occurring only occasionally, and usually at a late stage of design definition.

It could indeed be argued that transformative potential and agency lies in the very process of gender disaggregation. If correctly executed, it will unfold its own dynamic and point to transformation as the only way of overcoming constraints placed on the satisfaction of practical needs. Moser puts great trust in the integrity of institutional actors, but also de-links institutions from their political and socio-cultural context. Her arena for meaningful debate finds its location within the development agencies themselves, whereas the social actor of empowerment remains firmly outside the process. In other words, it declares institutions to be the actor of transformation.

Gender mainstreaming – concept and constraints

By the time of the Fourth World Women's Conference in Beijing, organized by the United Nations, all major development agencies had provided themselves with far-reaching definitions of gender mainstreaming, and professed to aim for agenda-setting and for impact on projects and programmes, including macroeconomic decision-making levels. In implementation terms, gender mainstreaming is defined as a two-pronged strategy. On the one hand, gender issues are to be identified and taken into account at all levels of development action. On the other hand, women-specific projects should continue to overcome the barriers and constraints pertaining particularly to women, which have been brought to the fore through gender analysis.

In contrast to these grand statements and on an operational level, the initiative for either strategy was left with the minuscule GAD units, which in turn were increasingly refocused on poverty alleviation. They sought to produce the range of documents required to actually integrate gender concerns into mainstream planning and implementation. They lobbied incessantly wherever internal lobbying was required, and that was almost everywhere; their particular concern lay with sector guidelines and central steering instruments, such as logical framework and project cycle management or instruments of quality control. They organized gender training, which usually remained optional, and tried to nudge reluctant staff into actual participation. The aid agency became their immediate and nearly exclusive terrain of action. Over time, the various tools and instruments reached a state of considerable refinement. They were complemented by a computer-supported indicator system developed by the Organisation for Economic Co-operation and Development, Development and Assistance WID Committee.

While the aims and objectives of the gender approach were systematically woven into the rhetoric of the existent planning and monitoring tools of development agencies, the small WID/GAD units found themselves going through the painful experience of an ever expanding rift between verbal reference and actual accommodation of their concerns. The 1990s saw a fair amount of academic reflection on that experience (Jahan 1995; Kabeer 1994; Macdonald 1994; Staudt 1997; Goetz 1995, 1997; Longwe 1997). The analysis focuses on two major constraints:

1. the direction of the mainstream, the effects of neoliberal structural adjustment and corporate-led globalization and their impact on gender relations;
2. the patriarchal structure of development institutions and bureaucracies as a major obstacle to gender mainstreaming.

Gender effects of macroeconomic policies Ever since the mid-1980s, attention has been drawn to the extent to which neoliberal policies entail systematic redistribution from bottom to top and a reckless plundering and destruction of limited natural resources. In the process, they contribute massively to impoverishing ever-larger segments of the population, in which women are markedly over-represented. While jobs and sources of a decent income become increasingly scarce commodities, the cost of living rises. Following the neoliberal creed of lean government and the benign effects of a private sector largely unencumbered by social or environmental considerations, or, for that matter, by discouragingly high taxes, governments withdraw dramatically from the provision of basic services. These have been shifted more and more into private households, where prevalent gender arrangements pile them on the shoulders of women. The phenomenon has been dubbed 'feminization of poverty' or 'feminization of responsibility'. In more economic terms, the flexibility of women's labour is thought of as an exploitable resource which has a long way to go before reaching its limits, and it is integrally built into the mechanisms of neoliberal policies. While the safety net of women's additional and excess labour is an indispensable component of present-day management of globalization, it is not reflected in national statistics; women are pushed back into invisibility (Elson 1991, Palmer 1994, Bakker 1994, Sassen 1996, Wichterich 2000).

Within this system, with its increasingly accentuated polarization of rich and poor, the relationship between economic and social/human development has ceased to be theorized. Neoliberal policies offer virtually no entry point for the needs, values and rights of women. The feminist proposal to integrate the economic and the political in a coherent concept with systematic links between macro-, meso- and micro-levels continues to be ignored. An opportunity structure for the unfolding of meaningful empowerment strategies does not exist. Empowerment is married to poverty alleviation – which has become the operative goal of GAD desks – and is entirely dissociated from growth strategies. Just as with the decline of the social infrastructure, where the poor are increasingly called upon to contribute to the limited basic amenities and social services available to them, women are pushed into a marginalized sphere where they struggle for survival, at best provided with micro-credits on market terms. Empowerment is redefined as the capacity to survive under the most inclement conditions.

Where the gender approach is properly applied and a thorough gender analysis is undertaken, more often than not the findings will point to gender imbalances disadvantaging women. GAD desks have found it virtually impossible to integrate these results into the mainstream of projects or programmes. Irrespective of the professed dual strategy of the gender approach, proactive action or additional programme activities designed to counteract constraints specific to women are usually perceived as causing additional costs in time and money, thereby falling outside the market logic of cost efficiency and of a concept of sustainability defined solely in financial terms. The chances of agenda-setting, of influencing the overall approach of a project or programme and of causing a redesign of structure and resource allocation are even more minimal.

Gender effects of bureaucracy Promising a dramatically new policy thrust, the integration of gender mandates into the basic policy statements of development agencies gave rise to great optimism. What remained to be done was to create organizational rather than GAD desk ownership of the gender mandate, and to firmly institutionalize the gender approach into the structure and culture of development organizations. The core issue at stake was how to integrate gender justice into the objectives, the mechanisms and procedures, the professionalism and the professional ethics of development agencies, so that gender issues would not become fragmented, instrumentalized or only rhetorically invoked – for this would reduce them to the status of marginal concerns, assigned to a 'women's corner' that carries little esteem and career potential. Using the insights of organizational sociology, administration theory, and state theory and its feminist critique, the process has been closely observed and analysed by feminist academics (Jahan 1995; Staudt 1997, 1998; Goetz 1995, 1997; Razavi and Miller 1995a, 1995b; von Braunmühl 1997, 1998).

As has been demonstrated, gender mandates cannot escape the

macroeconomic and macropolitical context into which they are integrated. In fact they are not supposed to – that is the very essence of mainstreaming. Effective agenda-setting and impacting on the course and direction of the mainstream has proven to be far beyond the power reach of those holding a stake in rebalancing the gender order. Furthermore, development agencies document the fulfilment of their policy mandates in quantitative terms, most prominently in the flow of funds. Redressing gender imbalances is a slow process. It tends to be allocated negligible resources, and often impact indicators have yet to be found and agreed on. In short, many conference speeches notwithstanding, management finds that actually living up to the gender mandate is an uninviting proposition that generates uncomfortable situations and offers all too few rewards. Not surprisingly, the operative maxim seems to have become 'add women and do NOT stir'.

A review of WID/GAD literature and inner-agency documents, and, surprisingly enough, of earlier writings by the feminist development community, reveals the somewhat astonishing assumption that the translation of the gender approach into agency action – including its transformative dimension – depends primarily on sufficiently convincing arguments being advanced in as non-confrontational and persuasive a fashion as possible. Feminist theory of the state and of bureaucracy has highlighted the patriarchal structuring of institutions. Organizations embody societal options, norms and practices that determine and express themselves in hierarchies, in chances of participation and decision-making. The fact that men are by and large liberated from reproductive work secures them a decisive participation advantage in institutions; this intertwines with the privileges in the private sphere as well as on the household level and reinforces them. The dynamics of decision-making and the mode of operation are deeply entrenched with and shaped by the patriarchal gender order, and mould prevalent norms, criteria for bestowing legitimacy, procedural requirements, career patterns, achievement criteria, expectations and informal cultural mores. This holds true for governmental as well as for non-governmental organizations. Some graphic research publication titles capture this effect forcefully. Jahan speaks of 'The Elusive Agenda' (Jahan 1995) and Longwe sarcastically portrays 'The evaporation of gender in the patriarchal cooking pot' (Longwe 1997). In recent years some hope has been invested in organizational development as a vehicle to directly aim at or to indirectly bring about gender-relevant change. However, time and again it has been found that committed and sustained advocacy is required, far beyond the clout and the possibilities of the small GAD units, in order to ensure the full application of gender instruments and, in the last instance, to redress gender imbalances in and through the complex and persistent system of patriarchal bureaucracies.

Patriarchal structures manifest themselves in a corresponding organizational culture. A male world-view is predominant; feminists have frequently mocked the mainstream as malestream. If at all acknowledged, gender disparities and imbalances are diagnosed only at a safe geographical distance and declared to be part of an unshakable and sacrosanct patrimony. Analysis of the intra-household allocation of power and resources remains rare, and agencies are at a loss about how to act upon the findings.

Gender training is supposed not only to equip those receiving it with suitable skills, but also to change attitudes and foster motivations for innovative action. All too frequently, however, gender issues are narrowed down again to women's issues and gender training participants are familiarized only with technical gender disaggregation methods, rather than with the critical content of the concept of gender. Subsequent action may result in activities designed to support and assist women in assigned roles, but it rarely addresses underlying gender relations. Training courses are optional and compete with others deemed much more relevant for career promotion, such as planning techniques, financial management or sector issues. Training programmes may open up genuinely novel perspectives for the male staff exposed to them, but their budgets never allow for the required thorough follow-up. Unlike other innovations, for example, introducing structural adjustment perspectives or logical framework skills, gender mainstreaming activities do not entail the provision of help desk functions. In short, the mainstreaming of the gender approach in terms of its institutionalization in the structures, procedures and the professional self-image and standards of organizations is for the time being an unattainable target.

In the transition from WID to GAD to gender mainstreaming, WID/GAD units lost their advocacy role. Their mandates and functions shifted from intra-institutional advocacy on behalf of and interacting with women, to bureaucratic engines assigned to drive a particular inner-agency innovation – the gender approach. The loss of the advocacy element and the importance of internal agency credibility and acceptability has increasingly placed a bonus on men as desk officers in GAD units, or on attaching a GAD mandate to the portfolio of male staff. While the GAD units are actually expected to perform the function of a task force, they continue to be seriously under-resourced. Research on the implementation of the gender approach unanimously comes to the conclusion that 20 years of gender mainstreaming have not brought gender concerns any closer to centre stage. A bureaucracy manifesting 'continuing indifference, ambivalence and active resistance' (Moser 1993: 180) has survived the onslaught of the gender approach unperturbed. Development policies have found the integration of women's empowerment into poverty alleviation strategies – firmly de-linked from neoliberal growth strategies – rather useful.

Gender mainstreaming and the social actor of transformation

Over time, WID and GAD practitioners and researchers have voiced fundamental criticisms regarding the gender approach and the efforts of gender mainstreaming in development agencies. The systemic and systematic constraints have been meticulously exposed, and time and again it has been argued that in practical terms mainstreaming is all about accessing as yet untapped resources of women's labour, pulling women into a context that is anything but benign to them, and modernizing gender inequalities.

No doubt all of this is sadly true. At the same time there are very few women professionals engaged in the field of development and women's organization who would want to forgo once and for all an opportunity to influence institutional policies on whatever level and to claim a share in the resources they command – one resource being access to crucial areas of social reality. Therefore, it remains entirely justifiable, and indeed absolutely necessary, to confront development institutions with the expectation of gender-just outcomes and with the installation of process mechanisms likely to produce such results.

By the same token, in recent years women engaged in action and research in the development community of the global North have found themselves caught in incessant struggles to overcome the resistance of bureaucratic structures and to challenge the hegemony of male-biased macropolitics. While they were refining their claims, they inadvertently placed their focus more and more on changes within the funding agencies and their administrations. There is a danger that one of the crucial experiences of early WID and GAD will be forgotten: without strong pressure on the part of the women's movement, the debate on women in development and on the relevance of gender relations in development policy would never have started in the first place. It was the continuing thematizing, organizing and networking propelled by the series of UN conferences that kept the issue in the limelight and the pressure on. The intense debate on gender mainstreaming is about to entrust empowerment-oriented agency primarily if not exclusively into the hands of development organizations, and to lose sight of the social actor of transformation – the women themselves and their organizations.

However, one of the early lessons learnt by the independent women's movements worldwide was that neither autonomy nor empowerment can be granted. Gaining control over their lives, deciding on which type of gender relations women want to live in, designing strategies and building alliances to get there: the realization of these aims may well be assisted by resources that would otherwise be unavailable, but it has to be wanted and enacted by the women themselves. The transformation of practical into strategic interests in turn requires discursive space, where the immediate experience of constraints and wants can be thematized by debating and politicizing the gender imbalances and injustices that manifest themselves in perceived deficits.

Therefore, if we accept that the desire for empowerment is grounded in individual experience, that it grows and is nurtured in exchange and reasoning on that experience (making sense of experience), and that it requires organizations, if we also come to recognize the systemic limits of 'entrist' strategies (Bangura 1997), it will be useful to explore the relationship between women's organizations and development institutions. The nature of their interaction, and the fate of the women's agenda in that interaction, may take us further in the quest for a strategy of transformation.

The debate on 'engendering democracy' in Latin America

In Latin America, the interaction of development and/or government agencies with the social actor of transformation of the given gender order, the organizations of the women's movements, has been reflected upon with particular depth and debated with great lucidity. This is closely related to the substantial investments women's organizations made in the democratization processes, in a range of Latin American countries. In the early phases of the democratization process most women's organizations nurtured great hopes that the democratic opening would provide an opportunity structure for effective gender mainstreaming on the macropolitical level. 'Engendering democracy' (Alvarez 1990) appeared to be both a viable prospect and a feasible strategy.

Over time, high expectations were somewhat moderated and the assessment of the gender transformation potential of democratization processes grew to be more differentiated. Critical and sceptical voices became more audible. The – not undisputed – desire of many women's groups and women's organizations to pursue empowerment strategies in collaboration and interaction with the newly constituted democratic governance structures led to a 'feminist NGO boom' (Alvarez 1999), but also produced disappointing and worrying results. There was growing concern about being led and/or imperceptibly moving away from genuinely feminist aims and objectives.

In contrast to much of the gender mainstreaming discussion revolving around the integration of the gender approach into development interventions, in Latin America the resulting critique and self-critique did not focus strongly on organizational sociology aspects. The different sets of parameters and horizons of legitimacy at work in bureaucratic institutions and in social movements, the highly dissimilar rhythms of bureaucratically mediated interventions and of movement action aiming at empowerment, were barely touched upon. From the outset, the focus of the analysis was on the formal and informal political agendas of either side, particularly, of course, on the fate of women's agendas as they interface with intervening governmental and/or developing agencies and the organizations of the larger women's movement.

Much of the debate on the experience with 'engendering democracy' is informed by the set of theoretical and methodological instruments developed by Molyneux and Moser. The dual nature of the category of gender is ever present, with acute awareness of the gender shortfalls of policies catering to women's interest, but not challenging the prevailing gender matrix. By the same token, charging ahead in quest of ambitious strategic objectives without firmly linking them to the given conditions and circumstances of women's lives and the way they define their interests in them, is recognized as a losing proposition and, for that matter, mere ideology. In this debate the dynamics of the transition from practical to strategic gender interests, about which Moser is so disconcertingly vague, are directly addressed and theorized. Furthermore, the debate is taking place in close connection with and reference to the experience of neoliberal and economic adjustment policies that newly democratized governments immediately embarked on.

This complex and demanding setting triggered off a remarkably differentiated and concisely articulated discourse of great interest to those in search of the possibilities and conditions for successful gender mainstreaming strategies. Into this debate Sonia Alvarez introduced the notion of hybridity, using it as a concept and as a measure to probe into the interaction of women's organizations with national and regional government structures and with international funding agencies. She is not worried by the NGO-ization of the organizations of the women's movements *per se*, but is much more concerned with the question of how the complex challenges emanating from this evolution are managed and acted upon:

Most newly professionalized feminist groups fashioned hybrid political strategies and identities – developing expertise in gender policy advocacy while
retaining a commitment to movement-oriented activities aimed at fostering
women's empowerment and transforming prevailing gender power arrangements. In collaboration with the 'global feminist lobby' local NGOs succeeded in pressuring many Latin American governments to enact a number
of feminist-inspired reforms – such as electoral quotas to enhance women's
political representation and legislation to combat domestic violence. (Alvarez
1999: 182)

After 20 years of experience with direct interaction between administrative units and the governmental apparatus addressing women's
concerns, as well as with international development agencies and organizations of the women's movement, Alvarez diagnoses with alarm:

I am suggesting that the above-outlined trends increasingly threaten to *de-
hybridyze* the heretofore-dual identity of most Latin American feminist
NGOs. And as I argued above, it is precisely that hybrid identity that up to
now has formed the mainstay of feminist NGOs' critical ability to contest
pathologized versions of neoliberal State policies 'with a gender perspective',
advocate for alternative understandings of women's rights, and promote
gendered social justice into the 21st century. (Alvarez 1999: 197)

The trends referred to by Alvarez will be considered in the following
pages. The focus will initially be on the process of repositioning of the
women's movements in the course of the democratic opening. It will
then move on to women-proactive shifts on parliamentary and administrative levels and the experience of interaction and collaboration with
the newly established governmental women's machinery. Finally, the
direct or indirect interfacing with international aid agencies ('donors')
will be discussed.

The experience of engendering democracy in Latin America

The political space opened up by the democratization processes in
Latin American countries offered greater opportunities for women to
be heard and listened to, not least because catering to women's interests
and demands promised to broaden the social basis of democratic parties
and to substantiate their claim to genuine and inclusive democracy.
Women engaged in the formation of new political parties or in the
reconstitution of the old ones. To the extent that the mass movement fighting for democracy left the streets, and the democratizing
momentum settled in conventional political parties within a system of

representative democracy, the element of mobilization necessarily also subsided (Blondet 1995; Frohmann and Valdés 1995; Lamas et al. 1995). This situation forced women's organizations to review their self-definition as autonomous organizations and to reposition themselves *vis-à-vis* the party political system.

The democratic political parties in power did pass legislation designed to improve the condition of women. Existing legislation was reviewed and amended to better accommodate the demand for civil equality of women. In addition, new legislation was introduced addressing issues specific to women in family law or concerning violence against women. A major contributory factor to these changes was the quota system, which women had vigorously fought for and which most political parties adopted (WEDO 1998; WLCA 1999). In fact, most of this legislation had either been introduced by women or owed its successful adoption to women's coalitions cutting across party lines (Jones 1996). Yet, from the perspectives of women's organizations, much remains to be done as regards the definition of legally relevant facts and circumstances. All too often the administrative implementation of potentially relevant legislation is found to lack vigour and conviction (Htun 1998).

Fuelled by the United Nations Decade for Women, as well as by the prodding of the WID/GAD desks of development agencies in pursuit of gender mainstreaming policies and their concomitant financial inducements, nearly all Latin American countries set up a women's machinery. Parliamentary women's commissions, regional women's councils, women's bureaux on state and communal levels, and, last but not least, women's police stations were established. Over time, most of them were not spared the fate of most 'national machineries' designed to address the situation of women. They remained marginal to the executive and political process, and the implementation of their programmes was largely left dependent on international funding sources (Goetz 1995, Byrne et al. 1996).

> In virtually all countries in the region, specialized State machineries charged with proposing and monitoring (though seldom implementing) gender-focused programmes and policies have been established. In some cases, such as those of Chile's SERNAM (*Servicio Nacional de la Mujer*) and Brazil's CNDM (*Conselho Nacional dos Direitos da Mulher*), significant sectors of the feminist movements actively advocated the creation of State women's offices – though the ultimate mandate, design and performance of the specialized agencies actually created typically fell far short of feminist expectations. In other cases, such as the *Consejeria para la Juventud, la Mujer, y la Familia* established in Gaviria's Columbia or Fujimori's recently created

PROMUDEH (*Ministério de Promoción de la Mujer y del Desarrollo Humano*), the founding of such women's State institutions appears to have been motivated by more pragmatic, when not outright opportunistic, considerations – such as the fact that bilateral and multilateral grants and loans, now often require evidence of government sensitivity to women's role in development (Alvarez 1999: 191).

Latin American women's organizations were thus interfacing with two types of institutional partners of co-operation. On the one hand, and much closer to home, there were the newly established governmental structures designed specifically to address women's issues. On the other hand, there was the 'donor community' with its equally recently adopted gender mainstreaming policies, which, since the Beijing Conference, tend to be argued increasingly in gender equality terms. Both types of agencies were more often than not connected through funding schemes, and both, in order to implement their policies, programmes and projects, required the co-operation and collaboration of feminist commitment, knowledge, competence and contacts. And it should not be forgotten that both offered women's organizations direly needed resources in terms of access to decision-making and to funding.

The newly established governmental women's machineries took up their function with hopeful acclaim and much enthusiasm from the great majority of women's organizations and feminist-inspired professional women. Some even saw an effective 'feminist subversion' (Alvarez 1997) at work, whereas others thought they detected merely a form of 'state feminism' and remained rather sceptical (Waylen 1997). The government machinery started a wide range of programme activities addressing women's concerns, funded in part by the national budget and in part by international sources. Most were in the field of food and nutrition, health, and education. In addition, women's information centres were set up in many places. Legislation was prepared to ensure that women could fully enjoy human and civic rights. Public campaigns condemning violence against women were mounted. For the purpose of designing and implementing these programmes, hitherto entirely autonomous women's centres and women's organizations were contacted and eventually contracted with. Well-known feminist professionals and highly renowned women activists were recruited for voluntary (board, council) or paid (staff) positions in the newly established women's machinery. Reputed feminists accepted public functions. Women's organizations took it upon themselves to monitor the execution of policies, legislation and programmes.

A couple of years and a world of hugely informative experience later there was a distinctly noticeable sobering. The budgets allocated to the women's machineries, national as well as international, continuously declined. Outspoken feminists found themselves crowded out of the very structures they had helped to build. By the same token, there was a growing incidence of women without any links to the women's movements being called into decision-making bodies, at times at the explicit behest of governmental or party political authorities (Soares et al. 1995).

The NGOs which had originated in the women's movements and over time had developed professionalism and a certain amount of institutionalization saw themselves increasingly framed in a neoliberal economic and political setting. They felt instrumentalized as proxies for civil society, without having the least chance to actually feed civil society political positions into decision-making processes and to have their concerns considered on macro-levels. Moreover, the extensive absorption of their most powerful and leading women into the governmental machinery substantially weakened the women's movement. Such appointments had reached significant numbers, and were rarely fully discussed with and endorsed by the organizations the women came from or were associated with. Almost imperceptibly the flow and direction of accountability shifted away from the inner-organizational democratic practices of the organizations of the women's movements to the rules, procedural requirements and conditionalities of the governmental bodies and the international agencies providing programme resources.

The assumption that basically gender-neutral governance structures equipped with women-specific mechanisms and instruments would easily produce effective new gender relations turned out to be facile and had to be reviewed. In addition, the political terrain, having been restructured within the dimensions of a neoliberal paradigm, seriously limited the space and scope for gender-transformative policies. The women and women's organizations involved in close interaction with public bodies increasingly saw themselves reduced to the execution of the dominant rationale. Access to public and international resources was subject to the terms and conditions of the neoliberal agenda. Feminist expertise was stripped of its 'superfluous' emancipatory commitment, with only the technical skills having a chance to be put into action. In analysing the loss of links and relationships to the women's movements on the part of the professionals and the women's organizations, Alvarez speaks of a 'gender technocracy' coming into existence (Alvarez 1999: 199). For obvious reasons, the capacity of such gender technocrats to actually monitor the action and the transformative

content of public policies was in danger of being seriously com-
promised.

As a result, and against the backdrop of the ongoing production of
poverty and of structural heterogeneity of neoliberal policy strategies,
women's organizations have found themselves confronting two developments which amount to the opposite of gender mainstreaming:

- While engaging in the public sphere with feminist agendas and
  commitments, women are more and more confronted with the
  neoliberal withdrawal of the state from large segments of provision
  of basic infrastructure and basic services. The links and relationships
  with grassroots women, carefully built and constructed with the
  perspective of empowerment policies, are instrumentalized and re-
  designed to serve as vehicles for the government and the society at
  large in shifting the burden of poverty alleviation on to the shoulders
  of the poor in general and women in particular. Poverty alleviation programmes have nothing to do with mainstreaming and
  empowerment. Rather, they are an invitation to the systematic self-
  management of a marginalized survival existence.

- The dual character of gender is definitely lost. Gender is understood
  in a very limited sense, having been narrowed down to address
  women in their assigned roles as family providers and nurturers.
  Poverty alleviation schemes, referring to empowerment, offer to
  assist women, preferably with small credits and income-generating
  programmes which in fact produce the dubious effect already
  discussed. Confined to incremental social gains, the 'gender technocracy' is forced to relinquish the transformative side of gender.

The situation is no different for the professional women who are
working more or less directly with international development agencies.
While generally 'unideological' gender experts tend to be preferred,
the occasional feminist, contracted for the execution of a gender mainstreaming policy mandate, may well be asked to involve herself in the
planning, implementation, monitoring and evaluation of projects and
programmes. But she will find herself in an operating environment
that places a premium on outcomes which can be quickly achieved and
easily demonstrated, requiring neither detours nor additional action,
and which absorb substantial amounts of money in a short period of
time – none of which an empowerment process can guarantee to
produce. As Soares says:

> There is lingering doubt as to the degree of subordination influencing the
> action of women's groups, particularly feminist NGOs, that deal with or

receive funding from international agencies to address gender issues. The question is to what extent our agenda, practice, discussion and exchange are being subordinated to decisions beyond our control. If the institutionalization of feminist groups permits them to negotiate as individuals or in small groups with international agencies, this could compromise the group's commitment to feminism and even put at risk the movement's principles of autonomy. (Soares 1995: 319ff.)

It may well be asked to what extent the dangers and tendencies Soares describes are due to collaboration with international funding agencies. Quite a number of project reports discreetly suggest that it is the reality shock of middle-class feminists encountering 'their' grassroots that expresses itself in such doubts – an encounter, for that matter, made possible only through the intervention of international funding agencies. Indeed, not infrequently, resistance against the strategic dimension of gender 'in the field' is articulated by female or male colleagues, not least by the men and women of the target group. An assessment of available options and conditions of choice and of the chances for influence and participation often leads women to consider carefully the investments required, the conflicts encountered and the risks entailed in strategies that challenged given gender arrangements. In such circumstances, insisting on stretching development action beyond the gender status quo may easily be accused of imposing an identity agenda, while those struggling to retain transformative elements may do so only at the cost of seriously endangering their own autonomy.

The experience in Latin America teaches us that feminists and women's organizations co-operating with public national or international bodies find it immensely difficult to retain control of their own agenda or even of the compromises they make. Whether this can actually be fully attributed to the neoliberal context – as, for instance, Alvarez suggests for Latin America – or whether neoliberal policies merely provide the contemporary backdrop and framework for resistance to rebalancing unjust gender arrangements, is not a question that must be answered here. Most disconcerting, however, is the fact that the involvement of the women's movement and its organizations as the social actor of transformation in gender mainstreaming policies evidently does disappointingly little to ensure gender-just policy outcomes.

The concept of hybridity

In her review of this experience, Sonia Alvarez uses the concept of hybridity and gives it the status of an analytical yardstick. She conceptualizes hybridity as the condition that allows women's organizations to balance bureaucratic demands and neoliberal rationales with the dynamics and perspectives of social movements in search of political, economic and social gender justice:

> The movement side of NGO identity is being challenged by their contractual relationship to States and donors who expect visible, short-term results on gender projects. Such exigencies may undermine NGOs' ability to pursue more process-oriented forms of feminist cultural-political intervention – such as consciousness-raising, popular education or other strategies aimed at transforming those gender power relations manifest in the realms of public discourse, culture and daily life – forms of gendered injustice that defy gender-planning quick fixes. (Alvarez 1999: 198)

Apart from providing an analytical tool, what is particularly interesting about the concept of hybridity in this context is that it allows for a perspective that may help to place agency back in the hands of women's organizations. 'To enhance their room for maneuver … feminists would have to devise *collective* strategies to resist the de-hybridization of NGOs and enable them perhaps to serve as more genuine intermediaries for larger civil society constituencies' (Alvarez 1999: 200).

In order to repoliticize the concept of gender by rediscovering and revaluing its transformative side, or, to put it in mainstreaming gender language, by re-emphasizing women's strategic interests, Alvarez proposes a strategy of research, reflection and differentiation. The heterogeneity of the origins of women's organizations in Latin America, the diversity of practices and the specificities of the hybrid identities that still characterize many feminist NGOs are to be closely studied. The interaction between an administratively mediated system rationale and the dynamics and aspirations of the women's movements needs to be explored in more detail, rather than prematurely discarded on the basis of an analysis that treats them as dichotomies.

Indeed, much is to be gained from an interface analysis that conceptualizes gender mainstreaming as negotiation space between actors of different social character. The factors of successful and of failed negotiation need to be scrutinized. Applying the concept of hybridity to such an analysis might be useful in order to better explore opportunity structures on the meso- and micro-levels. It could help women's organizations and feminist professionals to identify the conditions and circumstances most conducive to the introduction of strategic gender policy aspects, while closely monitoring their own capacity to retain that difficult and delicate balance of hybridity required for gender mainstreaming. However, one indispensable condition for the political success of such a research and reflection strategy lies in the willingness and the capacity of women's groups and individual women committed to gender justice to disclose and to share compromises, without running the danger of being instantly accused of having betrayed the cause.

Bibliography

Alvarez, S. E. (1990) *Engendering Democracy in Brazil: Women's Movements in Transition Politics*, Princeton, NJ: Princeton University Press.

— (1997) 'Contradictions of a "Women's Space" in a Male-Dominant State: The Political Role of the Commission on the Status of Women in Post-authoritarian Brazil', in Staudt, K. (ed.), *Women, International Development and Politics: The Bureaucratic Mire*, Philadelphia, pp. 59–100.

— (1999) 'Advocating Feminism: The Latin American Feminist NGO "Boom"', *International Feminist Journal of Politics*, Vol. 1, No. 2, September, pp. 181–209.

Bakker, I. (ed.) (1994) *The Strategic Silence: Gender and Economic Policy*, London: Zed Books.

Bangura, Y. (1997) *Policy Dialogue and Gendered Development: Institutional and Ideological Constraints*, UNRISD Discussion Paper 87, Geneva: UN Research Institute for Social Development.

Blondet, C. (1995) 'Out of the Kitchens and onto the Streets: Women's Activism in Peru', in Basu, A. (ed.), *The Challenges of Local Feminisms. Women's Movements in Global Perspective*, Boulder, CO: Westview Press, pp. 251–75.

Boserup, E. (1970) *Women's Role in Economic Development*, New York: St Martin's Press.

Braunmühl, C. von (1997) 'Mainstreaming Gender oder von den Grenzen, dieses zu tun', in Braig, M., U. Ferdinand and M. Zapata (eds): *Begegnungen und Einmischungen. Festschrift für Renate Rott zum 60. Geburtstag*, Histoamericana 4, Stuttgart: Heinz, pp. 375–94.

— (1998) 'Gender und Transformation. Nachdenkliches zu den Anstrengungen einer Beziehung', in Kreisky, E. and B. Sauer (eds), *Geschlechterverhältnisse im Kontext politischer Transformation*. Politische Vierteljahresschrift 38, Sonderheft 28, Opladen: Westdeutscher Verlag, pp. 475–90.

Byrne, B. et al. (1996) *National Machineries for Women in Development: Experiences, Lessons and Strategies for Institutionalizing Gender in Development Policy and Planning*, University of Sussex, Brighton: BRIDGE, Institute of Development Studies.

Commission for International Development (1969) *Partners in Development*, New York: Commission for International Development.

Elson, D. (1991) *Male Bias in the Development Process*, Manchester: Manchester University Press.

Frohmann, A. and T. Valdés (1995) 'Democracy in the Country and in the

Home: The Women's Movement in Chile', in Basu, A. (ed.), *The Challenges of Local Feminisms. Women's Movements in Global Perspective*, Boulder, CO: Westview Press, pp. 276–301.

Goetz, A. (1995) *The Politics of Integrating Gender to State Development Processes*, UNRISD Occasional Paper 2, Geneva: UN Research Institute for Social Development.

— (ed.) (1997) *Getting Institutions Right for Women in Development*, London, New York: Zed Books.

Htun, M. N. (1998) *Women's Rights and Opportunities in Latin America: Problems and Prospects*. Women's Leadership Conference of the Americas Issue Brief. Inter-American Dialogue/International Center for Research on Women, see http://www.iadialog.org.

Jahan, R. (1995) *The Elusive Agenda. Mainstreaming Women in Development*, London: Zed Books; Dhaka: Bangladesh University Press.

Jones, M. P. (1996) 'Gender and the Legislative Policy Priorities in the Argentine Chamber of Deputies and the United States House of Representatives'. Paper presented at the Annual Meeting of the Midwest Political Science Association.

Kabeer, N. (1994) *Reversed Realities – Gender Hierarchies in Development Thought*, London, New York: Verso.

Lamas, M. et al. (1995) 'Building Bridges: The Growth of Popular Feminism in Mexico', in Basu, A. (ed.), *The Challenges of Local Feminisms. Women's Movements in Global Perspective*, Boulder, CO: Westview Press, pp. 324–47.

Longwe, S. H. (1997) 'The Evaporation of Gender Policies in the Patriarchal Cooking Pot', in *Development and Patronage*, Oxford: Oxfam, pp. 41–49.

Macdonald, M. (ed.) (1994) *Gender Planning in Development Agencies. Meeting the Challenge*, Oxford: Oxfam.

Molyneux, M. (1985) 'Mobilization without Emancipation? Women's Interests, the State, and Revolution in Nicaragua', *Feminist Studies*, Vol. 11, No. 2, pp. 227–54.

Moser, C. O. (1993) *Gender Planning in Development. Theory, Practice and Training*, London: Routledge.

Moser, C. O. and L. Peake (eds.) (1987) *Women, Human Settlements and Housing*, London, New York: Tavistock Publications.

Palmer, I. (1994) *Social and Gender Issues in Macro-economic Advice*, GTZ, Eschborn: Gesellschaft für Technische Zusammenarbeit.

Razavi, S. and C. Miller (1995a) *From WID to GAD, Conceptional Shifts in the Women and Development Discourse*, UNRISD, Occasional Papers 1, Geneva: UN Research Institute for Social Development.

— (1995b) *Gender Mainstreaming. A Study of Efforts by the UNDP, the World Bank and the ILO to Institutionalize Gender Issues*, UNRISD, Occasional Papers 4, Geneva: UN Research Institute for Social Development.

Rogers, B. (1991) *The Domestication of Women. Discrimination in Developing Societies*, London: Routledge.

Rostow, W. W. (1960) *The Stages of Economic Growth: A Non-Communist Manifesto,* Cambridge: Cambridge University Press.

Sassen, S. (1996) 'Towards a Feminist Analytics of the Global Economy', *Indiana Journal of Global Legal Studies,* Vol. 4, No. 1, pp. 7–41.

Scott, G. (1979) *Recognizing the Invisible Woman in Development. The World Bank's Experience,* Washington, DC: World Bank.

Sen, G. and C. Grown (1987) *Development, Crisis and Alternative Visions. Third World Women's Perspective,* New York: Monthly Review Press.

Soares, V. et al. (1995) 'Brazilian Feminism and Women's Movements: A Two-Way Street', in Basu, A. (ed.), *The Challenges of Local Feminisms. Women's Movements in Global Perspective,* Boulder, CO: Westview Press, pp. 302–23.

Staudt, K. (1985) *Women, Foreign Assistance and Advocacy Administration,* New York: Praeger.

— (1997) *Women, International Development and Politics,* Philadelphia: Temple University Press.

— (1998) *Policy, Politics and Gender. Women Gaining Ground,* West Hartford, CT: Kumarian Press.

Waylen, G. (1997) 'Women's Movements, the State and Democratization in Chile: The Establishment of SERNAM', in Goetz, A. M. (ed.), *Getting Institutions Right for Women in Development,* London, New York: Zed Books, pp. 90–103.

WEDO (1998) *Mapping Progress: Assessing the Implementation of the Beijing Platform for Action 1998,* New York: Women's Environment and Development Organization.

Wichterich, C. (2000) *The Globalized Woman. Reports from a Future of Inequality,* London: Zed Books.

WLCA, Women's Leadership Conference of the Americas, Working Group Meetings on Women's Leadership and Corporate and Multilateral Development Bank Social Responsibility, February 1999, Rapporteur's Report, see http://www.iadialog.org.

CHAPTER 6

Reclaiming the Empowerment Discourse: A Challenge to Feminists

Carolyn Medel-Añonuevo

The popularization and institutionalization of empowerment

It is a cliché to say that empowerment is a fashionable term. Almost all papers on empowerment start with this caveat. True enough, everyone – from the grassroots woman organizer in the village, to World Bank staff in Washington, to the corporate world – has adopted this term in their respective field of work. The institutionalization of empowerment is also evident as one examines documents from the Beijing Platform of Action to United Nations reports, the Philippine Medium Term Development Plan and the action plans of NGOs.

Like many development terms, the popularization and institutionalization of empowerment could be seen as both a gain and a loss. On the one hand, it could be considered a victory for social movements, since the term that they introduced in the late 1960s is now part of the vocabulary of a wide range of groups. After all, as advocates of empowerment, aren't we interested in seeing the broadest base of the population adopt this term as their own? Don't we now have the tools to make governments accountable, now that they themselves have embraced this concept? On the other hand, we are caught in a dilemma, since the adoption of the term by different groups has also meant their appropriation of it for their own purposes. This means that these groups are redefining the term according to their own objectives and even appropriating its spirit. In the process, the term empowerment has been diluted and has therefore lost its sharpness as a concept advocating gender and social justice. Instead of a holistic perspective, the economic slant the term has taken has produced a fragmented meaning. For example, I have seen advertisements use the term empowerment to indicate the capacity to choose and buy a certain brand of product. It is no wonder that many feminists and other activists no longer use empowerment, since they believe that this word has been co-opted and is therefore no longer relevant.

I disagree, because I believe that, like similar concepts in many fields and areas, the term empowerment is a site of contestation and resistance. We cannot give it up simply because others have been creative enough to see its potential. The challenge to feminists and activists is to reappropriate the empowerment discourse by resharpening it so that it continues to be relevant for our work and our lives. To my mind, this entails a critical assessment of the concept at the same time as reflecting on our rich experiences of empowerment, and incorporating these practices in the discourse so that we can reclaim its original spirit and vision. These are the two areas I will discuss in more detail.

A journey through empowerment

The second cliché about empowerment is that it is difficult to define. The nature of empowerment itself presents some problems when one attempts to grasp it conceptually. But it is sufficiently exciting and controversial to have inspired many women and men to write books and articles describing, explaining and analysing its history and utility. I will not attempt to summarize what has been written or the issues that have been raised. Instead, I would like to share with you my own voyage in understanding and using the term. While personal, I believe that my story also carries many aspects of the history and evolution of empowerment.

Together with many activists in the Philippines, I started to use empowerment in the late 1980s in our popular education activities. For us then, consciousness-raising was a way of empowering women to unpack class and gender oppression. I do not recall any particular article or author who influenced us in using this term. It simply slipped into our vocabulary, and we used it in our talks and reports. Initially, participation was used side by side with empowerment, but later participation took a back seat as empowerment became the preferred term. Later, many of us feminists discovered Maxine Molyneux's discussion of practical and strategic gender needs and used this as one elaboration and operationalization of empowerment. The Sara Longwe empowerment framework introduced by the UN children's fund UNICEF and Caroline Moser's work (for example, 1993) also helped us in clarifying the history, context and elements of empowerment so that we could use it more clearly in our popular education work.

I took a more conceptual approach to and interest in the term when I started my field work with rural women in early 1990, as part of a multidisciplinary research team of the University of the Philippines where I was teaching. Having the luxury of being seconded to do field work, I was able to immerse myself in the rich conceptual discourse of empowerment that was developing both in the South and in the North. My organizing and education experience alongside women, with the possibility of doing conceptual work grounded in field research, provided me with an opportunity to connect the discourse with the practices, to unravel the limitations of the discourse as it tries to interpret the practices, and to use the practices to reconstruct the discourses.

Considering empowerment as both a means and an end, I described how it takes on a 'means' discourse when one is talking about the process of empowering and how it contributes to another objective. For example, John Friedmann (1992: 31) writes that 'alternative development involves a process of social and political empowerment whose long-term objective is to restructure the balance of power in society by making state action more accountable, strengthening the powers of civil society in the management of its own affairs, and making corporate business more socially responsible'. On the other hand, the 'ends' discourse is that which considers empowerment as an objective in many development projects, including those of women. For example, economic empowerment as a goal is referred to as that stage of development when ordinary people, particularly the poor, have direct control of economic life (NGO Orientation on Koop Work 1990).

Within these processes and goal discourses of empowerment, one still needs to look at the many dimensions (economic, political, social and psychological) of empowerment itself and the tendency of many definitions to approach it from specific perspectives. For example, there is a notion of empowerment as the transfer of political and economic power from one social class to another (NGO Report 1998). Kamla Bhasin (1990) talks about how people could consider empowering as the development of skills and abilities to enable rural women to manage better, have a say in or negotiate with existing development delivery systems; others see it as more fundamentally and essentially concerned with enabling rural people to decide on and to take actions which they believe are essential to their development.

In the 1990s we have seen a subtle shift from participation to empowerment. Is there any difference? Empowerment seems to be better than participation, because it expresses determination not to make just any kind of contribution. Participation meant taking part in the existing power structures, empowerment might mean transforming power relations through transforming oneself, changing relationships in society and changing cultural patterns. Indeed, the difference is in the word 'power'. In recent years, I have realized that the key to reclaiming the empowerment discourse is to put 'power' in the centre.

Power as the key concept in the empowerment discourse

Many women refuse to take power into their own hands. If possible, most women would prefer not to be concerned with the discussion of power as a concept. The lack of interest of women in taking up power or unpacking what it means is to a certain extent understandable. Living and experiencing a dominating, controlling and oppressive type of power has produced in many women an aversion to power. 'Power over' has been the most dominant and commonly practised power. Having control over economic resources, occupying political positions, having expertise and access to information, or simply being a man, could be some of the bases of this type of power. While men have been most prominent in practising this kind of power, women are not exempted. Having been mostly exposed to this model of power, it is not surprising that women, when put in positions or conditions of power, show their internalization of this dominant practice of it.

There is therefore a need to disseminate the other kinds of power which many women have been practising but which are not recognized as such. 'Power to' readily comes to mind. Due to their socialization, women have shown their fascinating range of abilities and capacities, from the power to listen, to the power to relate, to the power to do many things at the same time. The 'power to' as a power of agency is obviously the opposite of the 'power over', which strips women and men of their ability to act and take control of their lives. Yet it is clear that women and men practise and are surrounded by these two opposing types of power.

'Power with' is group/collective-based power which both women and men have practised, whether in the form of old boys networks or poor urban women organizing and successfully defying demolition teams. 'Power within' is more individually oriented, in the sense that it is more psychological and perhaps spiritual, as it refers to one person's internal resources. Harnessing both individual and collective resources is important, hence 'power with' and 'power within' are not mutually exclusive. The more relevant question is to what ends these resources are harnessed.

A preliminary analysis of the practices of 'power' would show that:

1. There are different bases of power – it can be economic, political,

cultural, social, religious (e.g., economic resources, positions and roles, access to information).

2. Power can have as many locations (e.g., within people themselves or in association with others; in institutions, in the family, in relations with others).

3. Given the multiple bases and multilocality of power, it could happen all at the same time with different consequences (e.g., concentration and monopoly of power, which is mostly in the hands of upper-class men, or diffusion of power as a result of contradictory power types, which is common to lower-class women who will have the 'power to' but could be overwhelmed by 'power over').

4. Power is relational, i.e., we are talking about power relations, something which is not static or permanent, but rather practised and constantly negotiated in relation to others.

Given this brief background on power, one could start to interrogate its implications for feminists in all arenas of work. It is therefore important to collect, compare, and analyse not only our concepts but, more importantly, our varied experiences. For example, we could consider how power is a key dimension in feminist education. First of all, women and men bring their own practices of power to the spaces of learning. The spaces themselves are thereby transformed into sites of practices of power. This means that in these created spaces, one could experience power over, power to, power with, and power within at different times, or perhaps two of them together at the same time. Educators, teachers, learners, students, participants and resource persons will be constantly practising, asserting and negotiating in these created spaces. How we structure educational programmes, what we include in the contents of the programme, the processes we use, how we conduct workshops, how participants react and relate to the programme, are in fact instances of the way power is being exercised and practised by the different agents.

If we take this as given, then one needs to ask how we could become more conscious in addressing the different kinds of power as they emerge. How could we use this informed understanding to articulate these different types and to interrogate them? How could we use these created spaces to question power and put it on the agenda? How do we use the spaces to transform the dominating and controlling type of power within people into an agency-facilitating type of power? The recognition and conscious articulation of such power types and tendencies is the first step. It is necessary to show that everybody has the potential for both agency and control power, and to understand that power is not simply out there in macro-structures (to be destroyed or grabbed), but is very much within us, in very intimate circumstances as well. Given that the spaces we create could be reproducing, affirming or negating different types of power, it is crucial that women and men who practise feminist education ask themselves questions about the kinds of power their processes promote.

Sharing practices of empowering education for women

At the UNESCO Institute for Education, we have been very fortunate to be able to work with women who have developed their conceptual frameworks of empowerment from actual experiences of activism. Sara Longwe (Zambia), Srilatha Batliwala (India) and Malena de Montis (Nicaragua), for example, have demonstrated how women across the world share the same concerns and are somehow working in the same direction. It is therefore important in our work to bring these women together to discuss, debate and develop strategies for how we could go forward. In 1993, we organized a seminar on 'Women's Education and Empowerment' to unpack what empowerment means for women who are learning to be literate. This was followed by a seminar on 'The Impact of Macroeconomic, Political and Social Changes on Women', where we examined the obstacles to empowering education and the strategies women use to overcome such obstacles. In our last seminar, we looked at how we could monitor and evaluate adult education from a gender perspective, asking how empowerment could be used as a variable to be analysed and what indicators were available.

It is clear that there is still a lot of sharing, analysing and mobilizing to be done, within communities and countries, across countries and between regions. Our experiences have shown that understanding the discourses of empowerment is not a solitary task. It is best done when the minds and hearts of women are able to come together, as they unravel the complexity of the power that rules their lives, but which also has the potential to transform their exclusion and marginalization.

The long-term goal of empowerment is to realize the vision of egalitarian societies. But as a process, it needs to contain participatory mechanisms that will already lay the groundwork for the transformation of individuals, relationships, communities and societies. Wherever we are working from, whatever space we choose to occupy and operate from, feminists have the possibility of contributing to a more sharpened understanding and use of empowerment.

Bibliography

Bhasin, K. (1990) *Towards Empowerment*, New Delhi: UN Food and Agriculture Organization (FAO).

Friedmann, J. (1992) *Empowerment: The Politics of Alternative Development*, Massachusetts: Blackwell.

Moser, C. O. (1993) *Gender Planning in Development. Theory, Practice and Training*, London: Routledge.

NGO Orientation on Koop Work (1990) *Proceedings of a Conference-Workshop on People's Co-operative*, Mindoro Oriental: Philippines.

NGO Report (1998) *Report on the Seminar Workshop on Strengthening NGO Participation in Cooperative Development*, Bagiuo City.

CHAPTER 7

Women's Interest in Social Policy – Rhetoric and Realities of Social Investment Funds

Renate Rott

Within the European tradition, any contribution on social policy would include a great number of specific topics: social security programmes for the labour force, labour regulations, health care, old age pension schemes, education, the quest for better living conditions, as well as human and civil rights; in general these are concepts of the 'classical' welfare state in Western industrialized countries. I have decided to concentrate on a more limited aspect: the introduction of Social Investment Funds (SIFs) as one of the most important projects of aid programmes in Latin American countries, including both those financed by international agencies such as the World Bank and the Inter-American Development Bank, and bilateral financing such as that of Japan and Germany. I have limited my observations to two Central American countries, Guatemala and Nicaragua. This chapter is structured in three parts. I begin with some explanations concerning the reasons why these funds have been implemented since 1985; I continue with a description of their performance and function, and end with some general remarks and observations.

The introduction and implementation of Social Investment Funds in Latin America

The debt crisis, which began in 1982 with Mexico declaring its moratorium, soon reached Argentina and Brazil. Country after country had to submit to the austerity programmes imposed by the International Monetary Fund (IMF). In addition to those austerity programmes, the implementation of structural adjustment programmes became a condition of specific agreements for rescheduling debt and for receiving loans from international financial institutions, most prominently the

IMF, the World Bank and the Inter-American Development Bank. Structural adjustment programmes with a neoliberal outlook included the general reduction of state intervention in the economy, the liberalization of trade and capital flows, the privatization of state enterprises, as well as new economic regulations and incentives for direct foreign investment. These austerity packages have led to rapid and deep cuts in social expenditure, especially in health care and education, with direct consequences and hardships for women.

Social policies in Latin America went through profound changes in the 1980s and 1990s. The new trend was the retrenchment of the state and market expansion in the financing, delivery and administration of social services. There is hardly any disagreement about the need for social policy reforms, but there is a wide divergence of opinion about their direction and focus. Even before the age of globalization and neoliberalism the coverage of social policies remained low in most Latin American countries, since the social security system was based mainly on employment in the formal sector of the economy. Latin American countries differed and continue to differ widely in their systems of social protection. Only six countries have built a system of social protection vaguely resembling a welfare state, covering more than 60 per cent of the economically active population with some form of social security as of 1980: Argentina, Brazil, Chile, Costa Rica, Cuba and Uruguay, plus three Caribbean countries – the Bahamas, Barbados and Jamaica (Mesa-Largo 1994: 22).[1] Given that the majority of women are still considered as working in the informal sector, their access to social security benefits has been rather limited, in the sense that benefits were for the most part available to them only as members of families, daughters or wives of men employed in the formal sector. While the economic performance of Latin American countries varies, in general terms it can be said that the period in question was characterized by 'great pains, no gains'.

The concept of SIFs started in the mid-1980s as a target-orientated special programme, a kind of safety net designed to cushion the worst consequences of the adjustment regulations and cuts in social expenditure. The first such case was seen in 1985 in Bolivia. Even though the first implementations were intended as a kind of short- or medium-term emergency programme, they are continuing and will eventually incorporate new forms of social policy-making in the future. As a senior World Bank functionary said: 'They are here to stay'. Since the mid-1980s and especially since the 1990s, the prevailing rhetoric and discourses of the international and national donors in their papers and project proposals reflect an intensified awareness of gender-related questions. The rhetorical codes also include catchwords like 'good governance', 'civil rights of ethnic groups', and 'co-operation with NGOs'; the all-embracing concept of 'civil society', the promise of modernity according to 'Western' standards, seems to have been especially prominent and of multifunctional use in the 1990s. This new type of vocabulary quite often seems to consist mainly of fashionable rhetorical codes used to fulfil the standards of political correctness in international relations. But the important questions are: How have these new rhetorical codes been implemented in the everyday reality of projects? Have gender-related aspects been included and has their realization been taken seriously?[2]

Performance and function of the social investment funds in Guatemala and Nicaragua

Guatemala has experienced 36 years of civil war. The peace treaty between the state and the guerrilla forces was signed only in December 1996, thanks to some important international intervention. The main victims of the civil war were the indigenous groups who make up more than 50 per cent of the population, and who are considered the poorest group within a country that is highly segmented on ethnic lines (Le Bot 1997). Nicaragua is the second poorest country on the continent after Haiti. Nevertheless, however disputed Sandinista policies may be today, the Sandinistas were quite successful in fighting illiteracy, especially among women (Randall 1994), whereas in Guatemala up to 80 per cent of the Mayan women in some regions are considered to be illiterate and only a minority speaks the dominant Spanish. It should be mentioned that the traditional organization of Mayan communities quite often explicitly excludes women from the public sphere.

Whereas formerly the international agencies usually loaned money to governments for specific purposes, the new 'demand-driven' approach is designed to concentrate on the basic needs of the poor or poorest part of the population. The donors act as intermediate financiers, and the programmes are administered by national agencies specially established for that purpose. The target groups – in this context, communities – are selected according to the available statistics, forming regions of intervention called 'poverty maps'.

In Nicaragua the SIF programme started in 1990 after the Sandinista government had lost the elections. In Guatemala the first agency (FONAPAZ, Fondo Nacional para la Paz) began organizing and co-financing the repatriation of refugees from the camps in Mexico in the early 1990s. The other most important fund, the FIS (Fondo de Inversión

Social), was set up to counterbalance the cuts in social expenditure in 1993; up to 1998 the FIS had a budget of approximately US$180 million. In Nicaragua the funds are administered by an organization called the FISE (Fondo de Inversión Social de Emergencia), which between 1991 and 1997 administered a budget of US$225.2 million. The planned budget for 1998 to 2001 was estimated at approximately US$162 million. Up to 1998 the German bilateral contribution within the general budget amounted to 20 per cent in Guatemala and 14 per cent in Nicaragua.

Due to their significant financial impact, the funds have a very high standing within the political hierarchy; the cabinet of the president or the vice-president is directly responsible for the funds. In order to reach a higher level of performance, national regulations of public adminis-tration are not applied to the funds. There are special staff regulations and much better salaries and promotion possibilities than in public administration. In both countries, the most important projects up to now have been realized within the fields of construction and infra-structure (water supply and disposal), and mainly in schools or health stations (*puestos de salud*) which have been built or repaired. Ministries as well as communities can apply for funding in order to realize projects within specific regions. In the future, such ministries will be responsible for staffing, whereas the communities will be partly responsible for maintenance. In Guatemala, communities had to form specific groups in order to take part in the competition for the projects. For the poor indigenous villagers, finding their way through the bureaucratic mire proved to be a very hard and barely comprehensible process, and their influence was limited to the early planning period. This has been the case in Nicaragua too.

Since the mid-1990s donors have forced national agencies to con-centrate on more than construction and infrastructure. In order to foster civil society, they have asked them to include new topics like civil participation, community development and planning, and co-operation with NGOs. Within the rhetorical codes of the fight against poverty, women have always been explicitly included. But in 1997 an American female consultant for the World Bank made an evaluation in Guatemala stating clearly that in the projects she had visited, women were absolutely invisible both in the planning and the execution of the projects. An evaluation made one year later on behalf of the German contribution once again documented – even more drastically – that nothing had been done to include women as citizens, and that there had been no programme for poor women in the countryside. The only exceptions to this discrimination against women could be witnessed in the stove projects, in which cooking stoves are given to families in the countryside. These stove projects – at one time a favourite of German development aid – were originally developed as an instrument to cut down the use of firewood. The stoves are relevant both to the ecological and the gender-related aspects that have been established by the funding agencies. For various reasons the stoves, which are distributed to select communities, are rather inappropriate: they take up too much space and overheat the small Indian huts, and they are much too expensive when one takes into account the general standard of living (BMZ, October 1998: 71). It should also be mentioned that there are very few women working in responsible positions in the fund headquarters. In the whole country, only one female employee was working in one of the regional offices.

Nicaragua's situation, in comparison to that of Guatemala, looks much better on the surface. In the rural villages women are actively participating in the school and health committees, very often still called after the Sandinista term, *brigadas*, which gives us a clue as to why there may be a problem with the agencies of the government of President Aleman. Anti-Sandinista personnel have been hired to administer the SIFs. As far as construction work is concerned, they have built up an enterprise that works efficiently, but the supervising engineers are hardly qualified for the newly required type of 'social work'. To overcome this shortcoming, the new tasks are given on a contract basis to so-called NGOs, which are selected according to their professional experience. Employees of these NGOs then go out to the communities, giving lectures on community planning and administration, co-operation and other topics. I use the term 'NGOs' with some caution, because many of these new types of NGOs are in reality mainly consulting firms (*consultorias disfrazadas*). Regional or locally based NGOs, which are very often still related to groups abroad, are hardly involved or permitted to participate. As one of the engineers involved remarked: 'More than 90 per cent of them are Sandinistas' (BMZ, October 1998: 70); this was not meant as a compliment.

Whereas in Guatemala construction work has been done by unpaid members of the community (taking advantage of the Mayan spirit and cultural heritage and saving money as well), the unskilled work in Nicaragua has been paid, but only men have been employed. No special programmes have been developed for women. Even so, the evaluation report written in 1997 for the German financing agency, the KfW (Kreditanstalt für Wiederaufbau), stated: 'In the first place, women and children have been the foremost beneficiaries of the projects, because they are the ones who preeminently will benefit from the schools, health stations and portable water installations' (BMZ, October 1998: 71).

Apparently the male consultant who wrote this could only imagine women in their reproductive functions and in their role as mothers. Without doubt, housework and child-rearing were made a lot easier with the availability of portable water and with the building of a health station nearby; but even so, it is hoped that the men will also use the water supply regularly and that the responsibility of caring for children will also be shared.

Undoubtedly, many NGOs in both countries are trying actively to include women, and they have already established ethnic, transethnic, national, transnational and even international relations with other NGOs. One could even call it an 'NGO boom'. Notwithstanding this boom and the new forms of networking and South–South relations, in general the relationship between NGOs and the state agencies is a difficult one on both sides. In both countries the governments and their agencies consider NGOs to be somehow 'left-wing'. On the other hand, the human rights rhetoric used by most of the NGOs hardly seems to be a basis for any reciprocal understanding, especially when one considers that the engineers working on the projects have a time schedule in mind. The new aspects of participation and community development emphasized since the mid-1990s by the donors are enforcing a new type of professionalization on the part of the NGOs: the transformation of NGOs into small consulting firms, which could lead to divisions within the NGOs. The independent NGOs themselves – or at least quite often their financiers abroad – speak of the danger of co-optation, and say that they want to participate as partners, not as servants of the government or international agencies. Another complex multi-dimensional problem also confronts the NGOs: especially in Guatemala, women-orientated NGOs are still struggling to translate the codes and concepts currently used by international agencies or feminist groups into the codes of Mayan culture, to adapt them to the necessities of everyday life, and to overcome the suffering and traumatic experience of the civil war (Commission for Historical Clarification 1999).

General remarks and observations

1. In the 1990s the prevailing rhetoric of the international and national donors reflected an intensified awareness of women- and gender-related questions. The rhetorical patterns of representation came to include catchwords or codes like 'good governance', 'governability', 'participation', the 'need to form new coalitions', the 'civil rights of ethnic groups', 'co-operation with NGOs', and the 'empowerment' of the poor and of women, and they emphasized the all-embracing

concept of 'civil society'. These rhetorical codes, as I have called them, are the result of international discussions, of the great conferences organized by the UN and the pressures of the nationally or internationally organized NGOs, of feminist movements and networks. And there are even some women struggling within the bureaucratic mire of the big banks and development agencies – especially within the UN – to advance the empowerment of women.[3]

2. In both Guatemala and Nicaragua the SIFs have a high political standing and are administered without any broader or even parliamentary control; they are operated with much discretion and can thus be used for partisan politics. Only donors can exercise control over budget and performance, which makes the political concept of 'civil society' rather questionable. Donors have established a set of regulations that applies to all Latin American countries. Even so, it should be stated that the national performance is filtered through, and depends on, the prevailing national conditions, political framework and cultural heritage.

3. Women as well as the relevance of gender aspects have been verbally included in the design of the funds. However, in reality the presence of women has been practically invisible in the case of Guatemala, and has been tolerated but not especially supported at the community level in Nicaragua, where there would have been an active possibility.

4. The term 'gender', which describes the social construction and performance of sexual categories and the relationship between the sexes, is by now known in more sophisticated circles involved in the development discussion. It has been introduced in order to overcome the former women-related Women in Development (WID) approach (Moser 1993). I am not the first, and will not be the last, to observe that it quite often still seems to be preferable to make special mention of the existence and the needs of women, or at least to combine the categories of women and gender. The banal daily commonplace use of 'gender' makes it easy to declare that almost every type of development project is gender-related, for example the construction of infrastructure, highways and airports and the modernization of the fishing industry.

5. One sceptical remark concerning the relevance of discourse analysis, which is so prominent in the academic field today. Without question, one can use sophisticated methodological approaches to analyse the discursive patterns and rhetorical codes used in the development agencies. One may find a high level of political correctness, new codes and many inconsistencies, shortcomings and arguments that

merely 'paper over' the underlying conflict, but even so one will learn little about the real performance and acceptance of the projects.

6. The intensive ongoing national, transnational and international discussion of gender and empowerment, and the professionalization of urban feminist groups that is occurring in Latin American countries, have given a certain legitimacy to feminist positions. But this legitimization – as already mentioned – will always be filtered, as the case of Nicaragua shows clearly, through national politics, cultural heritage, and the ethnic and class divisions which also still exist between women.

Notes

1. For extensive treatments of the emergence, nature, crisis and reforms of systems of social protection in Latin America, see Huber (1996, 1999) and Laurell (2000); for the ongoing pension privatization on a mandatory basis see Müller (2000) and Bertranou (2000).

2. It should be mentioned that all international as well as national donors have established guidelines regarding the awareness of gender-related topics; monitoring procedures (evaluations) have been established to supervise the performances. Even so, as the cases of Guatemala and Nicaragua demonstrate, little or nothing has been implemented in reality.

3. For the participation of women in social movements, see Escobar and Alvarez (eds) (1992), Tinker (1999), Alvarez (1998, 2000), and Aguilar T. et al. (eds) (1997). For the discussion within international agencies, see Staudt (ed.) (1997).

Bibliography

Aguilar T., A. L., B. E. Dole, M. Herrera, S. Montenegro, L. Camacho and L. Flores (1997) *Movimiento de mujeres en Centroamérica*, Managua, Nicaragua: Programa Regional la Corriente (et al.).

Alvarez, S. E. (1998) 'Latin American Feminisms Go Global: Trends of the 1990s and Challenges for the New Millennium', in Alvarez, S. E., E. Dagnino and A. Escobar (eds), *Cultures of Politics/Politics of Culture: Re-visioning Latin American Social Movements*, Boulder, CO: Westview Press, pp. 293–324.

— (2000) 'Translating the Global. Effects of Transnational Organizing on Local Feminist Discourses and Practices in Latin America', unpublished paper.

Arbeitskreis Armutsbekämpfung durch Hilfe zur Selbsthilfe (1996) 'Weltbankpolitik und Armutsbekämpfung. Das Konzept der Sozialfonds in Zentralamerika'. Dokumentation des Fachkolloquiums, Bonn v. 21–22 February, unpublished paper.

BMZ (Bundesminsterium für wirtschaftliche Zusammenarbeit und Entwicklung) (1998) 'Hauptbericht über die Evaluierung des Instruments der Sozialinvestitionsfonds in Lateinamerika, Phase II. Länderstudien Guatemala und Nicaragua', Bonn im Oktober, unpublished paper.

Bertranou, F. M. (2000) 'Pension Reform and Gender Gaps in Latin America: What are the Policy Options?' Universidad Siglo 21 and UNcuyo, Argentina, April 17, unpublished paper.

Commission for Historical Clarification (1999) *Guatemala. Memory of Silence. Tz'inil na'tab'al*, Report of the Commission for Historical Clarification, Conclusions and Recommendations, Ciudad de Guatemala: CEH.

Escobar, A. and S. E. Alvarez (eds) (1992) *The Making of Social Movements in Latin America: Identity, Strategy, and Democracy*, Boulder, CO: Westview Press.

Huber, E. (1996) 'Options for Social Policy in Latin America: Neoliberal versus Social Democratic Models', in Esping-Andersen, G. (ed.), *Welfare States in Transition: National Adaptations in Global Economies*, London, Thousand Oaks, CA: Sage, pp. 141–91.

— (1999) 'Globalization and Social Policy Developments in Latin America'. Unpublished paper prepared for the conference on 'Globalization and the Future of Welfare States: Interregional Comparisons', Brown University, 22–23 October.

Laurell, A. C. (2000) 'Structural Adjustment and the Globalization of Social Policy in Latin America', *International Sociology*, Vol. 15, No. 2, June, pp. 306–25.

Le Bot, Y. (1997) *La guerra en tierra mayas. Comunidad, violencia y modernidad en Guatemala (1979–1992)*, México, D.F.: Fondo de Cultura Económica.

Mesa-Largo, C. (1994) *Changing Social Security in Latin America: Toward Alleviating the Social Costs of Economic Reform*, Boulder, CO: Westview Press.

Moser, C. (1993) *Gender Planning and Development. Theory, Practice and Training*, London, New York: Routledge.

Müller, K. (2000) 'Pension Privatization in Latin America', *Journal of International Development*, Vol. 12, December, pp. 507–18.

Randall, M. (1994) *Sandino's Daughters Revisited. Feminism in Nicaragua*, New Brunswick, NJ: Rutgers University Press.

Staudt, K. (ed.) (1997): *Women, International Development, and Politics: The Bureaucratic Mire*, updated and expanded edn, Philadelphia: Temple University Press.

Tinker, I. (1999) 'Nongovernmental Organizations: An Alternative Power Base for Women?', in Meyer, M. K. and E. Prügl (eds), *Gender Politics in Global Governance*, Lanham, MD: Rowman & Littlefield Publishers, pp. 88–104.

PART III

Instrumental Silence? Women and Gender in Conflict Management Theory and Practice

Engendering the Field of Conflict Management: Why Gender Does Not Matter! Thoughts from a Theoretical Perspective

Cordula Reimann[1]

Silences are the loudest voices.[2] (Steve Smith)

A glance through the literature and current debates in the field of conflict management will suffice to show that this field – like the discipline of International Relations (IR) until the late 1980s – remains by and large silent about 'gender'. As a result, sophisticated gender-specific or gender-related in-depth analysis of conflict management is still noticeably absent. However, by the late 1990s some policy-related institutions of conflict management practice had started slowly but surely focusing on a more 'gender-sensitive' approach: international governmental organizations (IGOs) like the UN,[3] OSCE,[4] and EU[5] have produced a substantial body of wide-ranging policy recommendations on the position of women in violent conflicts and on the mainstreaming of 'gender' into policies related to post-conflict rehabilitation, development and peacebuilding.[6] By the same token, non-governmental organizations (NGOs) like OXFAM,[7] International Alert,[8] and others have begun stressing the 'gender' dimension of conflict and its implications for the peacebuilding process and for their own work during the last few years. However, conflict management as theory remains resistant to gender-related issues, not to mention to a gender-sensitive analysis of its theoretical implications. Hence the intriguing question that arises is not so much why gender actually matters,[9] but *why it still does not (appear to) matter* in the overall field of conflict management. In other words, what are the main reasons for the persistent and pertinent gender blindness in conflict management? For the sake of clarity, I will distinguish between more conflict management-related reasons on the one hand and more feminism-related reasons on the other. Finally, I try to draw some preliminary conclusions. My intention is to paint in rather broad strokes and to offer some initial provocations for further debate and research. Given the overall theme of this volume, much of the argument that follows has an analytical focus derived from feminist critiques of international relations.

What does 'engendering' mean, and how do we define 'conflict management' and the 'field of conflict management'? 'Engendering' refers – in varying degrees – both to ongoing projects of feminism, the *deconstruction*[10] of gender-biased knowledge claims (that is, revealing androcentrism in fundamental categories, in empirical studies and in theoretical perspectives; locating 'invisible' women; and incorporating women's activities, experience and understanding)[11] and the *reconstruction* of a gender-sensitive theory and practice (that is, exploring the theoretical implications of taking gender seriously).[12] Gender is defined here as the social construction of social relations between 'women' and 'men'.[13] As such, gender must be seen in terms of the *individual gender identity* (social norms and the socially constructed individual identity), the *symbolism of gender* (classification of stereotypical gender dualisms)[14] and the *structure of gender* (the organization and institutionalization of social action in the public and private spheres).[15]

The term 'conflict management' is used inconsistently throughout the literature in the field of conflict management. In fact, this field consists of a plethora of different theoretical approaches and conceptual frameworks that may be, especially for newcomers to the field, rather irritating if not confusing at times. To keep it simple, this chapter uses a rather broad definition of 'conflict management' which embraces all proactive forms of conflict handling including conflict settlement, conflict resolution and conflict transformation approaches. For the purposes of this chapter, all three approaches to conflict management will be used interchangeably,[16] with two exceptions. When the analytical focus is on the process-oriented approach to solving a conflict, I will call it 'conflict resolution/transformation'; when the emphasis is more on an outcome-oriented approach, I will use the term 'conflict settlement'. The overall 'field of conflict management' as theory and practice is best understood as a rather complex, multidisciplinary field drawing on different disciplines such as (international) law, psychology, philosophy, International Relations, conflict/peace research, political science, economics and social anthropology. When I speak of the theory of conflict management, I have in mind different theoretical and empirical approaches to conflict management. When I talk of the practice of conflict management, I refer to the actual, concrete conflict management practice. This may include formal strategies (like negotiation) and informal ones (such as

problem-solving/facilitation workshops or grassroots peacebuilding initiatives).

The problem: the male/mainstream[17] of conflict management

First of all, one could argue that, given its multidisciplinary nature,
the gender blindness of conflict management comes as no surprise: it
'just' reflects the gender-blind spots of its underlying disciplines. However, in the last two decades or so, in most disciplines feminists have
started *deconstructing* and, to a lesser extent, *reconstructing* the discipline-
specific gender-blind spots.[18] The question of why the engendering
process of conflict/peace research including conflict management has
been rather marginal, particularly in contrast to development studies,
cannot be tackled here at any great length. What seems to matter most
is that by the end of the 1980s/early 1990s gender had become a central
category in Development Studies.[19] Since then a huge body of evidence,
both theoretical and empirical, has been presented on the 'gendered'
nature of development aid/policy implying its 'male bias',[20] both at the
conceptual level of structural adjustment programmes and in their
operation and outcomes.

By the mid-1980s, the vast majority of structural adjustment programmes had turned out to be insufficient in alleviating poverty and
achieving sustainable economic and social development in developing
countries. As such '... the *efficiency concerns* of the *practitioners* in
development planning and *policy-making* ... could no longer afford to
ignore women or gender relations'.[21] In other words, the imperative for
engendering development aid came very much from policy-related
concerns: to achieve (more) efficiently a self-sustaining development
process in developing countries, gender inequality had to be addressed
in all areas of development including the informal sector, the formal
sector, the household, etc. By contrast, within IR and in conflict/peace
studies, including the field of conflict management, a clearly defined
and agreed-on policy arm concerned with pressuring efficiency concerns
and social change is clearly missing. This suggests that *the very lack of a
legitimate and clearly defined policy arm* constitutes a straightforward and
unobjectionable reason for the slow and marginal engendering process
of conflict/peace research and IR.[22]

This argument has great surface plausibility. However, it is also
deceptive. It obscures the distinctiveness of the engendering process of
IR compared with that of conflict/peace research, including conflict
management. In contrast to the – albeit slow – engendering process of
International Relations in the last few years, conflict/peace research

and conflict management theory's overall silence on 'gender' has remained striking – even more so in the light of their focus on both
'high' and 'low politics' in contrast to IR's (earlier) emphasis on 'high
politics'.[23] Clearly, conflict/peace research's focus on the macro- and
micro-level should render it more open to a gender perspective related
to the sphere of 'low politics'. So why is the gender blindness of conflict
management rather persistent and pervasive?

The most obvious place to look for gender-blind spots seems to be
the specific research agenda of conflict management theory.[24] In conflict
management theory, a great deal of attention has been devoted to the
analysis of the contextual and process variables of interpersonal/social
and international conflicts, such as the sources and nature of the conflict,
third-party characteristics etc., which may lead to conflict management.[25]
The very little empirical, but not necessarily feminist, research considering 'gender issues' relates 'sexual difference' and subsequent differences
in negotiation styles to the effectiveness of conflict management.[26]
Gender in its threefold dimension (individual gender identity, symbolism
of gender and structure of gender) is neither an analytical category nor
an integral part of different approaches to conflict management. To
illustrate and exemplify the gender blindness of conflict management
theory, I will examine three distinctive approaches to conflict management. These are conflict settlement, conflict resolution and conflict
transformation.

Conflict settlement

Like early IR, the realist approach to conflict management – conflict
settlement à la Zartman and Bercovitch – was heavily preoccupied with
the notion of 'negative peace' (peace without social justice), or precisely
the 'cult of power' from which women have been excluded. The world
of IR scholars like Zartman and Bercovitch is one of international
conflicts defined as results of 'incompatible interests' and 'competition
over rare resources'.[27] Their analytical focus is an outcome-oriented one:
it is necessary to wait for a 'ripe moment'[28] in order to end violent
conflict and to agree on, for example, a cease-fire. Official third-party
interventions in the form of arbitration, peace negotiations, 'power
mediation', or 'carrot and stick' (the use of leverage or coercion in the
form of promised rewards and threatened punishments) indeed represented and reflected 'male hegemony' in so far as most practitioners –
diplomats and scholars of conflict management – were (and still are!)
men. The analytical focus was very much on assumptions of rational
and autonomous male selves that were taken for granted. Not only did

conflict settlement subscribe to a stereotypical understanding of men, it also – implicitly and explicitly – denied social relationships in general and women's agency in particular.

One could therefore argue, as Jacqui True has done for the IR context,[29] that in conflict management theory the understanding of human agency is imposed by taking the standpoint of men as somehow generic. Women and their social interests, ideas and experience were considered simply irrelevant to the analysis of conflict management and, in turn, were 'hidden'[30] or made 'invisible'.

Conflict resolution

John Burton's pluralist, transnational approach to IR sets the terms of reference for a more process-oriented, conflict resolution approach.[31] In contrast to Zartman and Bercovitch, Burton stresses that conflicts in international relations primarily arise out of the failure to satisfy human needs. Seen in these terms, the origins of a conflict can be found in the underlying needs (like security, identity, participation, recognition, distributive justice etc.) of the conflict parties. The aim is to eliminate the violent and destructive manifestations of conflict which are based on the unsatisfied needs and fears of the conflict parties. The key is to translate the interests and positions of the parties involved into their underlying needs for identity, security, and participation. To facilitate and promote 'controlled communication'[32] between the conflict parties, Burton introduced the concept and tool of the 'problem-solving workshop'. This is an academically based, unofficial third-party approach, bringing together representatives of parties in conflict for direct communication. Based on human needs theory,[33] a problem-solving workshop aims at reframing the conflict as a shared problem with mutually acceptable solutions.[34] As such, the aim of a 'problem-solving workshop' is the satisfaction of the parties involved and hence increased co-operation and improved communication between them.

Burton's broadening of the agenda of conflict management (and IR with his 'world society approach') to include questions of distributive justice and the satisfaction of needs renders his approach more open to theorizing about gender than its realist counterpart. However, the hierarchical power structures of society, women's needs, the allegedly non-political 'private sphere' and, most importantly, the gendered notion of international conflict, are 'neutralized': violent conflict *and* its management in particular are basically seen as 'gender neutral', that is they are considered as having no effects on the position and role of 'women' and 'men' in society. However, women may be discussed and 'brought into' the problem-solving workshop as an additional category next to ethnonational and religious groups. Structural notions (like the gender-specific distribution of labour in most conflict situations) and symbolic features of gender (like questions of shifting identities of masculinity and femininity in conflict situations) which might prevent women from participating in problem-solving workshops are excluded, and hence indirectly reinforced.

Conflict transformation

John Paul Lederach's idea of conflict transformation moves far beyond conflict resolution and conflict settlement. According to Lederach, peacebuilding is best understood as a *long-term, multi-dimensional and dynamic process.*[35] The aim of this process should be not only to include a multiplicity of peacemakers from the grassroots level in the top leadership, but also to create an infrastructure for social empowerment. In contrast to theorists in conflict resolution and conflict settlement, the scholar-practitioner Lederach challenges the notion of simply transferring conflict management techniques across cultures with little or no understanding of the cultural knowledge and resources available in the conflict setting.[36] The underlying assumption is that the potential for peacebuilding already exists in the particular region or community, and hence is rooted in its 'traditional culture'. To build on local struggles for social change then means to be aware of the already existing traditional ways of conflict handling in a given society. Along these lines, Lederach has influenced the recent debate on conflict management theory. He has criticized most approaches to conflict management theory – in both the realist and the pluralist vein – for their culture blindness, that is, their theoretical and practical bias to a Westernized model of conflict handling.

Clearly, Lederach's focus on social empowerment and transformation seems most favourable to theorizing about gender. However, I would argue that in this model women seem mainly of empirical interest: women *qua* women's groups may be an integral part of grassroots groups or local peace constituencies, but with what gender-specific consequences and in which gendered context of conflict remains unclear. The diverse and even shifting identities and roles of women (and men) are dismissed. In other words, gender as 'women's issues' may be *subordinated* to the culture question. This becomes strikingly obvious when Lederach discusses local peacemaking NGOs and their 'indigenous' peacemaking techniques and methods. He dismisses the fact that most indigenous customs of conflict handling are based on notions of gender inequality (like stereotypical notions of masculinity and femininity), and as such may be understood as the reasons for domestic and social conflict. An illustrative example is the system of the Somali elders who, as all-male members of the community, have the traditional authority to coerce the conflict parties into settling a conflict and accepting an agreement.

Given that all three approaches are much more complex in theory and practice than this snapshot may suggest, any attempt to classify various approaches to conflict management theory must fall short of this complexity. However, the brief analysis of these three approaches highlights some of the gender-blind gaps in the theory. The male social character seems hegemonic, in a Gramscian sense, in so far as the absence of women seems somehow 'natural'.[37] In this context, V. Spike Peterson and Jacqui True's characterization of the mainstream/malestream IR research community may also hold true for conflict management theory, namely, that it manifests a 'simultaneous reliance on and refusal to theorize hegemonic masculinities'.[38]

This leads us to another reason for the persistent gender blindness of conflict management theory: 'academic machismo'. The 'added value' of a gender dimension still seems to be unclear to most 'male-/mainstream' practitioners and scholars in the field of conflict management. It seems fair to say that there is marginal, if any, understanding of feminist theory.[39] Under the 'veil of ignorance', most scholars claim their work has 'no gender dimension',[40] since women – invisible or not – simply do not matter for their analysis of 'hard core' questions related to high-profile negotiations, unsatisfied human needs, or culture-sensitive bottom-up approaches.[41] The point here is not so much that most scholars and practitioners ignore the gender dimension of their work on purpose; more important seems to be the fact that gender is not purposefully included. One could argue that this form of 'gender blindness' reflects a bias towards 'academic machismo'[42] in the form of academic and disciplinary paternalism, and hence 'a deep fear of looking at the microstructuring of masculinity/ies'.[43] Related to this is the fear of losing control over academic resources, agendas and policies, since the advocacy of gender issues seems to be considered a 'win/lose' scenario. It seems safe to say that feminist interventions in conflict management, like those in IR, are often portrayed as 'male-bashing'.[44] This misunderstanding refers to the malestream's misinterpretation of 'gender issues' as 'women's issues'. Gender, defined as the social construction of social relations, should be of as much interest and concern to men as to women. The rather limited and half-hearted understanding of feminism within the field of conflict management has to be seen in the wider context of the recent dismissal of critical theory, post-modern-ism/post-structuralism, and social constructivism.[45]

This, in turn, leads us to the role of theory and notions of self-reflexivity in conflict management theory. The field of conflict management is far removed from the theoretical and methodological discussions that have taken place in IR during the last 40 years. In contrast to conflict management, IR as a discipline, especially in the Anglo-American research community, has come a long way from the analytical and 'practical' backwardness of a research community that was virtually silent on questions of ontology (what is being analysed) and epis-temology (how it is analysed). Not only did the so-called fourth debate[46] foster questions on ontology and epistemology, it also promoted 'critical perspectivism'[47] as a form of critical self-reflection. In order to avoid methodological and theoretical closure and incarceration,[48] this debate provided a stronger impetus for dialogue with developments in social/political theory such as critical theory,[49] historical sociology,[50] post-structuralism/post-modernism,[51] and feminism.

By contrast, a study of the relevant literature in the field of conflict management suggests that dominant approaches are 'theory-light', that is to say they remain rather shy of 'theorizing' with regard to both conflict and conflict management. In fact, the field of conflict management seems to have 'significantly surpassed theory building'.[52] Most conflict management approaches or strategies are not based on a broad theoretical concept of conflict or an explicit theory of conflict.[53] There is 'no real theoretical justification for *when, (who)* and *why* to use (what) conflict intervention techniques'.[54] By contrast, one may find '... a number of processes which are dependent upon the expertise of the individual practitioner'.[55] Most of them turn out to be rather static models which are '... inductive descriptions of core components of practice, with some prescriptive guidelines for interventions'.[56] The most noteworthy example here may be the work of the Harvard Negotiation Project.[57] Others, like the realist Bercovitch, aim at developing regu-larities, if not causal explanations, about 'effective' conflict management. Bercovitch's research comes in the form of large-scale systematic studies of 'effective' conflict management, or more experimental and laboratory approaches to third-party intervention. Such large-scale systematic studies receive particular analytical attention as they are considered to produce the most policy-relevant findings for political decision-makers.[58]

The understanding of theory adopted in the field of conflict management is thus very much reduced to the explanation of observable or personal experience, defined in terms of cause–effects logic or policy recommendations. The ultimate test of theory is its usefulness and technical applicability in guiding and orientating policy towards given ends, such as the settlement of violent conflicts. Confronted with this criticism, a lot of scholar-practitioners in the field point out half in self-defence, half in despair, that their focus is on practice, 'the real world out there'. Why should they care (so much) about theory? Apart from anything else, this indicates a rather limited understanding of theory. Most conflict management research seems (more implicitly than explicitly) to work exclusively with the understanding of theory as an empirical tool.[59] That is, theory is expected to offer first and foremost some framework to analyse and describe (and sometimes predict) the 'real world'. While it is beyond the scope of this chapter to spell out the (striking) methodological differences between the work of the mainstream approaches to conflict management theory, what seems to matter most here is that all of them subscribe to *objectivism*. This is the view that objective knowledge of the 'real world out there' is possible whether or not this knowledge is grounded in subjective experience. Based on a (strict) subject–object and fact–value distinction, scientific, 'objective' findings not only sharply contrast with value judgements, which are considered to be highly subjective, but are given epistemological priority. Only a few scholars like Adam Curle reject this view and subscribe to Galtung's definition of 'objectivity as an inter-subjective dialogue based on explicit premises *i.e. values*'.[60]

The prime analytical focus of conflict management research is on empirical evidence, without explicitly considering that theoretical notions already inform the practice of conflict management itself. Most past research in the field, especially in the Anglo-American research community, has focused on the detached analysis of third-party strategies and behavior, the nature of conflicts etc. Burton's credo to get 'from subjectivity to theory-based objectivity'[61] turns out to be

> inappropriate because any analysis of the social world will be infused with the values of the analyst. In a world of competing values, the merits of any particular model, therefore, are not self-evident. No model is free from ideology. Since John Burton wishes to change the world, he has no alternative but to make the argument for change in ideological terms. It is counter-productive to dress one's values in natural science garb. A non-ideological model of social order is a chimera which it is a mistake to claim or pursue.[62]

By subscribing to theory as an empirical tool most theoretical or conceptual approaches to conflict management turn out to be what Robert Cox has called 'problem-solving approaches',[63] that is to say, they work with and within a given dominant framework of institutions and social relations.[64] By definition, a 'problem-solving approach' 'takes the world as it finds it, with the prevailing social and power relationships and the institutions into which they are organized, as the given framework for action'.[65] Furthermore, a 'problem-solving approach' does not critically reflect on the very framework of social order/status quo, which involves elements like its gendered nature or its androcentric (male-centred) universality and objectivity.

This may also explain why most of the existing conceptual and explanatory frameworks of conflict management theory work with an implicit, taken-for-granted agreement about the nature of social justice and (positive and negative) peace.[66] An explicit normative theoretical foundation essential for evaluating and understanding 'success' in conflict management is missing.[67] Lewis Rasmussen, Nadim Rouhana and Joy Rothman stress that most evaluation of successful conflict management is done poorly, mainly because 'the theoretical grounds on which an intervention has been built have not been clarified'.[68] Therefore, largely unstated and 'hidden' values define what 'success' means in conflict management. Given these premises, the idea of an 'effective' outcome seems in itself subjectively constructed: to label an effort in conflict management a success is a value judgement.[69] This critique is partly taken up in the ongoing discussion on 'Peace and Conflict Impact Assessment' (PCIA) in the field of conflict management and development. PCIA aims to offer a conceptual framework for systematically anticipating and evaluating the potential and actual peace-building (or peace-inhibiting) impact of development projects in war-prone areas, and vice versa.

In conclusion, it is obvious that gender blindness is only the final straw in the overall refusal to take into account ontological and epistemological considerations in the field of conflict management. Due to a rather limited understanding of theory, scholars have largely focused on the 'reality' of conflict management practices, without reflecting how far these have themselves been informed by highly normative but taken-for-granted assumptions about the legitimacy, power and 'neutrality' of the third party, of universal and generic human needs, of the unequal distribution of power among the parties, and so on. This is because most research in the field of conflict management has been based on flawed dichotomies, such as objectivity/subjectivity, fact/value, public–private. Conflict management theory's implicit commitment to the public-private split has rendered the private sphere, and thus women, 'non-political' and 'invisible'. This, in turn, may explain most scholars' reluctance to address the 'gendered' features of violent conflict and of the post-settlement phase. The increase in domestic violence, rape and changes of the family structure and social structures is regarded as somehow 'natural'. Most conflict settlements and many bottom-up approaches take the form of 'gendered deals':[70] formal and informal peace negotiations and initiatives tend to *exclude* women from the relevant decision- and policy-making bodies and from the implementation of the resulting agreements.

The solution? Feminism and its difficult relationship with conflict management

Given the overall absence of women and feminists in international conflict management the silence on gender in conflict management seems less striking, but it is still particularly ironic in view of feminism's longstanding association with pacifism.[71] In the anglophone research community, most female scholars and feminists who get involved in 'gender and conflict' have an academic or practical background in development studies/co-operation.[72] This comes as no surprise for two reasons. First, as mentioned earlier, in development studies a huge body of evidence on the 'male bias'[73] of development aid has been gathered since the mid-1980s – both at the conceptual level of structural adjustment policies and at the empirical level, that is, of their operation and outcomes. Second, many current development co-operation projects take place in violent conflict situations. Hence they have to deal with the social and economic effects of crisis escalation and post-settlement peacebuilding in one way or another.[74]

Both the empirical and the theoretical body of evidence on 'women/ gender and conflict'[75] concentrate very much on emergency situations in the 1980s and 1990s. There is little reference to the post-settlement peacebuilding process *or* to an explicit 'non-gendered peace deal'. Most current peace deals, for example the Oslo Peace Accords or the Dayton Agreement, do not take into account the gendered nature of conflicts as reflected in features such as the gendered distribution of labour before and after the conflict.[76]

For most of these scholars, conflict management theory and the practice of conflict management has not been of primary analytical concern. By the same token, the terms 'conflict analysis', 'peacebuilding' and 'conflict resolution' (interrelated but distinctive areas of interest both in substance and in emphasis) are often used interchangeably, if not synonymously.[77] While one could argue that this reflects a lack of coherent conceptual and theoretical rigour in some feminist work, I would suggest that it points to a more general problem touched on earlier. Given the multidisciplinary and complex nature of the field of conflict management in theory and practice, it seems safe to say that feminism may somehow find it difficult to situate itself. One could argue that feminist approaches to the underlying disciplines of conflict management theory like law, psychology, philosophy, International Relations, politics, economics, etc. are still preoccupied with the reconstruction and deconstruction of these gender-blind disciplines. Along these lines, feminist approaches which are busy with *deconstructing* and *reconstructing* the discipline-specific gender-blind spots of conflict management theory's underpinnings *implicitly* engage in conflict management. However, these scholars are simply too busy to *explicitly and deliberately* focus on the 'gender blindness' of conflict management theory and practice. At the same time, the distinctiveness of the 'gender blindness' of conflict management theory and practice seems to be the part and parcel of the rather limited feminist interest in conflict management.

On the one hand, the co-operative and non-adversarial features of the theory and practice of conflict resolution (John Burton) and conflict transformation (John Paul Lederach) run in tandem with the essentialist notion of 'women as peacemakers'. Indeed, the essentialist equation of women with peace *and* its building fits somehow too nicely into Herb Kelman and John Burton's idea of the mediator as associated with patience, empathy and non-violence.[78] Some feminists might therefore argue that the practice of conflict resolution just incorporates inherently female characteristics such as compassion, empathy and co-operation as a matter of course. In this way, conflict resolution in theory and practice stresses the stereotypical female attribute of the necessity 'to sustain life'. And in a gender-friendly reading of Burton's work, women may become the 'female mediators'. So why be critical of conflict resolution, which is based on allegedly inherent female characteristics and implicitly seems to support the equation of 'woman with the peaceful sex'? This equation goes back to the old debate in feminism on questions of war and peace and women's involvement in them.[79]

On the other hand, in the last 30 years, international conflict management has not done much to portray itself as an exciting 'new' enterprise distinctively different from mainstream/malestream IR. In fact, until recently, introductory textbooks on conflict management theory either did not exist, or failed to stress its multidisciplinary approach.[80] Apart from material with an exclusively psychological perspective, most of the academic literature on conflict management theory was written from a realist or an institutionalist/pluralist IR perspective. Most international conflict management theorists are still either IR scholars or psychologists. Many feminists may have read conflict management theory and practice as a prime example of another form of 'masculine hegemony'[81] and the perpetuation of a 'power cult' as in early IR: from a (standpoint) feminist perspective the whole 'enterprise' of international conflict management appears first and foremost to be one of domination. International conflict management, both in theory and practice, remains a 'man's world'. In contrast to those engaged at the domestic and local level in efforts to build peace, most of the practitioners and academics involved in international conflict management are still men.

One could thus argue that the field of conflict management perpetuates and enforces the exclusive power structures and power hierarchies of a patriarchal society. Some feminists might argue that most third-party interventions tend to suppress social conflicts like gender inequality. All third-party interventions such as mediation or negotiation are based on principles of confidentiality and privacy, far removed from any form of public influence and participation. One has to ask to what extent there is a danger that, in the push for privacy, women's interests are once again marginalized or co-opted. This goes to the heart of the problem: is there a 'wolf in sheep's clothing', that is to say, do we change the symbols but subscribe to the 'old' principles and practices of patriarchy in the 'new' post-settlement social order?[82]

By managing or 'continually resolving conflicts',[83] conflict management remains caught in the logic and practices of *management* and so neglects the underlying power arrangements of its own initiatives, such as gender inequality. This suggests that most international conflict management turns a blind eye to an understanding of violent conflicts as positive moments of radical social change. During violent conflict situations, many women take over traditionally male-defined responsibilities and tasks and – notwithstanding gross human rights violations and everyday brutality – break with the old social order. As Esmeralda, a woman from El Salvador, puts it: '... I feel we have learnt something about what living in this country is about ... how some people have more opportunities than others and how people from poor classes live ... I also learnt how to work ... I have stopped being scared. [I've learnt] to speak out in front of people, to know more things, about others as well as myself.'[84]

In the light of their survival of violence and of social and economic deprivation, women may challenge traditional gender stereotypes by taking on non-traditional roles, such as becoming combatants or heads of households, and by gaining (more) self-confidence and new economic and political skills. This was clearly the case in Liberia, where Liberian women, being traditionally not very powerful, returned empowered from the refugee camps in Nigeria and Ghana. In Sri Lanka, Tamil

women actively participate in the war between the Sri Lankan government and the Liberation Tigers of Tamil Eelam (LTTE) as LTTE fighters
and suicide bombers. Due to the ongoing war, many households have
turned into female-headed households. Women became the dominant
breadwinners and took over 'traditional' male roles and duties. Women
who were subjected to social and cultural restrictions, sexual abuse and/
or domestic violence in the pre-violent conflict situations may perceive
violent conflicts as moments of empowerment and true liberation.

The ending of a violent conflict not only promotes changes in the
division of labour, in the political (trans)formation and women's involvement in them, it may also lead to (radical) changes in gender relations.
However, one cannot stress strongly enough that all these changes need
not necessarily be permanent and empowering for women in the long
term. And one should keep in mind that civilians – here predominantly
women and children – are both targets and the most vulnerable victims
of all 'internationalized' conflicts like those in Sri Lanka, Liberia or El
Salvador. What seems to matter most is to see the ambiguous character
of violent conflicts for most women. While some violent conflicts may
indeed represent intermediate catalysts for women's empowerment,
wars are first and foremost experienced as devastating human tragedy,
gross atrocities and large-scale ('gendered') human rights violations
(sexual violence, rape and forced prostitution). Therefore, when discussing women's agency in violent conflict and the management of
conflict, one has to keep in mind the uneasy tension between women's
'vulnerability/victimhood' on the one hand and women's 'empower-
ment/emancipation' on the other, without prioritizing one over the
other.

Following the argument above, one could assume that it would be a
straightforward and crucial task to decode conflict management's
'gender-blind' spots both on a conceptual and empirical level. However,
violent conflicts *and* their management as 'gendered' social phenomena
have remained by and large unquestioned and rather under-theorized in
feminism. Indeed, these aspects have received very little attention in
past and most current NGO work, and academic research mainly focused
on the impact of conflict on women (and on men and gender relations).
A case in point may be the growing body of work analysing women's
diverse activities and 'new experiences' in the course of a conflict that
may have social, political and economic consequences for the post-
settlement peacebuilding process.[85] While portraying the great variety
of *active* roles played by women during violent conflict and in the wider
peacebuilding process, this approach obscures the complex nature and
dynamics of 'gender', and its relevance to international conflict in

general and to the theory and practice of international conflict management in particular. It remains, for instance, by and large unclear to what extent conflict management is based, if not even dependent, on certain gender arrangements in the private or public sphere and on stereotypical notions of masculinity and femininity. This is to say, too, that most of this work has fallen short of an analysis of the *impact of gender relations on conflict in general and on conflict management in particular.* Most of the research has not, for example, considered the possibility that local methods or customs of conflict resolution which are based on gender inequality might even foster conflictual patterns in society. In fact, most indigenous customs of conflict handling are based on stereotypical notions of masculinity and femininity. The system of the elders in Somalia who, as all-male members of the community, have traditional authority to coerce the conflict parties into settling a conflict and accepting an agreement, may serve as an illustration. However, the events in Somaliland in the early 1990s may be a rather positive example of a gender- and culture-sensitive intervention. In Somaliland, indigenous methods of conflict handling were part and parcel of the peacebuilding process from the very beginning, and the attempt to stop the fighting was successful.[86] Locally based reconciliation conferences acknowledged the contributions of women to peacebuilding and reconciliation.[87] This is to say, too, that claims for cultural sensitivity are used as an excuse for political inaction on gender issues. The example of Somaliland may teach us that cultural boundaries are indeed less fixed, but porous and flexible – and gender-sensitive approaches can take advantage of this. Not only does the culture/gender 'double bind' raise crucial questions about the notions of (im)partiality, power and a more partisan approach to conflict transformation, it also poses some serious challenges in respect of how to get the culture and gender dimensions of conflict management sufficiently and equally considered in theory and practice.

On a more positive note, one has to keep in mind that gender (identity) is made up by other important variables such as class, age, religion and ethnicity, hence any analysis of peacebuilding activities in a specific region and at a specific time has to be seen against this background. In other words, a gender analysis has always to take into account the wider constraining social, economic and political forces involved in rebuilding society after a violent conflict. This, in turn, clearly speaks to the importance of more contextualized in-depth analyses, comparative case studies, and 'lessons learned' studies of *gender relations and their impact on post-war peacebuilding activities.* How far is international and inter-group conflict and its management based, even dependent on, certain gender arrangements? How far are different theoretical and practical approaches to conflict management based on similar (or even the same) gendered concepts, underlying gendered imagery and symbolism found in mainstream IR? What is discussed, and what is left out in the gender-neutral language in the field of conflict management? How are masculinity and femininity defined in the broader peacebuilding process, compared with wartime?

From gender blindness to engendering conflict management

In a field as heterogeneous and dynamic as conflict management, the above discussion does not represent an exhaustive account of the rich tradition and complexity of different approaches and their theoretical and empirical interpretation – both inside and outside the anglophone research community. Such a brief analysis can do no more than highlight the most crucial aspects of the gender blindness of conflict management as theory and practice. However, focusing on the reasons for the gender blindness of conflict management, the following analytical gaps and disjunctions became evident:

- 'Gender blindness' as the inherent fundament of other disciplines.
- Lack of a legitimate and clearly defined policy arm which is concerned with efficiency pressures.
- Gender-neutral understanding of conflict and its management.
- Early focus on the 'cult of power' from which women have been excluded.
- Half-hearted or limited inclusion of feminism within/by the mainstream suggests 'academic machismo' on the one hand and academic paternalism on the other.
- Misunderstandings encountered about feminism in conflict management.
- Limited understanding of theory and refusal of normative considerations.
- Limited attention paid to wider debates within social/political theory.
- Predominance of 'problem-solving' approaches within conflict management in the light of limited self-reflexivity.
- Research community's failure to readdress the fact-value split.
- Difficult and ambiguous relationship between feminism and conflict management.

Given that most theory of conflict management remains gender-blind, the most crucial impetus coming from this chapter should be to avoid a theoretical and empirical framework that continues to be couched in gender-neutral terms. Therefore, what seems to matter most is the gender-sensitive *deconstruction* and *reconstruction* of the gendered imagery employed, and of the categories and institutions – both in positivist and in the latest post-positivist approaches to conflict management as theory. This, in turn, must address misunderstandings about feminism (and the meaning of gender!) commonly encountered in the field of conflict management.

A more thorough engendering process of conflict management will be highly dependent on the openness of conflict management practitioners and scholars, most likely the very few feminists among them, to bringing into the open the gender blindness of conflict management as theory and practice. The underlying, albeit highly controversial, assumption among some feminists is that there *is* indeed a place for a gender-sensitive analysis in this extremely androcentric field. I would argue that a gender analysis with its three-fold definition of gender (individual gender identity, symbolism of gender and structure of gender) is an important entry point for understanding and situating the complex internal power dynamics of conflict management activities, and for promoting social justice in peacebuilding activities. Apart from anything else, this is mainly due to three distinctive reasons that point to three rather neglected areas in the field of conflict management.

First, most analysis of conflict management works with a rather simplistic and static notion of identity. While John Burton, E. Azar[88] and others have stressed the identity group as the most relevant unit of analysis in the study of 'protracted' or 'intractable' social conflicts, their work does not account for shifting and constructed identities and their connections with violence in most violent conflicts.[89] Because of its explicit emphasis on the individual, a gender analysis encourages the scholar/practitioner to focus on the individual and his/her changing identities, roles, needs and interests in the pre- and post-conflict situation.

Second, by its very definition a gender analysis intermediates between the individual and the structural level. That is, it addresses essential linkages between the micro-level (the individual) and the macro-level (the organization of social action in the private and public spheres), by taking into account the meso-level (symbolism of gender such as certain notions of masculinity and femininity). At the same time, it synthesizes the analysis of the private (the individual and the household) and the public sphere (the community, the state and the international arena). A gender analysis enables us to analyse the impact of violent conflicts on individuals, how they suffer, what underlying constraining factors (like violent forms of masculinity *and* femininity) may drive them to (incite others to) use violence. In fact, a gender analysis has the potential to generate closer-knit linkages between different levels of analysis and different categories of actors.[90] It addresses the question of how far the individual motivation may be shaped and constrained or fostered by the (gender) symbolism and structure of the community level and beyond. By the same token, it may help us to shed light on male and female violence, with neither being the result of purely individual motivations, but generated by a particular configuration of gender symbolism and structure (embodied in social institutions that promote certain notions of femininity and masculinity). In a word, looking at conflict management through 'gender lenses' may bring into the open the shifting identities of women and men, together with the underlying symbolism of femininity and masculinity and its structural manifestation, i.e., the organization and institutionalization of social action in the public and private spheres, during and after conflict management processes.

Third, a gender analysis is a tool enabling us to directly address dichotomous, dualist theorizing in the field of conflict management. Gender, by its very definition, informs about and criticizes the very organization and institutionalization of social action based on the 'colonizing dichotomies'[91] of masculinity (associated with objectivity/reason/power/violence/fact etc.) and femininity (equated with subjectivity/feeling/powerlessness/non-violence/value, etc.). This argument, carried further, suggests that with the ongoing analytical lack of attention to gender in the theory of conflict management, any kind of dichotomous, dualist theorizing cannot be successfully challenged and transformed, but, on the contrary, will be further reinforced.

At the same time, there is still a great need for sophisticated gender-specific or gender-related in-depth analysis of conflict management, for example with regard to the culture/gender 'double bind' in most conflict management processes, or women's inclusion in and exclusion from formal negotiations. The very exclusion of women from, for example, the UN-organized, -facilitated and -sponsored peace conferences in Somalia helped to enhance the legitimacy and authority of the warlords, who are often strangers to the local communities. But what would have been different if women had been included in the formal and informal negotiations from the very beginning? Would women have made a difference in the peace conferences?

If one accepts that the (albeit slow) impetus for a stronger analytical focus on gender issues in the field of conflict management comes very much from the more engendered field of development,[92] the next question is how to apply gender-sensitive 'lessons learned' studies of development aid to the field of conflict management. This also seems highly timely, given the current debates on Peace and Conflict Impact

Assessment (PCIA) both in the field of conflict management and in development co-operation.

The field of development co-operation has produced and developed a large number of gender frameworks and gender-sensitive tools during the last ten years. These include the Harvard Analytical Framework/ Gender Roles Framework (GRF) and, derived from it, the Capacities and Vulnerabilities Analysis (CVA), the Development Planning Unit Framework (DPUF) and the Social Relations Framework (SRF). While none of these conceptual frameworks has been specifically developed to address and explain the conflict situation and its distinctive pre- and post-crisis features, all have been applied in emergency/crisis situations. The intriguing challenge is then to show to what extent the field of crisis prevention and conflict management can actually learn from the field of development. The question is *how, to what extent,* and *which* gender frameworks of the development field may, *if at all,* be successfully applied to and integrated into the field of conflict management.

My final conclusion is that what is needed are further steps to embed and institutionalize the benefits of feminist and non-feminist 'cross-fertilization' in the form of journals, working groups, etc. within the conflict management community. Otherwise we will repeat and re-create discussions on 'women or gender and conflict' and, on a happy and sunny day, even on 'women or gender and conflict management', on a rather *ad hoc* basis, which may not go beyond academic paternalism and goodwill declarations. This also means that the engendering process will always remain partial and marginal if gender-aware analysis and research is considered as 'surplus work' on 'women's issues' by the malestream research community, or remains highly dependent on the 'tyranny of the urgent' in form of policy pressures!

Notes

1. The author would like to thank Sarah Perrigo and Norbert Ropers for comments on an earlier version of this chapter.

2. Smith, S. (1995), p. 2.

3. See for example, United Nations (1995), UNIFEM (1995, 1996).

4. See OSCE (1999, 2000) and http://www.osceprag.cz.

5. See European Commission (1996a, 1996b).

6. Gender mainstreaming is understood here as a strategy to promote gender equality. It has two dimensions: on the one hand, the inclusion of a gender analysis as an integral part of any design, implementation, monitoring and evaluation of all policies, projects and programmes, and on the other hand, initiatives to consult women and men equally and integrate their needs,

views and concerns in all decision-making processes across all issues in question.

7. See El-Bushra, J. and E. Piza Lopez (1993).

8. See International Alert (1997, 1998a and 1998b). International Alert also initiated the international campaign, 'From the Village Council to the Negotiating Table. Women in Peacebuilding', in October 1999 with the aim to strengthen the role of women in peacebuilding and conflict transformation processes. See also International Alert (1999).

9. I have discussed elsewhere the question of why gender does matter; see Reimann, C. (1999).

10. Note that the use of 'deconstruction' in connection with this feminist 'project' is not derived from Jacques Derrida and has as such no post-modernist or post-structuralist significance.

11. V. S. Peterson, 'Introduction', in Peterson, V. S. (ed.) (1992), p. 6 (his emphasis).

12. Ibid., p. 2. The feminist reconstruction is based on the results of the deconstruction project. At their best, feminist deconstruction and reconstruction are complementary and interrelated. As such, engendering constitutes the first step in the wider 'gender mainstreaming' approach.

13. In the following, I will use 'men' and 'women' without quotation marks. I do so without posing the 'gender' categories as fixed, permanent and essential. Rather, I consider both terms as socially constructed and manipulated subject statuses, which emerge from a politicization of slightly different anatomies in labour, work, etc. As such, these two terms are not necessarily mutually exclusive categories.

14. Stereotypical gender dualisms are classified by different dichotomies which have little in common with sexual difference. Masculinity, for example, is associated with objectivity/reason/autonomy/subject/production/culture in contrast to femininity equated with subjectivity/feeling/dependency/object/value/reproduction/nature. To be feminine is to be not masculine.

15. Harding, S. (1986).

16. I am aware that the term conflict management is a rather unhappy one, because, for example, conflict transformation approaches move far beyond the 'logic of management'. In the absence of a 'better' alternative, I use conflict management as an umbrella term, while being aware of its definitional pitfalls. In my reading of the literature, the term 'conflict resolution' – especially in the anglophone research community – is too heavily associated with the work of John Burton, Herb Kelman and Ronald Fisher.

17. The term 'malestream' defines the male-dominated discipline of conflict management. 'Malestream' need not necessarily be mainstream (think of the gender blindness of critical theory, for example) and vice versa (female peace researchers doing mainstream research). If 'mainstream' can be used interchangeably with 'malestream' it is obvious and indicated as such.

18. By the mid-1990s a reasonable number of feminist articles and books had brought new insights and conceptual frameworks into the discipline of

International Relations. For an excellent and comprehensive introduction to feminist encounters with IR, see Steans, J. (1998).

19. See for example, Wallice, T. and C. March (eds) (1991), Subrahmanian, R. (1996) and Moser, C. O. N. (1993).

20. See Elson, D. (ed.) (1995).

21. Pankhurst, D. and J. Pearce (1998), p. 156 (emphasis Reimann).

22. See Ibid.

23. The term 'high politics' refers to questions of national security, particularly the strategic interests of the states. 'Low politics', by contrast, points to questions of social welfare and socio-economic issues.

24. The categorization does not pretend to be definite or exhaustive.

25. See for example, Bercovitch, J. and J. Z. Rubin (eds) (1992), pp. 1–29, and Frei, D. (1975).

26. See Weingarten, H. R. and E. Douvan (1985); Burrell, N. A. et al. (1988); Wall, V. D. and M. L. Dewhurst (1991); Maxwell, D. (1992) and Stamato, L. (1992).

27. See Zartman, W. I. (1985, 1987); Bercovitch, J. and J. Z. Rubin (eds) (1992); Bercovitch, J. (ed.) (1996) and Zartman, I. W. (ed.) (1995).

28. Zartman, I. W. (1985). Critiques of 'ripeness' can be found in the work of, for example, Mitchell, C. (1995) and Kleiboer, M. (1994).

29. See True, J. (1996), p. 228.

30. See Halliday, F. (1988).

31. See Burton, J. W. (1972).

32. See Burton, J. W. (1969).

33. John Burton's human needs theory is based on the work of A. Maslow and Paul Sites.

34. See Burton, J. W. (1987, 1990a).

35. See Lederach, J. P. (1997).

36. See Lederach, J. P. (1995).

37. For Gramsci's notion of hegemony in the context of international relations, see Cox, R. W. (1983).

38. Peterson, V. S. and J. True, '"New Times" and New Conversations', in Zalewski, M. and J. Parpart (eds) (1998), p. 15.

39. I am aware that in conflict/peace research some male peace researchers actually try to include feminist perspectives in their academic work. See Krippendorff, E. (1988); Galtung, J. (1996). However, their encounters with feminist theory take the form of academic goodwill declarations rather than of a thorough analysis of feminist theory. The German peace researcher Tordis Batscheider comes to the same kind of conclusion; see Batscheider, T. (1993), p. 13.

40. See for example, Carver, T. (1996), p. 4.

41. In this day and age of political correctness most male peace researchers,

of course, are less explicit about their gender blindness. Here I would agree with Betty A. Reardon that 'what is said around coffee tables in research institutes often is more truly revealing than what is said around seminar tables'. See Reardon, B. A. (1985), p. 5.

42. Zalewski, M., 'Introduction', in Zalewski, M. and J. Parpart (eds) (1998), p. 7.

43. Murphy, C., 'Six Masculine Roles in International Relations and their Interconnection. A Personal Investigation', in Zalewski, M. and J. Parpart (eds) (1998), p. 103. To demonstrate this assumption conclusively tends, of course, to be difficult. As a matter of fact, biases tend to be assumed rather than explicitly argued for. However, a cursory look at the literature will show that such a bias is indeed implicit in most writings of the scholars referred to.

44. For a similar observation on the discipline of IR, see Tickner, J. A. (1997). While J. Ann Tickner sums up 'troubled engagements between feminists and IR theorists', she leaves somehow open and vague how to resolve these misunderstandings.

45. Exceptions here may include the work of Jabri, V. (1996), Fetherston, A. B. and A. C. Parkin (1997), and Fetherston, A. B. (2000).

46. The anglophone research community mainly refers to three 'Great Debates' based on a chronological view of the evolution of IR: the first debate between idealism and realism, the second between traditionalism and behaviourialism, and the third between neorealism, pluralism, and globalism. I prefer to speak of four debates, the fourth being the one between positivism and post-positivism (like parts of feminism, critical theory, post-modernism, etc.). The distinction matters in so far as otherwise the fourth debate appears to be part of the third debate, which gives a rather different ontological and epistemological twist to the self-presentation of IR. I am aware that this classification is tentative and contentious at best. Moreover, the development of, for example, the German-speaking IR research community followed from the very beginning a different but related research agenda.

47. Lapid, Y. (1989), pp. 241–3.

48. See George, J. (1994), pp. 197–234.

49. See for example, Linklater, A. (1990) and Campbell, D. and J. George (1990).

50. See for example, Mann, M. (1986, 1993).

51. While some scholars explicitly refer to post-structuralism, others prefer the term post-modernism. However, one has to stress that there are striking differences between post-modernism and post-structuralism, which are beyond the scope of this paper. See for example, Dillon, M. (1996), George, J. (1994), and Walker, R. B. J. (1993).

52. Wall, J. A. and A. Lynn (1993), p. 182.

53. See for example, Scimecca, J. A., 'Theory and Alternative Dispute Resolution. A Contradiction in Terms?', in Sandole, D. J. D. and H. van der Merwe (eds) (1993), pp. 211–21.

54. Scimecca, J. A., 'Theory and Alternative Dispute Resolution', p. 217 (emphasis and brackets added by Reimann). The promotion of universal, handy techniques of conflict resolution without any theoretical basis whatsoever is most striking in the work of Roger Fisher and William Ury. See for example, Fisher, R. and W. Ury (1981).

55. Scimecca, J. A., 'Theory and Alternative Dispute Resolution', p. 214. See for example, Zartman, I. W. and M. R. Berman (1982), Burton, J. W. (1987), Lederach, J. P. (1995, 1997).

56. Fisher, R. J., 'Interactive Conflict Resolution', in Zartman, I. W. and J. L. Rasmussen (eds) (1997), p. 261.

57. See for example, Fisher, R. and W. Ury (1981).

58. Bercovitch, J., 'Mediation in International Conflict', in Zartman, I. W. and J. L. Rasmussen (eds) (1997), p. 133.

59. See also Zalewski, M. (1996), pp. 341–4.

60. Galtung, J. (1996), p. 16 (emphasis Reimann). See for example, Curle, A. (1971), p. 5.

61. Burton, J. W., 'Conflict Resolution as a Political Philosophy', in Sandole, D. J. D. and H. van der Merwe (eds) (1993), p. 57.

62. Little, R. (1984), p. 95.

63. One should not mistake Robert Cox's idea of a 'problem-solving approach' for John Burton's idea of a 'problem-solving approach/workshop' or the Harvard's School's understanding of a 'problem-solving approach'. In fact, Burton is one of the few who takes up and discusses in some length the shortcomings of what Cox calls 'problem-solving approaches' – Burton calls them 'puzzling-solving approaches'. See Burton, J. W. (1979), especially pp. 3–6.

64. Cox, R. (1981), p. 129.

65. Ibid.

66. Zartman, I. W. et al. (1996), pp. 79–98.

67. See also Kleiboer, M. (1996), p. 377. While Bush and Folger concentrate their analysis very much on domestic conflict resolution, and here particularly on the Alternative Dispute Resolution (ADR) movement in the US, they offer some initial provocations for further discussion on assessing conflict management success. See Bush, B. and J. Folger (1994).

68. Folger, J. P. (1999), p. 214.

69. Ibid., p. 219.

70. Pankhurst, D. and J. Pearce (1998), p. 161.

71. Berg, E. Z. (1994), p. 326.

72. Scholars with a development background, among others, may be Judy El-Bushra, Eugenia Piza Lopez, Ruth Jacobson and Donna Pankhurst. See for example, El-Bushra, J. and E. Piza Lopez (1993); El-Bushra, J. (1998); El-Bushra, J. and J. Abuah (1999); El-Bushra, J. (2000); Jacobson, R. (1999); Pankhurst, D. and J. Pearce (1998).

73. Elson, D. (ed.) (1995).

74. See also Anderson, M. B. (1996, 1999).

75. See for example, Ridd, R. and Callaway, H. (eds) (1987); Cockburn, C. (1998); Byrne, B. (1996); Cooke, M. and A. Woollacott (1993); Korac, M. (1998); Turshen, M. and C. Twagiramariya (eds) (1998); Urdang, S. (1989), World Vision International (1996), and O'Connell, H. (ed.) (1993).

76. For the gendered nature of, for example, the Dayton Agreement, see Lithander, A., Kvinna Till Kvinna Foundation (ed.) (2000).

77. See for example, GOOD (1998), El-Bushra, J. and J. Abuah (1999), and El-Bushra, J. (2000).

78. Herbert Kelman is one of the leading conflict resolution scholar/ practitioners who has extensively written on and engaged in problem-solving exercises in a variety of conflicts.

79. The feminist literature on the war/peace issue is rather elusive. For one of the classic, perhaps most influential and impressive contributions, see Elshtain, J. B. (1987). For an excellent reader, see Lorentzen, L. A. and J. Turbin (eds) (1998).

80. For one of the few exceptions, see Miall, H., O. Ramsbotham and T. Woodhouse (1999). This gap may also be filled by the *Berghof Handbook for Conflict Transformation*. See Berghof Research Center for Constructive Conflict Management (ed.) (2000).

81. This expression is borrowed from Robert W. Connell. See Connell, R. W. (1987), especially chapter 8 and Connell, R. W. (1995).

82. Northrup, T. A. (1996), pp. 13–15, p. 19.

83. Nordstrom, C., 'Contested Identities/Essentially Contested Powers', in Rupesinghe, K. (ed.) (1995), p. 106.

84. See Bennett, O., J. Bexley and K. Warnock (eds) (1995), p. 203 (their emphasis).

85. See for example, Cockburn, C. (1998); Cooke, M. and A. Woollacott (1993); El-Bushra, J. and E. Piza Lopez (1993); Jacobson, R. (1999); Lentin, R. (ed.) (1997); Ridd, R. and H. Callaway (eds) (1987); World Vision International (1996); International Alert (1999).

86. See for example, Drysdale, J. (1994), pp. 129–48.

87. Duffey, T. (1998), p. 182.

88. Edward Azar was a conflict resolution scholar/practitioner who developed a theory of protracted conflict and its management, and briefly worked with John Burton on theory development and problem-solving exercises.

89. See also Pankhurst, D. and J. Pearce (1998), p. 157.

90. See El-Bushra, J. and J. Abuah (1999), p. 14 and El-Bushra, J. (2000).

91. I borrowed this term from Maria Mies. See Mies, M. (1986), p. 210.

92. See Pankhurst, D. and J. Pearce (1998), pp. 161–2.

Bibliography

Anderson, M. B. (1996) *Do No Harm, Supporting Local Capacities for Peace Through Aid*, Cambridge, MA: Development for Collaborative Action.

— (1999) *Do No Harm: How Aid Can Support Peace – or War*, Boulder, CO: Lynne Rienner.

Batscheider, T. (1993) *Friedensforschung und Geschlechterverhältnis. Zur Begründung feministischer Fragestellung in der kritischen Friedensforschung*, Marburg: BdWi-Verlag.

Beckett, G. R. (1997) 'Social Theory and the Theory and Practice of Conflict Management', in Broadhead, L.-A. (ed.), *Issues in Peace Research 1997–98*, Bradford: University of Bradford, Department of Peace Studies, pp. 59–85.

Bennett, O., J. Bexley and K. Warnock (eds) (1995) *Arms to Fight. Arms to Protect. Women Speak Out About Conflict*, London: Panos.

Bercovitch, J. (ed.) (1996) *Resolving International Conflicts. The Theory and Practice of Mediation*, Boulder, CO: Lynne Rienner.

Bercovitch, J. and J. Z. Rubin (eds) (1992) *Mediation in International Relations. Multiple Approaches to Conflict Management*, London: St Martin's Press.

Berg, E. Z. (1994) 'Gendering Conflict Resolution', *Peace & Change*, Vol. 19, No. 4 (October), pp. 325–48.

Berghof Research Centre for Constructive Conflict Management (ed.) (2000/2001) *Berghof Handbook for Conflict Transformation*, http://www.b.shuttle.de/berghof/.

Burrell, N. A. et al. (1988) 'Gender-Based Perceptual Biases in Mediation', *Communication Research*, Vol. 15, No. 4, pp. 447–69.

Burton, J. W. (1969) *Conflict and Communication. The Use of Controlled Communication in International Relations*, London: Macmillan.

— (1972) *World Society*, London: Macmillan.

— (1979) *Deviance, Terrorism and War. The Process of Solving Unsolved Social and Political Problems*, Oxford: Martin Robertson.

— (1984) *Global Conflict. The Domestic Sources of International Crisis*, Brighton: Wheatsheaf.

— (1987) *Resolving Deep-Rooted Conflicts: A Handbook*, Lanham, MD: University Press of America.

— (1990a) *Conflict. Human Needs Theory*, London: Macmillan.

— (1990b) *Conflict. Resolution and Prevention*, Houndmills: Macmillan.

Bush, B. and J. Folger (1994) *The Promise of Mediation. Responding to Conflict Through Empowerment and Recognition*, San Francisco, CA: Jossey-Bass.

Byrne, B. (1996) 'Towards a Gendered Understanding of Conflict', *IDS Bulletin*, Vol. 27, No. 3, pp. 31–40.

Campbell, D. and J. George (1990) 'Patterns of Dissent and the Celebration of Difference. Critical Social Theory and International Relations', *International Studies Quarterly*, Vol. 34, No. 3, pp. 269–95.

Carver, T. (1996) *Gender is Not a Synonym for Women*, London: Lynne Rienner.

Cockburn, C. (1998) *The Space Between Us. Negotiating Gender and National Identities in Conflict*, London: Zed Books.

Connell, R. W. (1987) *Gender and Power. Society, the Person and Sexual Politics*, Palo Alto, CA: Stanford University Press.

— (1995) *Masculinities*, Berkeley: University of California Press.

Cooke, M. and A. Woollacott (1993) *Gendering War Talk*, Princeton, NJ: Princeton University Press.

Cox, R. W. (1981) 'Social Forces, States and World Orders. Beyond International Relations Relations Theory', *Millennium. Journal of International Studies*, Vol. 10, No. 2, pp. 126–55.

— (1983) 'Gramsci, Hegemony, and International Relations. An Essay in Method', *Millennium. Journal of International Studies*, Vol. 12, No. 2, pp. 162–75.

Curle, A. (1971) *Making Peace*, London: Tavistock.

Dillon, M. (1996) *Politics of Security. Towards a Political Philosophy of Continental Thought*, London: Routledge.

Drysdale, J. (1994) *Whatever Happened to Somalia? A Tale of Tragic Blunders*, London: HAAN.

Duffey, T. (1998) *Culture, Conflict Resolution and Peacekeeping. An Analysis with Special Reference to the Operations in Somalia*, Bradford: Department of Peace Studies/University of Bradford (unpublished PhD Thesis).

El-Bushra, J. (1998) *Gendered Interpretations of Conflict: Research Issues for COPE*, London: ACORD (RAPP).

— (2000) 'Transforming Conflict. Some Thoughts on a Gendered Interpretation of Conflict Processes', in Jacobs, S., R. Jacobson and J. Marchbank (eds), *States of Conflict. Gender, Violence and Resistance*, London: Zed Books, pp. 66–86.

El-Bushra, J. and J. Abuah (1999) 'Digging In: Why aren't Gender Analysts and Conflict Analysts Speaking to Each Other and What Might They Learn if They Did?', paper presented to the conference on 'NGOs in a Global Future' at Birmingham University (January 1999).

El-Bushra, J. and E. Piza Lopez (1993) *Development in Conflict. The Gender Dimension. Report of a Workshop Held in Thailand*, Oxfam Discussion Paper 3, Oxford: Oxfam Publications.

Elshtain, J. B. (1987) *Women and War*, New York: Littlefield.

Elson, D. (ed.) (1995) *Male Bias in the Development Process*, Manchester: Manchester University Press.

European Commission (1996a) *The European Union and the Issue of Conflicts in Africa. Peacebuilding, Conflict Prevention and Beyond*, Brussels: European Commission Publications.

— (1996b) *Linking Relief, Rehabilitation and Development*, Brussels: European Commission Publications.

Fetherston, A. B. (2000) *From Conflict Resolution to Transformative Peacebuilding: Reflections from Croatia*, Working Paper 4 (April 2000), Bradford: University of Bradford, Department of Peace Studies.

Fetherston, A. B. and A. C. Parkin (1997) 'Transforming Violent Conflict. Contributions from Social Theory', in Broadhead, L.-A. (ed.), *Issues in Peace Research 1997–98*, Bradford: University of Bradford, Department of Peace Studies, pp. 19–57.

Fisher, R. and W. Ury (1981) *Getting to Yes. How to Negotiate without Giving In*, London: Arrow Books.

Folger, J. P. (1999) 'Evaluating Evaluation in Ethnic Conflict Resolution. Themes from, and Commentary on, the Haverford-Bryn Mawr Conference', in Ross, M. H. and J. Rothman (eds) (1999) *Theory and Practice in Ethnic Conflict Management. Theorizing Success and Failure*, London: Macmillan, pp. 209–39.

Frei, D. (1975) 'Erfolgsbedingungen für Vermittlungsaktionen in internationalen Konflikten', *Politische Vierteljahresschrift*, No. 16, pp. 447–90.

Galtung, J. (1996) *Peace by Peaceful Means. Peace and Conflict, Development and Civilization*, London/Oslo: Sage Publications/PRIO.

George, J. (1994) *Discourses of Global Politics: A Critical (Re)Introduction to International Relations*, Boulder, CO: Lynne Rienner.

GOOD (1998) *Gender Perspectives in Conflict Prevention and Resolution*, Report of 1997 Annual Conference (24–25/9/1997 in Lyngby/Denmark).

Halliday, F. (1988) 'Hidden from International Relations. Women and the International Arena', *Millennium. Journal of International Studies*, Vol. 17, No. 3, pp. 419–28.

Harding, S. (1986) *The Science Question in Feminism*, Milton Keynes: Open University Press.

International Alert (1997) *Capacity-Building Workshop for Women in Decision-Making in Rwanda (9–13/1/1997)* (co-organized by Forum des Femmes Parlementaires du Rwanda and International Alert), report, London: International Alert.

— (1998a) *Training of Trainers on Gender and Conflict Transformation. Capacity Building for Women's Peace Movements in Burundi (7–12/4/1997)* (co-organized by Search for Common Ground, UNIFEM and International Alert), report, London: International Alert.

— (1998b) *Code of Conduct. Conflict Transformation Work*, London: International Alert.

— (1999) *Women, Violent Conflict and Peacebuilding. Global Perspectives*. International Conference, 5–7/5/1999 in London, London: International Alert.

Jabri, V. (1996) *Discourses on Violence. Conflict Analysis Reconsidered*, Manchester: Manchester University Press.

Jacobson, R. (1999) 'Complicating "Complexity": Integrating Gender into the Analysis of the Mozambican Conflict', *Third World Quarterly*, Vol. 20, No. 1, pp. 175–87.

Keller, E. F. (1985) *Reflections on Gender and Science*, New Haven, CT: Yale University Press.

Kleiboer, M. (1994) 'Ripeness of Conflict. A Fruitful Nation?', *Journal of Peace Research*, Vol. 31, No. 1, pp. 109–16.

— (1996) 'Understanding the Success and Failure of International Mediation', *Journal of Conflict Resolution*, Vol. 40, No. 2 (June), pp. 360–89.

Korac, M. (1998) *Linking Arms, Women and War in Post-Yugoslav States*, Uppsala: Life and Peace Institute.

Krippendorff, E. (1988) 'Militär und Geschlecht. Haben wir genügend Erkenntnisarbeit geleistet?', *DIALOG. Beiträge zur Friedensforschung*, Vol. 3, No. 4, pp. 7–21.

Lapid, Y. (1989) 'The Third Debate: On the prospects of International Theory in a Post-Positivist Era', *International Studies Quarterly*, Vol. 33, No. 3, pp. 235–54.

Lederach, J. P. (1995) *Preparing for Peace. Conflict Transformation across Cultures*, Syracuse, NY: Syracuse University Press.

— (1997) *Building Peace. Sustainable Reconciliation in Divided Societies*, Washington, DC: United States Institute of Peace Press.

Lentin, R. (ed.) (1997) *Gender and Catastrophe*, London: Zed Books.

Linklater, A. (1990) *Beyond Realism and Marxism. Critical Theory and International Relations*, Basingstoke: Macmillan.

Lithander, A., Kvinna Till Kvinna Foundation (ed.) (2000) *Engendering the Peace Process. A Gender Approach to Dayton and Beyond*, Stockholm: Kvinna Till Kvinna Foundation.

Little, R. (1984) 'The Decision-Maker and Social Order: The End of Ideology or the Pursuit of a Chimera?', in Banks, M. (ed.), *Conflict in World Society. A New Perspective on International Relations*, Brighton: Wheatsheaf, pp. 78–95.

Lorentzen, L. A. and J. Turpin (eds) (1998) *The Women and War Reader*, New York and London: New York University Press.

Mann, M. (1986) *The Sources of Social Power. Vol. 1: A History of Power from the Beginning to 1760 AD*, Cambridge: Cambridge University Press.

— (1993) *The Sources of Social Power. Vol. 2: The Rise of Classes and Nation-States 1760–1914*, Cambridge: Cambridge University Press.

Maxwell, D. (1992) 'Gender Differences in Mediation Style and their Impact on Mediator Effectiveness', *Mediation Quarterly*, Vol. 9, No. 4, pp. 353–64.

Miall, H., O. Ramsbotham and T. Woodhouse (1999) *Contemporary Conflict Resolution*, Cambridge: Polity Press.

Mies, M. (1986) *Patriarchy and Accumulation on a World Scale. Women and the International Division of Labour*, London: Zed Books.

Mitchell, C. (1995) *Cutting Losses. Reflections on Appropriate Timing*, Fairfax, VA: George Mason University.

Moser, C. O. N. (1993) *Gender Planning and Development. Theory, Practice and Training*, London: Routledge.

Northrup, T. A. (1996) 'The Uneasy Partnership Between Conflict Theory and Feminist Theory', Syracuse University, unpublished paper.

O'Connell, H. (ed.) (1993) *Women and Conflict*, Oxford: Oxfam Focus on Gender 2.

OSCE (1999) *Gender Issues*. Final Report of OSCE Supplementary Implementation Meeting (14–15/6/1999) ODIHR.GAL/24/99/ (24/6/1999), Vienna.

— (2000) *Action Plan for Gender Issues.* Preamble (1 June 2000), SEC. GAL/12/00/Rev.7.

Pankhurst, D. and J. Pearce (1998) 'Engendering the Analysis of Conflict: A Southern Perspective', in Afshar, H. (ed.), *Women and Empowerment. Illustrations from the Third World,* London: Routledge, pp. 155–63.

Peterson, V. S. (1992) 'Transgressing Boundaries. Theories of Knowledge, Gender and International Relations', *Millennium. Journal of International Studies,* Vol. 21, No. 2, pp. 183–206.

— (ed.) (1992) *Feminist (Re)Visions of International Relations Theory,* Boulder, CO: Lynne Rienner.

Reardon, B. (1985) *Sexism and the War System,* New York: Columbia University Press.

Reimann, C. (1999) *The Field of Conflict Management – Why Does Gender Matter?* AFB-Report (October), Bonn: Information Unit Peace Research Bonn.

Ridd, R. and H. Callaway (eds) (1987) *Women and Political Conflict. Portraits of Struggle in Times of Crisis,* New York: New York University Press.

Rupesinghe, K. (ed.) (1995) *Conflict Transformation,* London: Macmillan.

Sandole, D. J. D. and H. van der Merwe (eds) (1993) *Conflict Resolution Theory and Practice. Integration and Application,* Manchester and New York: Manchester University Press.

Schmid, H. (1968) 'Peace Research and Politics', *Journal of Peace Research,* Vol. 5, No. 3, pp. 217–32.

Smith, S. (1995) 'The Self-Image of a Discipline', in Booth, K. and S. Smith (eds), *International Relations Theory Today,* Cambridge: Polity Press, pp. 1–37.

Sørensen, B. (1998) *Women and Post-Conflict Reconstruction. Issues and Sources,* WSP Occasional Paper No. 3 (June) (http://www.unrisd.org/wsp/op3/toc.htm).

Stamato, L. (1992) 'Voice, Place, and Process. Research on Gender, Negotiation, and Conflict Resolution', *Mediation Quarterly,* Vol. 9, No. 4, pp. 375–86.

Steans, J. (1998) *Gender and International Relations,* London: Polity Press.

Subrahmanian, R. (1996) *Institutions, Relations and Outcomes. Framework and Tools for Gender-Aware Planning,* Brighton: University of Sussex (Institute of Development Studies).

Tickner, J. A. (1997) '"You Just Do Not Understand." Troubled Engagements Between Feminists and IR Theorists', *International Studies Quarterly,* Vol. 41, pp. 611–32.

True, J. (1996) 'Feminism', in Burchill, S. and A. Linklater et al., *Theories of International Relations,* London: Macmillan, pp. 210–51.

Turshen, M. and C. Twagiramariya (eds) (1998) *What Women Do in Wartime,* London: Zed Books.

UNIFEM (1995) *African Women for Peace.* Activities of the African Women for Conflict Resolution and Peace Project of UNIFEM/AFWIC (July), Nairobi: UNIFEM.

— (1996) *Looking at Peace Through Women's Eyes* (June), Nairobi: UNIFEM.

United Nations (1995) *Platform for Action*, Beijing, New York: United Nations Publications.

Urdang, S. (1989) *And Still They Dance. Women, War, and the Struggle for Change in Mozambique*, London: Earthscan.

Walker, R. B. J. (1993) *Inside/Outside. International Relations as Political Theory*, Cambridge: Cambridge University Press.

Wall, V. D. and M. L. Dewhurst (1991) 'Mediator Gender. Communication Differences in Resolved and Unresolved Mediations', *Mediation Quarterly*, Vol. 9, No. 1, pp. 63–85.

Wall, J. A. and A. Lynn (1993) 'Mediation. A Current Review', *Journal of Conflict Resolution*, Vol. 37, pp. 160–94.

Wallice, T. and C. March (eds) (1991) *Changing Perceptions. Writings on Gender and Development*, Oxford: Oxfam Publications.

Weingarten, H. R. and E. Douvan (1985) 'Male and Female Visions of Mediation', *Negotiation Journal*, Vol. 4, pp. 349–58.

Woodhouse, T. (ed.) (1991) *Peacemaking in a Troubled World*, Oxford: Berg.

World Vision International (1996) *The Effects of Armed Conflict on Girls*, Geneva: World Vision.

Zalewski, M. (1996) '"All These Theories Yet the Bodies Keep Piling Up": Theories, Theorists, Theorising', in Smith, S., K. Booth and M. Zalewski (eds), *International Theory. Positivism and Beyond*, Cambridge: Cambridge University Press.

Zalewski, M. and J. Parpart (eds) (1998) *The 'Man' Question in International Relations*, Oxford/Boulder, CO: Westview Press.

Zartman, I. W. (1985) *Ripe for Resolution. Conflict and Intervention in Africa*, New York: Oxford University Press.

— (1987) *Positive Sum. Improving North–South Negotiations*, New York: Transaction Publishers.

— (ed.) (1995) *Elusive Peace. Negotiating an End to Civil Wars*, Washington, DC: The Brookings Institution.

— et al. (1996) 'Negotiation as a Search for Peace', *International Negotiation*, Vol. 1, pp. 79–98.

Zartman, I. W. and M. R. Berman (1982) *The Practical Negotiator*, New Haven, CT: Yale University Press.

Zartman, I. W. and J. L. Rasmussen (eds) (1997) *Peacemaking in International Conflict. Methods and Techniques*, Washington, DC: United States Institute for Peace.

CHAPTER 9

Making a Difference? The Inclusion of Gender into Institutional Conflict Management[1] Policies

Donna Pankhurst

Gender issues came late to Conflict Resolution (CR) and associated policy areas, as Cordula Reimann outlined in Chapter 8, but have certainly arrived with intensity! In the space of a few years we have witnessed a change in international discourse from barely a mention of gender issues to one in which a focus on the plight of women in conflict is commonplace. In taking analytical accounts of gender issues from Development Studies (DS) and International Relations (IR), CR is confronting a sophisticated set of ideas and a huge range of policy experience and evaluation. In the face of this confrontation, CR has not yet adapted very much in institutional or policy terms at an international level, although significant changes are taking place. Like other policy changes in large organizations, there are also variations in local experience, as reforms filter down to the implementation level at differential rates.

I begin by identifying the main policies and institutions under scrutiny. *Peacebuilding*, an evolving term (still sometimes written as peace-building or peace building), basically refers to activities that take place after a conflict has reached some sort of ending. The term is used to cover many different activities, with various objectives. It is a policy area which has become increasingly attractive to international non-governmental organizations (INGOs) and official aid agencies, particularly in Africa. As with other areas of development policy, such agencies bring to this area sets of assumptions and values about what is desirable and achievable, some of which are more overtly stated than others.

The term is also closely linked with Conflict Resolution, an area which has similarly soared in popularity with many international actors, ranging from the UN and regional security organizations (of which

there are several in Africa), through official military and political interventions by individual governments, to INGOs engaging directly or
giving support to other actors. CR also has a vast range of different
meanings. Its central business is often thought to be the achievement
of *negative peace*, that is, the removal of organized violence or war, but
it also has a wider use, connoting activities to reduce differences of
interest and to increase understanding and tolerance in any context.
The latter activity is seen as part of peacebuilding, and typically includes
training and activities in mediation.

Women as actors, and gender issues in general, are persistently
marginalized in analyses of conflicts, in policies intended to bring about
an end to conflict, and in new constitutions or other mechanisms to
facilitate post-conflict settlements. Some changes in approach have
occurred, such as the international recognition of rape as a war crime;
the recognition by the UN that (male) soldiers often behave in an
exploitative and violent way towards women in the populations they
are supposed to protect; and greater attention being paid to the needs
of women as refugees. Nevertheless, these changes have not as yet led
to a significantly greater participation of women or to any great weight
being given to gender issues. By contrast, policies and international
policy statements for ('post-conflict') peacebuilding, increasingly pre-
sume a central importance for women. It is worth reflecting on how
these contrasting approaches have come about.

The engendering of conflict resolution

CR and conflict analysis 'discovered' gender later than DS or IR, for
rather intriguing reasons (Pankhurst and Pearce 1997). The process of
gender being taken more seriously is also remarkably slow, and something which is being noted and analysed by an increasing number of
writers (Reimann 1999). One explanation which I still find quite plausible
became clear to me when making a comparison with DS (and a similar
contrast can be drawn between the slow process of mainstreaming
gender in IR and what happened in DS).

In short, there was an efficiency imperative[2] to take gender issues
seriously. Basically, many development policies often failed because they
ignored women, and it became apparent (through the theoretical and
empirical work of feminist academics and practitioners) that if gender
issues were taken into account, a far greater degree of success could be
achieved. This is a complex story, as we saw in the chapters on development, but the point is that change did occur, so that gender has become
more or less mainstreamed in many areas of DS. If this explanation is

correct, then in order for a similar push to occur for CR (or IR, for that matter), a related 'policy-wing' would need to benefit in some way by taking gender seriously. Until recently this was not perceived to be the case; settlements could be found to conflicts not only with no involvement of women, but also at the cost of women as a gender, where settlements were clearly not to their advantage.[3] It was thought to make no difference to the ability to find a settlement, or the chances of that settlement holding, if women were completely ignored or disadvantaged.

More recently, with the extension of so-called CR into post-conflict policies, gender issues and the activities of women are seen to be far more central, and directly to affect the *efficacy* of peace settlements and attempts at peacebuilding, even as women still remain marginalized at the point of brokering a settlement. This shift of attention is based on a set of assumptions about the nature of women and about gender stereotypes, and is subject to an increasing amount of criticism (Jacobs et al. 2000). Nevertheless, there is a view widely held in international, and African, policy circles that there is something worthwhile in this approach; that many women are well placed to take on the work of preventing conflict at a local level; and that they can even be helped to play a much greater role in reducing or even ending violence and conflict. Making and building peace has thus been added to 'women's work' (Jacobs et al. 2000). Conflict resolution training workshops are more often organized by INGOs for women than for mixed groups in many African countries, for instance. I would like to emphasize, however, that very few international organizations have changed their practice in terms of giving (or even seeking) a greater role for women in the process of negotiating, brokering or mediating settlements to large-scale violent conflicts. The work allocated to women seems much more to be identified with what happens after this point.

Gender, conflict resolution and peacebuilding in Africa

Increasing attention is drawn in international academic and NGO literature to the important roles that women often play in African societies in mobilizing men to fight, in sanctioning violence and – most commonly – in intervening to stop fighting or to limit violence (El-Bushra 2000). This last experience is often identified as holding the potential for changing the nature of CR and peacebuilding, although most organizations have held back from intervening to support women directly in such ventures. Where outside intervention has occurred, it has been by INGOs trying to shape and support women's initiatives to stop or prevent fighting in a subtle way, and on a very small scale.

By contrast, there is a significant and growing international presence (both INGO and official) in a number of African locations which is primarily geared to the rather vague objective of peacebuilding once a 'post-conflict' moment has been identified. Whereas it is rather difficult to identify things to spend money on which are clearly geared to promoting peace, there has been a growing fashion for identifying and promoting so-called 'traditional' methods of conflict resolution (in the sense for searching for an end to organized violence) and of post-conflict mediation and reconciliation. Increasing amounts of money are being used in this way, in contexts where INGOs have multiple, and often unclear, objectives and where there is commonly considerable confusion about what exactly is being promoted.

So-called 'traditional' mechanisms can include long, stylized discussions; various types of rituals; and acts of property and labour transfer (both individual and collective). It can be intended to achieve a range of outcomes between different parties, including a shared understanding of different points of view, retribution, compensation, forgiveness and trust building. These contrasting intentions may exist in the same country – even in the same communities – but are increasingly being packaged within an international terminology of peacebuilding, not least to access funding from international donors. Some such mechanisms have been in constant use for several generations. More commonly, others are recently resurrected from the memories of elderly people (and reinvented); while others are actually being invented for the first time. This is not in itself surprising, in countries where the invention and/or reinvention of tradition has a long history in the hands of political leaders as a tool for mobilization and strengthening legitimacy (Ranger 1983; Howard and Jacobs 1987). The term 'traditional' is therefore often misleading, but tends to have the effect of placing the process off-limits to outsiders, where intervention could easily be cast as cultural imperialism. Instead, very local politics determine what actually happens.

A striking feature about such mechanisms is that they are nearly all determined and carried out by men, with men and for men. One cannot read from this what the outcomes are for women; they certainly vary, as was apparent from detailed field work in Uganda this year. Nevertheless, the way in which these activities are conceived and analysed by outsiders is in great contrast to that of the CR and mediation activities, which are commonly promoted as the quintessential business of women! They also stand out as quite separate from other kinds of rehabilitation and recovery policies which are part of peacebuilding, in which women's particular needs are increasingly being acknowledged and addressed (such as health services, for instance).

A clash of discourses

Two distinct discourses are gaining prominence in politics in a number of African countries, arising directly from these different policy approaches to peacebuilding. The ideology of so-called tradition is promoted as an effective arena for the promotion of peace, and commonly includes highly unequal gender relations and at least a marginalization of women's gender interests. At the same time, new, innovative, and *often imported* methods of mediation and conflict resolution are being geared towards women (typically through training courses and workshops), with the expectation that peace is women's work. Imported with these approaches is also a good deal of international feminist discourse.

It is not uncommon, then, to find organizations and individuals in African capital cities which deploy highly sophisticated *feminist* analyses of their own societies, economies and international locations. It is normal, however, for this to take place within contexts where gender inequality is extreme and well-defended – and perhaps made virtually untouchable – in the name of tradition. The interaction between these two poles appears to me to be limited to a clash, followed by a stand off at the moment. Increasing awareness of feminist analyses is not leading to widespread changes in local politics (or therefore in some efforts at peacebuilding), and the promotion of women as peacemakers is not widely challenging the value placed on so-called tradition.

El-Bushra (2000) has observed the same phenomenon and concluded that the problem is that women in such African contexts often do not recognize or desire the political agenda which is implicit in feminist analyses and policy proposals around peacebuilding. She suggests that women identify the need for 'mutual respect' as paramount, which she explains as referring to a reconstruction of gender relations in which both men and women are able to resurrect social roles and divisions of labour that are acceptable to the majority of society's members, even where these are evidently unequal and exploitative. El-Bushra extends this analysis to development policies, and suggests that analyses from DS are responsible for the promotion of policies which contain the potential to promote a feminist agenda that many women do not want.

The comparison with Development Studies (DS) is worth considering further in the light of the 'efficiency imperative' I identified earlier. Many feminists within DS have regarded the mainstreaming of gender as highly problematic, particularly because what was lost, as their analyses were taken on board by policy-makers, was the emancipatory project for women; making women efficient producers of cash crops, for instance, was not their prime objective! Criticisms made of the assumptions behind the 'women as peacemakers' model are made from a similar perspective. In both cases, it is the larger, more transformatory, political project which is lost, or at least obscured. El-Bushra suggests that it is this project itself which is rejected by many women in Africa (perhaps because it is premature), but at least part of the problem, I suggest, is that it is, in fact, not usually articulated.

In post-conflict peacebuilding in Africa there is often no language to describe what it is that people want to achieve politically, other than peace, in the sense of Galtung's *negative peace*. What is desired, or aimed for beyond this, is not clearly articulated, and so can easily be obscured or ignored. A persistence, or even an increase in social violence, including specific violence against women, for instance, offers no inherent threat to negative peace, even though for many it is evidently something which should be reduced or removed.

Debates about democracy, civil society and good governance continue in Africa and all go some way towards attempting to fill this gap (Pankhurst 2000), but such debates are rarely extended in situations of fragile peace, much less integrated with discussions about inequalities or conceptualizations of how to improve gender relations. Actors in the 'international peace industry' have no common agenda of what post-conflict societies should be transformed *to*, and many have no agenda to support transformation *at all*, because hanging on to conditions of negative peace dominates all other agendas. In this context different discourses and values, shaped locally and internationally, tend to collide, rather than interact; to co-exist, rather than transform. For the moment at least, it is unclear what major policy shifts might be possible in this area in the foreseeable future, even if we regard the ultimate transformation of gender relations as inevitable.

Notes

1. In this context, 'conflict management' includes activities also referred to as conflict resolution and peacebuilding.

2. This was an observation first made by Elson (1995).

3. Jenny Pearce and I have called this the 'gendered deal', which is sometimes made between warring parties with the consent of peace brokers (Pankhurst and Pearce 1997: 160).

Bibliography

El-Bushra, J. (2000) 'Transforming Conflict: Some Thoughts on a Gendered Understanding of Conflict Processes', in Jacobs, S., R. Jacobson and J. Marchbank (eds), *States of Conflict. Gender, Violence and Resistance*, London: Zed Books, pp. 66–86.

Elson, D. (1995) *Male Bias in the Development Process*, Manchester: Manchester University Press.

Howard, T. and S. Jacobs (1987) 'Women in Zimbabwe: Stated Policy and State Action', in Afshar, H. (ed.), *Women, State and Ideology. Studies from Africa and Asia*, London: Macmillan, pp. 28–47.

Jacobs, S., R. Jacobson and J. Marchbank (eds) (2000) *States of Conflict. Gender, Violence and Resistance*, London: Zed Books.

Pankhurst, D. (1999) 'Issues of Justice and Reconciliation in Complex Political Emergencies', *Third World Quarterly*, Vol. 20, pp. 239–56.

— (2000) 'Women. Gender and Peacebuilding', Centre for Conflict Resolution, Working Paper 5, Department of Peace Studies, University of Bradford.

Pankhurst, D. and J. Pearce (1997) 'Feminist Perspectives on Democratization in the South. Engendering or Adding Women in?', in Afshar, H. (ed.), *Women and Politics in the Third World*, London: Routledge, pp. 40–47.

— (1998) 'Engendering the Analysis of Conflict: Perspectives from the South', in Afshar, H. (ed.), *Women and Empowerment*, Basingstoke: Macmillan, pp. 155–63.

Peel, J. D. Y. and T. O. Ranger (1983) *Past and Present in Zimbabwe*, Manchester: Manchester University Press.

Ranger, T. O. (1983) 'Tradition, and Travesty: Chiefs and the Administration in Makoni District, Zimbabwe, 1960–1980', in Peel, J. D. Y. and T. O. Ranger (1983) *Past and Present in Zimbabwe*, Manchester: Manchester University Press, pp. 20–41.

Reimann, C. (1999) *The Field of Conflict Management – Why Does Gender Matter?*, AFB-Report (October), Bonn: Information Unit Peace Research Bonn.

CHAPTER 10

. . . .

War in Empty Rooms and the Sudanese Women's Union

Fatima Ahmed Ibrahim

Sudan and the long-neglected war

Sudan is the largest country in Africa and one of the richest in natural resources. Sudanese people come from many different races, and have many cultures and religions. In the North, there is a mixture of Arab and African people, most of whom are Muslims. In the South, the majority are of pure African descent and many are Christians, while others have tribal beliefs.

From 1821 to 1956 Sudan was under colonial rule: first under Turkish-Egyptian and then from 1898 to 1956 under British-Egyptian rule, when Sudan was a *de facto* British colony. During their stay in our country, the British made all necessary arrangements to ensure that their policies and economic interests would be preserved long after their departure. Our country would continue to be a cheap source of manpower and raw materials, and a market for their manufactured products. The British administration developed only the Northern part of Sudan and neglected the South. In fact, it pursued the political and cultural separation between the North and the South. This policy instilled hatred between the people in the South and North, and it deepened their ethnic and religious divisions. Thus the British succeeded in making the people in the South fight against the government in the North. As a result civil war broke out in 1955, just one year before the departure of the British administration in 1956.

After independence in 1956, the new Sudanese government made no effort to abolish racial discrimination against the South or to bring about social justice in order to stop the war. Thus the civil war continued. In 1957 the USA offered financial aid to Sudan, which was rejected by all political parties and by the trade unions. The majority of politicians preferred to adopt a policy of self-reliance and of developing our national resources. To avoid exposing himself to charges of failure if he accepted the American aid, the prime minister of the ruling *Umma* party handed over power to the military leader, General Aboud, in 1958. It was later revealed that the USA had planned and executed that military coup (Agee 1975: 82). The new military regime accepted the American aid and banned all political parties, trade unions and later the Sudanese Women's Union. Many American economic advisers came to Sudan and started to dominate government policies, in particular economic policy. This is an obvious indication that, soon after Sudan had gained political independence, a new type of colonialism found its way into our country.

In October 1964 the Sudanese people overthrew the military regime and restored democracy. But in 1969 Nemeri, an army officer, seized power in yet another military coup. After a peace agreement with the South in 1972, his government granted the South limited autonomy status in cultural affairs and local administration. The 1970s were therefore marked by a period of peace in Sudan. In 1983 Dr Turrabi, the leader of the Islamic Front Party, joined the Nemeri government, which then started to implement Islamic law in Southern Sudan. As a result, the civil war flared up again. In 1985 a popular uprising took place and the Nemeri regime was overthrown by military leaders, and in 1986 the military handed over power to a coalition of different parties.

In 1988, army officers presented a memorandum to the Supreme Council demanding an immediate end to the war and the reversal of Islamic policies and laws in Southern Sudan. All political parties and representatives of the army, trade unions and the Sudanese Women's Union prepared a peace agreement to be signed in July 1989. The only party which refused the peace agreement was the National Islamic Front. In June 1989 it seized power in a military coup, and immediately started the war again under the new slogan, 'The Holy Islamic War'.

A war in the name of Islam is a violation of democracy and human rights and also a violation of Islamic principles. Islam is a religion of peace. Muslims have to pray five times a day, and at the end of each prayer they have to repeat the sentence 'Peace upon you'. So, killing innocent children, women and civilians in the name of Islam is a crime.

The government has continued the enforcement of Islamic laws and traditions up to the present. It is clear that this government is waging this war to force the Southerners into separation from the North. Hundreds of thousands of people have been killed on both sides and several million people displaced. Hundreds of millions of dollars are spent on this war, while our children in the South and North are dying from famine. The government used to kidnap students and young people and send them to the war zone without adequate training. This war, which has continued for 34 years, is completely neglected by the international community, and especially by the regional and international peace movements. It is a war against poor people. It is a war that is not present in the media or on the agendas of international political decision-makers. It is a war in empty rooms.

Twice invisible: women's human rights violations

The Sudanese Women's Union was founded in 1952, before independence, with the aim of emancipating women. Women were disadvantaged and discriminated against. The discrimination was reflected even in the family home, where the largest and most beautiful rooms were reserved for the man and his guests. The practice of circumcising girls during their early childhood to control sexuality and ensure virginity still continues today. Young women were denied the right to choose their husbands, and in most cases they were not consulted about their marriage. Moreover, family laws were designed to favour men. As mothers, women did not enjoy the same rights as fathers. Even today, the man has the right to marry more than one wife and the right to divorce his wife or wives at any time. In the event of divorce, the Law of Obedience forced the wife to go back to her husband if he changed his mind, irrespective of her interest and desire. Family law granted mothers custody of their sons up to the age of seven and of their daughters up to the age of nine. Until a few years ago, there was no law to make fathers pay maintenance for their children after divorce.

Ironically, even in the Southern Sudan, where some of the population is Christian, men also marry more than one wife, the reason being that women are an important economic force. Women provide valuable labour in agricultural and food production. Thus, the more wives the man has, the greater his wealth and the number of his children, which gives him higher social status. This shows that traditions and economic benefits are stronger causes of discrimination against women than religious factors. Socio-economically, women also face repression. The percentage of women's illiteracy is higher than men's, and the number of girls enrolled in school is less than half that of boys.

In the 1960s only a tiny minority of women went out to work, and their work was confined to nursing and education. Women used to earn 80 per cent of men's wages for the same kind of work and with the same qualifications. Women were not equal to men in terms of their professional opportunities, training, promotion or pensions. Women did not have the right to paid maternity leave. They worked on the basis of monthly contracts, which forced them to leave their jobs after marriage and made them vulnerable to being fired at short notice. In agricultural areas, women's work was, and still is, considered part of the men's work and hence they are not paid for their work in the fields. In Western Sudan, for example, women do all the agricultural work and men do none. But after the harvest, husbands take all the income and marry another wife. This is why the number of wives killing their husbands is growing today. In Eastern Sudan, the situation is even more backward. Mentioning a women's name in public is considered a disgrace to her family.

The Sudanese Women's Union: strategies for women's equality and peace in Sudan

At the start of the Sudanese Women's Union in 1952 we set up an executive committee, which included a member from the South and a woman representative from the trade unions. This was important to encourage trade unions to fight for the equality of working women and to strengthen the links between trade unions and our women's union in order to fight together for that aim. From the very beginning, it was clear to us that we had to keep our organization independent of any party or government, in order to build it into a mass movement reaching women and wives in all the villages of all regions of Sudan. So we formed branches in many parts of Sudan, including the South. Our committees in the towns helped to reach women in their homes and trained young women to become cadres in the town districts. We also used to have committees in many of the girls' secondary schools and girls' student leagues in all the universities. We organized special training courses for the young cadres.

Building branches in the villages was difficult and sensitive. So we used to approach the chief of the village and the male and female community leaders, including the Imam of the mosque. We were careful to include men in our activities and conferences. Under the leadership of a member of the executive committee, we formed special programme committees among our grassroots members. These committees were responsible for their own programme design and implementation, and they helped to involve many members in the union's leadership.

At the beginning, and because of lack of experience, the Sudanese Women's Union started by promoting reformism and charity work. But it was soon realized that these types of activities would not solve women's problems, nor would they eradicate illiteracy among them or promote equality. Also, charity would not be able to satisfy the needs of the poor. Hence it would not be able to eradicate poverty or discrimination against women, because it does not address its root causes. As a result, our union introduced changes to its approach and programmes. We started to conduct a peaceful campaign alongside our regular work. The goal was to pressure the government into changing its policies and laws affecting women. In 1953 we launched a campaign demanding that women should be granted the right to vote. Through their right to vote, we wanted to transform women's voices into a political force that all parties would compete to win. To raise the consciousness of women, I together with some of my colleagues started publishing the *Women's Voice Magazine*. Our magazine took the following positions:

- Emancipation does not mean copying Western women. It also does not mean abandoning our valuable traditions, good behaviour and religious beliefs. It means emancipation from ignorance, poverty, all kinds of discrimination and exploitation, disease and backward traditions.
- Equality does not mean copying men. It is the right of any woman to be as she likes to be.
- Personal and sexual freedom will never eradicate women's discrimination or achieve equality with men, or stop rape and child sexual abuse.
- There are causes and symptoms of discrimination against women. Concentrating on symptoms will never eradicate the disease. Rape, violence and circumcision are symptoms of discrimination and not causes. So we have to concentrate on involving women in politics and making them a strong political force.
- In Western countries women are still not equal to men either in rights or in decision-making (according to UN statistics), in spite of the fact that Western countries are considered civilized, democratic and defenders of human rights. This is because their democracy is not based on social justice and human rights. This is why in the West there is discrimination against women, racial discrimination and class exploitation.
- Not all men as males are responsible for women's discrimination, because there are a lot of men who are themselves discriminated against and exploited.
- Islam is not responsible for discrimination against Muslim women and their inequality, because there are women who are not Muslims, and yet are discriminated against and not equal to men.
- Therefore the ruling political regimes are responsible for all kinds of

discrimination and violations of human rights. These are the direct results of their policies and legislation, which affect the life and situation of the people.

Success of our campaign

As could be expected, the union's demand for women's political rights in the 1950s was met with strong opposition from the Islamic Front (which is in power today) and other Islamic groups, on the grounds that Islam does not allow women's equality in general. We realized that the best way to respond to that attack was to base our arguments for the defence of women's rights on Islam. By studying the Qur'an we showed that Islam does not prohibit women's rights, equality, or women's involvement in politics. Furthermore, it does not permit polygamy, and there is no provision for an Islamic state.

We took part in the struggle against the military regime and at the same time succeeded with our campaign: women achieved the right to vote and to stand for elections in 1964. Two women stood as candidates: the Muslim sister who had opposed our demand for women's political rights, and myself. She failed and I succeeded and became the first woman member of parliament in Sudan, Africa and the Middle East. In 1965 we introduced to parliament a draft for the Act on Equal Rights for Working Women. In support of the draft, the Sudanese Women's Union formed the Working Women's Equality Committee, which consisted of representatives from trade unions, students and youth organizations. They organized a broad campaign in support of women's equal rights, and particularly of the Act to be passed in parliament. As a result, women achieved the following rights in 1969:

1. The right to enter all economic spheres: women were then able to enter the judiciary (and even to become Islamic judges), diplomatic service, armed forces, police, etc.
2. Equal pay for equal work, and equal chances in training and promotion, equal pensions.
3. Fully paid maternity leave of eight weeks and for breast-feeding hours during work time.
4. The abolition of the monthly contract work arrangements for women after marriage.

Another success of the campaign was changes in the family law:

1. An act was adopted giving girls the right to be consulted before marriage.

2. Abolition of the Obedience Law.
3. Women were given the right to divorce in case of proven abuse, also in the case of no longer wishing to live with their husbands. However, the law provided that any dowry paid had to be given back after the divorce.
4. Mothers were allowed custody of their sons up to the age of 17, and of their daughters until marriage.
5. Children were given the right to maintenance by their fathers in the event of divorce, provided that it did not exceed half of the father's income.

For these achievements, the United Nations awarded our union the UN Human Rights Prize in 1993. Thus the Sudanese Women's Union became the first, and so far the only, women's organization in the whole world to be awarded this prize.

Setbacks under Islamic military rule and our continuous resistance

Unfortunately, as soon as the present Islamic military regime took power in 1989, it banned the Sudanese Women's Union together with political parties, trade unions and all other organizations. Tens of thousands of women and men were dismissed from their work. The regime imprisoned political and trade union leaders and other leading personalities. It dismissed all women judges, diplomats, police and army officers, and women serving in high-level civil service posts. It abolished all women's rights, especially all the previous achievements in family laws. A new family law was introduced depriving women of their rights. For example, one law gives the father the right to marry off his daughter even if she is under age, and to stop her marriage in court if he does not consent to it, irrespective of her wishes. The Islamic government made it compulsory for women to wear the *hijab*. If a woman does not wear it, she can be flogged in public and be dismissed from her school or job. Women in the Southern region and the Nuba Mountains in Western Sudan are suffering even more, because they and their children are facing death, disaster, disease, famine and displacement as a result of the civil war. In addition there is the enslavement of and trade in human beings as slaves in the South.

As a result of this dictatorship and the war, Sudanese people are suffering from high inflation, famine, lack of health care and social services, shortages of clean water and electricity. So far, about seven million people, most of them educated professionals, intellectuals and political leaders, have left Sudan to seek asylum in other countries.

On top of all that, the government has implemented IMF structural adjustment programmes. This has led to further economic hardship for our people. In 1976 one Sudanese pound equalled US$3, but today you have to pay 2,500 Sudanese pounds for US$1. This has caused complete economic destruction. Consequently, big changes took place in our society, which is still based on an agricultural economy. A wealthy parasitic capitalist minority class emerged within the new ruling regime. Its members exploit Sudanese gold and oil resources, export them to buy weapons, and keep the rest of the profit for themselves. Our middle class has disappeared, and the vast majority of our population is in complete poverty, particularly women and children.

In spite of all this suffering and difficulties, our union has succeeded in uniting all women's groups under the Women's Alliance, to work together to mobilize and organize the mass of women to take part in opposition activities against the regime, in order to restore democracy based on social justice, human rights and peace. Outside our country, we organize the union's members in different countries, issuing our magazine *Women's Voice*. In London we formed the Sudanese Committee Against Violation of Women's, Youth and Students' Human Rights. We organize campaigns, go picketing and present memorandums to the British Prime Minister and the United Nations, drawing attention to human rights violations in Sudan, in order to gain support for the struggle of our people for democracy and peace. In December 1996, we organized a peace caravan to the liberated areas in South Sudan, starting from Nairobi in Kenya on International Human Rights Day – December 10 – and returning one week later. A large number of representatives of human rights organizations, journalists and mass media from Western countries took part. We also organized another peace caravan to The Hague Appeal for Peace Conference in 1999. We plan to organize a peace caravan through Europe to gain the support of the European peace movement, in order to put pressure on the Sudanese government to stop the war immediately.

Petition of the Sudanese Committee

Both women and men suffer from the civil war, which has been neglected by the outside world. But women suffer in two distinct ways: from the war and from their oppression as women. Their suffering has been made even more invisible; there is silence about violations against Sudanese women in the international community. And there is no political space in the international community to fight for the end of the war in Sudan – a war in empty rooms.

Dear readers, on behalf of our children, women, youth and students, and the Sudanese people, who are facing hunger, disease, and death, I appeal to you to give us your support and help. There is a painful tragedy taking place in Sudan, especially in the South, the Nuba Mountains and the East of our country. We are in urgent need of your help:

1. We are in need of access to the media.
2. We need help to convince European governments to stop any support to this Islamic military regime, which has been condemned twice by the UN General Assembly and the UN Human Rights Commission in December 1992 and in April 1997. There is even a report by the Canadian investigators of the UN Commission on Human Rights who visited Sudan recently, and proved that the Sudanese military regime is violating human rights. President General Omer El Basheer recently announced that the regime would never stop applying Islamic laws. They have admitted that their war planes bombed schools in the South, killing teachers and pupils. Many European governments support this Islamic regime. European governments should oppose the Sudanese government and not buy gold or oil from it.
3. We are in urgent need of financial help for our Sudanese Women's Union both inside Sudan and for our work outside Sudan.
4. We need signatures for our memorandum to the United Nations, the European Parliament and European governments to support the Sudanese people by putting pressure on the Islamic military regime to stop the war and human rights violations immediately and unconditionally.
5. I need your support for a proposal for a worldwide campaign to convince families not to buy war toys for their children, and for appeals to the mass media to stop violent films.
6. Lastly, I appeal to you to support our effort to organize a campaign to stop the UN General Assembly from accepting military regimes as members of the UN. This will help to put an end to military coups.

Note

Fatima Ahmed Ibrahim can be contacted via the editors.

Reference

Agee, P. (1975) *Inside the Company: CIA Diary*, London: Allen Lane.

....

PART IV

Women's Human Rights – New Spaces for Women's Activism?

CHAPTER 11

Global Women's Politics: Towards the
'Globalizing' of Women's Human Rights?

Uta Ruppert[1]

'In many ways the global women's movement is the strongest, most inclusive, most dynamic and viable of global movements operating in the world arena today.' This statement by Ellen Dorsey (1997: 336) appears in an article on the global women's movement and women's human rights written just a few months after the 1995 World Conference on Women in Beijing. The following is her prognosis for the future of the women's movement at that time: 'The last several years of the 20th century may prove to be critical to whether the emerging movement capitalizes upon its efforts towards greater coherence in advancing a global culture of women's human rights or breaks down on philosophical, organizational, or strategic lines' (ibid.).

Now, more than five years after Beijing and several months after the Beijing + 5 Conference in New York, her assumptions still seem relevant enough to be used as a starting point for reflections on the role of the women's human rights approach in the politics of the international women's movement(s), or rather, the women's movement as a global political actor.[2] One should, however, be careful when assessing the achievements of the global women's movement in the 1990s, as these were often perceived rather enthusiastically shortly after Beijing. Scepticism with regard to an over-optimistic view of the women's movement and to analytical exaggerations of social movements' political influence may serve as a precaution against the scientific construction of social myths, as well as against political frustration and disappointments. Nevertheless, according to my line of reasoning, Dorsey's text provides the inspiration for an elaboration of the following three assumptions, which might help to provide an analytic frame within which to look at the women's human rights approach as a central tenet of global women's politics.

First of all, I consider it empirically and conceptually appropriate to use the term 'global women's politics' for what is commonly referred to as 'international women's politics', and consequently to speak of 'global' instead of 'international' women's movement(s).[3] Second, it is my assumption that the women's movement's shift from an international to a global orientation is closely tied to the women's rights approach. In my opinion, 'globality', understood as an explicit political aim of the women's movement, and the political process of 'globalizing' the women's human rights framework, are interdependent and have ultimately given rise to each other. Third, I therefore agree with Dorsey's assumption that the future of global women's politics cannot be seen as separate from the women's human rights framework. During the years following Beijing, it has probably been one of the most important strategic bonds, one of the central connecting reference points, and at the same time the fundamental ethical standard of the global politics of women's movements.

From international to global politics of the women's movement(s)

In contrast to conventional international politics of nation states, the self-perception and practice of the international women's movement during the last 25 years was never characterized by the typical concept of how inter-state systems interact. None of the movement's activists, nor feminist scholars of International Relations, would ever describe the political relations between national women's movements and their activities in terms of simply crossing the borders between nation states. Lines of conflict between women and women's movements from different regions and countries often run parallel to nation-state borders, as, for example, they did and to a certain extent still do in regard to the conflict between Israel and Palestine. However, national alliances were never a priority concern within the international women's movement.

On the contrary, since the beginning of the United Nations Decade for Women the international women's movements' most important political strategies and objectives have always been located *below* and *above* the *nation-state* level. On the one hand, it could be said that the movements' spheres of activity are located below the state level, that is, at the socio-political level, in the non-public, allegedly private sphere, where social conditions are determined by everyday life. On the other hand, women's movements are active above state levels, that is, on the institutional and organizational levels of international governance.

The international women's movements have never restricted their politics and policies to the official public levels of politics. They have always politicized the concrete everyday living conditions of women (and men), as well as the whole range of diversities and different levels of cultural, social and political conditions which produce and reproduce these concrete living conditions. This is why social and political processes at a local and regional level have always played an important role in the movements' understanding of international politics. Examples that have most often been quoted within the movement(s) to demonstrate this are women's poverty and violence against women within their specific contexts, including the entire spectrum of women's strategies and political processes in combating these problems (see, for example, Basu 1995; Nelson and Chowdhury 1994).

Transcending in this way the traditional notions of political spheres and levels of action, international women's movements have made visible all the different local and allegedly private dimensions of international relations. This distinct difference from conventional perceptions of the term 'international' and from conventional international politics is what I propose to call a *characteristic orientation towards the global and global politics* of the international women's movement.

Thus, the attribute 'global' expresses in this context a double meaning: the notion of generality, and simultaneously, the concept of *contextualization*. In contrast to traditional Western thought about universality, the idea of global politics also stresses *difference and diversity*. It is more open to comprehending the general, which includes the particularities of local or regional contexts as well as those of the many levels of 'public' and 'private' contexts of political action. In order for this project to be successful, it needs to be founded on the process of 'constantly identifying and re-establishing the interfaces between the specific and the general in each and every context', as Richard Falk (1995: 242) rightly puts it.

In practical terms, and indeed since long before this perspective became fashionable in international politics and in International Relations, the political process of the international women's movement has been shaped by the insight that international politics does not simply take place at the inter-nation-state level, but also encompasses multi-centric and multilevel processes. Thus the movement's multidimensional political understanding, which is sensitive to differences, almost pre-destined it to become the most global of all social movements of the 1990s. This is why Ellen Dorsey (1997: 336) called it 'a model and a vision of global governance'. After the end of the Cold War, when the importance of globalization and global politics became more apparent not only to social movements and NGOs but also to state actors, the women's movements had already acquired diverse practical experience of how to pursue global politics.

Networking, for example, the political cure-all of the late 1990s for NGOs' global policies and for global governance more generally, has long been one of the women's movements' top priorities. It has been on the movements' political agenda since the Third World Conference on Women in Nairobi in 1985. Accordingly, the women's movement was able to present itself as a well-prepared, well-organized and rather coherent actor in the World Conference NGO forums of the 1990s.[4] The second example is the caucus system, which the women's movement installed as an exemplary tool for global negotiations. Already utilized in the early 1990s during the 1992 Earth Summit in Rio de Janeiro (UNCED), the caucus system is designed to be an inclusive participatory form of mediation and communication between the movement's grassroots and the official negotiation structure. With the women's caucus, the women's movement is the only political force in the process of global politics that has developed a concrete answer to the serious problems around the question of democracy that grow out of the global governance scenario.[5] Of course, the caucus system is not a general solution to obscure, confusing and hierarchical decision-making structures, nor is it an answer to the absence of democratic authority and control. These problems are far from being solved within the women's movements themselves. But it is another example of the movement's drive and capacity for innovation in developing tools for global politics.

Interdependencies between 'globality' in the movement's sense and the 'globalizing' of the women's human rights framework

In addition to the women's movement's perception of world politics as multicentric and multilevel, a second component was required to develop a global discourse inside the movement itself, and to make the movement a truly global political actor. Pluralism and the recognition of complexity and diversity are not enough to hold together, on a long-term basis, such a broad and diverse movement as the women's movement. Similarly, the concept of global governance is not a sufficiently strong political basis for the movement to navigate within the various arenas of world politics, even though it offers more possibilities for interaction than the classic idea of inter-state relations (see Ruppert 2000). Global politics and governance instead of government are by no means a guarantee of the success of women's political objectives, as was seen during the Beijing + 5 Conference (see Chapters 3 and 4).

The second component, which in my opinion was essential for the women's movement to become an effective global actor, was the movement's shift towards aiming for 'globality' as a main objective. Even though there has never been an explicit discourse along these lines, the movement's political practice suggests a conceptual differentiation between three different political approaches on the global level:

1. Criticizing and combating globalization as a neoliberal paradigm (for example Wichterich 2000).
2. Utilizing global politics, or rather global governance, as tools for governance under the conditions of globalization (for example Meyer and Prügl 1999; Holland-Cunz and Ruppert 2000).
3. Specifically creating 'globality', which the women's movement has aimed for and worked towards as an important factor in women's global politics.

'Globality' is scarcely noticed in feminist analysis of women's human rights policies. One reason why I consider this question to be more important than commonly recognized is that I see the political creation of 'globality' as strongly interwoven with the women's human rights policies of the movement. From a feminist perspective, 'globality' means – at least to me – everything that global politics or global governance should be based on or directly accompanied by. This includes, in particular, the political creation and establishment of global norms for world development and global ethics for industrial production, such as (social and gender) justice, sustainability and peace, based on the creation of globally valid fundamental human rights. As early as 1991, the women's movement(s) had clearly and powerfully demanded all this in the 'Women's Action Agenda 21', which it developed in connection with the UNCED process.

Thus, even before the 1993 World Conference on Human Rights in Vienna, the women's movement had already successfully taken a first major step towards the global 'shift from basic needs to basic rights'.[6] Then, as is well known, it took a second major step during the transition from Vienna, via the Cairo World Conference on Population and Development 1994, to Beijing 1995. The women's movements used the preparatory process for the Vienna Conference as an opportunity to publicly promote and politicize their demand for the comprehensive protection of women's human rights within the official framework of the United Nations. This demand called for a double shift in thinking: on the one hand it expressed the idea of equal human rights for women, as illustrated by the slogan 'human rights are women's rights', and on the other hand, there was the recognition of women's specific rights as human rights, which was summarized in the slogan 'women's rights are human rights' (see Wichterich 1999: 57–9). With this, the notion of women's rights, which had been introduced a decade earlier with the Convention on the Elimination of All Forms of Discrimination Against Women (CEDAW), was once again resolutely presented to the world public, now within the general human rights framework.

The process by which the women's movements succeeded in gaining recognition of their demands by the UN at the Vienna conference in 1993 is widely known. Its groundbreaking success in Vienna was to bring about a decisive 'feminist extension' or 'redefinition' of the Western human rights principle of universality (see Gerhard 2000: 19). Since the Vienna Conference, different forms of violence against women, which had previously been considered 'private', have been internationally recognized as human rights violations. What had been central to the practice of the international women's rights movement for over two decades, and for which women's rights movement(s) had demanded recognition, was no longer to be ignored at the UN level: the personal is political at the local, the national *and* the international level. Or, to put it another way, it can be concluded that the global is always personal.

The movement's success in Vienna has been thoroughly analysed and discussed in feminist theory (for example, Cook 1994; Peters and Wolper 1995). But one important aspect of this success story has, as far as I know, rarely been mentioned. It is the process of becoming a global movement, which runs parallel to the political creation of 'globality'. I am convinced that the women's movement formed a global movement by agreeing upon the women's human rights approach during the period between Vienna and Beijing, at least in the sense that:

1. It turned into a collective actor in global politics, particularly on the level of international politics.
2. It works towards establishing global standards and ethics.
3. Its understanding of women's human rights as a core normative reference point can, in fact, be called global.

This means that women's human rights are above all – at least in principle – inclusive and indivisible. Despite the conflicts about political priorities within its different branches, for instance along the North–South divide, the movement has been strongly committed to the indivisibility of the different human rights categories. It has rejected the idea of ranking the different concerns expressed in political rights, social rights and the right to self-determined development in a hierarchical manner, which is a typical Northern practice.

Meanwhile, even critical mainstream authors in International Relations have come to the conclusion that the strength of the women's movement was essential for the international recognition of the 'necessity of the interdependence and indivisibility of human rights' (Hamm 1999: 441) during the Vienna Conference and its follow-up. Similar to critical mainstream concepts, which are based on the idea of social justice and the protection of basic human needs, the women's movement also 'consistently linked all categories of rights to the structural conditions that discriminate against women and produce profound patterns of inequality and violence', as Ellen Dorsey (1997: 343) aptly puts it.

This normative and political 'globalizing' of women's human rights was essential in bringing about the advancement of global women's politics and policies in the 1990s. Since Vienna, the women's human rights approach has provided a connecting framework for the separate fields of international and global women's policies. The majority of the movement's issues, most notably development policies and peace-making, like those discussed in this book, can be united under this one thematic umbrella and – even more importantly – this one normative frame. Simultaneously, the global concept of women's human rights can be utilized in different institutional contexts to pursue the objectives of women's politics. And in addition, the women's human rights norm can, of course, be strengthened through its own ability to consolidate the women's movements' power by bringing together and offering a normative focus for the disparate, but increasingly overlapping, fields of global women's politics.

The best example of these interdependencies is the global issue of empowerment. Women's empowerment is one of the most important requirements for women's human rights, and at the same time one of its central objectives. Without the discussions about empowerment and its political processes within the movement, which were initiated by DAWN in 1985 in Nairobi (DAWN 1985 and Medel-Añonuevo, see Chapter 6), we could not conceive of a global woman's human rights concept today. Moreover, empirical studies, like those by Birte Rodenberg and Christa Wichterich (1999) on women's projects funded by the German Heinrich Böll Foundation, have begun to show that the women's human rights approach gives important impulses to the empowerment processes of the countless women's organizations and projects around the globe which are working at different levels of women's social and political organization.

Today's women's rights politics became possible only after the different approaches of international women's politics moved towards 'globality'. In this process empowerment, as characterized by DAWN, has been pivotal to globality. The Earth Summit in Rio was the location where its potential for political transformation gained worldwide visibility. Hence, the women's movement's self-perception, and its claim to be a global movement in global politics, were prerequisites for the process of globalizing women's human rights. Only within this framework was CEDAW – having been adopted in 1979 and entered into force in 1981 – finally able to become a more effective instrument to be used by women's NGOs (see Pansieri 2000).

Interfaces between the advancement of global women's politics and the women's human rights approach

The Beijing + 5 Conference has made feminist activists and scholars all over the world aware of how limited the women's movements' influence is and how limited their social as well as political scope of action. Restrictions are imposed by the economic realities of globalization, which seem to represent insurmountable obstacles to the improvement of the living and working conditions of the majority of women worldwide. Simultaneously, feminists are confronted by political products of the globalization process, such as fundamentalism and cultural relativism, which are hindrances to the advancement of women's rights. Caught between these two forces, the women's movement is looking for allies within the ranks of the governments who at least show some interest in the movement's issues. However, this interest is often based on the condition that no monetary or political costs will be incurred.

The fact that the women's rights approach has only a limited scope of action does not, however, mean that the globalizing of women's human rights should not be prioritized. On the contrary, it even strengthens the case for prioritizing this issue. There is no doubt that the most lasting success of the movement's politics in the last ten years has been made in the arena of human rights politics. Violence against women is, and will remain recognized as, a human rights violation. This will not change, even though there were heated disputes over basic women's rights during the Beijing + 5 Conference in New York, and even though the movement was not able to achieve full recognition of its position – a position that had already been accepted by the United Nations in Cairo in 1994. These continuous disputes about resolutions that had already been agreed upon justifiably produce a lot of political anger and frustration among the movement's activists and observers. It also demands a lot of political strength and staying power. But, from an analytical viewpoint, the recurring debate over what has already been achieved is not surprising.

Despite the discussions that continually develop around definitions and details of the concept of violence against women and around the human rights of women to self-determination – especially in reference to their own bodies and sexuality – the ever recurring international disputes must not necessarily be considered a defeat. On the contrary, this could even be considered a success for the movement's global politics, at least in some respects. I regard it as proof of the success of the movement that in Vienna in 1993, the women's movement fully succeeded in at least breaking open the constitutive norms of international politics once and for all, because it put the feminist concept of global human rights permanently on the United Nations agenda. In addition, this is helpful to women's movements in countries whose governments persistently refuse to recognize women's basic rights (see for example, Oloka-Onyango and Tamale 1995, Kuenyehia in Chapter 12 and Wölte in Chapter 13). Although this is less than the comprehensive recognition of the global principle of women's human rights that the women's movement had hoped for after the Vienna Conference, it is still a lot if one considers the precarious starting position and fundamental obstacles faced by international/global women's politics (see, for example, Pettman 1996 and Zalewski in Chapter 2). If it is true, as feminist international relations theories claim, that gender relations represent basic patterns of power, and simultaneously express constitutive norms at a national as well as at an international level (Ruppert 2002), then making the renegotiation of gender relations a permanent issue in international politics is a large step on the way to 'engendering global politics'.

The development of global women's politics is, of course, not a rosy success story, but rather a double-edged sword. On the other side of the more or less successful story, political costs threaten to arise. To pursue 'globality' and the movement's process of becoming global may, for example, increase the risk of glossing over core conflicts within the movement, like those about the unequal distribution of power and resources, or racist structures of subordination. The aim of creating global standards may turn into the contrary and thwart pluralism, that is, the need to politicize differences (see Chapters 3 and 4).

In addition, the arenas of international politics where women's human rights are negotiated are not identical to the arenas of international high politics. The women's human rights approach just brushes and barely challenges prevailing norms or ruling interests concerning so-called hard issues such as security and economic policies. These are situated within the traditional power-based arenas of international high politics, where civil society's participation is inconceivable. Thus, implementing a shift in interests in international politics by transforming constitutive norms is not only politically risky, but also an uncertain tactic. What other path actually open to international and global women's politics, however, is more promising than the global women's human rights path? Despite all justified scepticism towards 'law-based or legal-style activity' (Miller 1999: 175), I still do not see many alternative strategies for success.

To sum up briefly: while not wanting to sound overly optimistic, or to ignore the political risks and costs of the whole process, I believe that up to now the global women's movement has rather productively utilized the opportunities available to it in global politics. It was gradually able to extend the social and political scope of its action on the international level. With the women's rights approach, it developed a political framework which it has conceptually filled with meaning during the last ten years.

First of all, in much the same vein as the empowerment approach, the women's rights approach has been able to produce stability in the movement. It is also able to form a conceptual connection within the movement and to offer a basis for its fundamental standards of ethics.

Second, by consolidating the different concerns of the women's movement under this one thematic umbrella, the women's rights approach may function as a factor strengthening women's politics, and actually does so already.

Third, because the human rights norms are generally valid, that is, locally as well as nationally and internationally, they increase the ability of women's movements in all existing forms to navigate inside institutional politics on all levels of political action. Simultaneously they are – at least in principle – compatible with radical visions of world development or the global transformation of world politics.

Fourth, in dealing with the human rights frame as the only global norm in international politics, it challenges other constitutive norms of international politics such as legally accepted sexual violence against women during war. Hopefully this will, in turn, affect the development of norms on other political levels in the medium-term future.

Finally, the women's human rights approach may also serve as a bond to reinforce the interconnections with the three different strategies of global women's politics, which are:

- combating neoliberal globalization.
- navigating within the arenas of global governance.
- establishing political globality.

Notes

1. Special thanks to Seanna Doolittle for her help with translating the first version of this paper, and many thanks for constructive discussions and productive comments to Marianne Braig, Christa Wichterich and Sonja Wölte.

2. I use the term women's movement in two senses. One corresponds to the existence of diverse women's movements as actors on all levels of political activities. The second sense, which is used more frequently in the context of this chapter, refers specifically to the women's movement as a collective and coherent international and/or global actor with regard to international politics.

3. For a more detailed summary of my views on the development from international to global politics and movements, see Ruppert 1998a and b; I have tried to develop a more precise distinction between global women's politics and global women's movement(s) in Ruppert 2001; interfaces between feminist and mainstream perspectives on global politics are discussed in Ruppert 2000.

4. For critical feminist comments on the global governance process, see, for example, Runyan 1999 and Stienstra 1999.

5. One of the most interesting mainstream perspectives on democracy in global governance is put forward by Rosenau 1997; for an elaborated feminist view see Holland-Cunz 2000.

6. Christa Wichterich (see, for example, 1999: 57) has been a major promoter of this subject in Germany. For a synopsis of the Women's Human Rights debate in Germany in the late 1990s, see Braig and Gerhardt 1999.

Bibliography

Basu, A. (ed.) (1995) *The Challenge of Local Feminism. Women's Movements in Global Perspective*, Boulder, CO: Westview Press.

Braig, M. and U. Gerhard (eds) (1999) *Dokumentation des Workshops: 'Frauenrechte sind Menschenrechte'*, Frankfurt: Zentrum für Frauenstudien und die Erforschung der Geschlechterverhältnisse an der Johann Wolfgang Goethe-Universität.

Cook, R. (ed.) (1994) *Human Rights of Women. National and International Perspectives*, Philadelphia: University of Pennsylvania Press.

DAWN (1985) *Development, Crisis and Alternative Visons. Third World Women's Perspectives*, Stawanger: DAWN.

Dorsey, E. (1997) 'The Global Women's Movement: Articulating a New Vision of Global Governance', in Diehl, P. F. (ed.), *The Politics of Global Governance. International Organizations in an Interdependent World*, Boulder, CO: Lynne Rienner, pp. 335–59.

Falk R. (1995) *On Human Governance. Toward a New Global Politics. A Report to the World Order Models Project*, Cambridge: Polity Press.

Gerhard, U. (2000) 'Für ein dynamisches und partizipatorisches Konzept von Grund- und Menschenrechten auch für Frauen', *Das Argument*, Vol. 234, pp. 9–23.

Hamm, B. (1999) 'Menschenrechte und Demokratie', in Hauchler, I., D. Messner and F. Nuscheler (eds), *Globale Trends 2000. Fakten, Analysen, Prognosen*, Frankfurt/M: Fischer, pp. 439–61.

Holland-Cunz, B. (2000) 'Politiktheoretische Überlegungen zu Global Governance', in Holland-Cunz, B. and U. Ruppert (eds), *Frauenpolitische Chancen globaler Politik. Verhandlungserfahrungen im internationalen Kontext*, Opladen: Leske + Budrich, pp. 25–44.

Holland-Cunz, B. and U. Ruppert (eds) (2000) *Frauenpolitische Chancen globaler Politik. Verhandlungs im internationalen Kontext*, Opladen: Leske + Budrich.

Meyer, M. K. and E. Prügl (eds) (1999) *Gender Politics in Global Governance*, Boulder, CO: Rowman & Littlefield.

Miller, A. M. (1999) 'Realizing Women's Human Rights: Nongovernmental Organizations and the United Nations Treaty Bodies', in Meyer, M. K. and E. Prügl (eds), *Gender Politics in Global Governance*, Boulder, CO: Rowman & Littlefield, pp. 161–76.

Nelson, B. and N. Chowdhury (eds) (1994) *Women and Politics Worldwide*, New Haven, CT: Yale University Press.

Oloka-Onyango, J. and S. Tamale (1995) '"The Personal is Political" or: Why Women's Human Rights are Indeed Human Rights. An African Perspective on International Feminism', *Human Rights Quarterly*, Vol. 17, pp. 691–713.

Pansieri, F. (2000) 'Global Governance for the Promotion of Local Governance. The Case of CEDAW', in Holland-Cunz, B. and U. Ruppert (eds), *Frauenpolitische*, pp. 105–16.

Peters, J. and A. Wolper (eds) (1995) *Women's Rights, Human Rights: International Feminist Perspectives*, New York: Routledge.

Pettman, J. J. (1996) *Worlding Women. A Feminist International Politics*, London: Routledge.

Rodenberg, B. and C. Wichterich (1999) *Empowerment, A Study of the Women's Projects Abroad Supported by the Heinrich Böll Foundation*, Berlin, Heinrich Böll Foundation, available at http://www.boell.de.

Rosenau, J. (1997) *Along the Domestic–Foreign Frontier. Exploring Governance in a Turbulent World*, Cambridge: Cambridge University Press.

Runyan, A. S. (1999) 'Women in the Neoliberal "Frame"', in Meyer, M. K. and E. Prügl (eds), *Gender Politics in Global Governance*, pp. 210–20.

Ruppert, U. (1998a) 'Geschlechterverhältnisse in der Internationalen Politik. Eine Einführung', in Ruppert, U. (ed.), *Lokal bewegen – global verhandeln. Internationale Politik und Geschlecht*, Frankfurt/M: Campus, pp. 7–24.

— (1998b) 'Perspektiven internationaler Frauen(bewegungs)politik', in Ruppert, U. (ed.), *Lokal bewegen*, pp. 233–55.

— (2000) 'Global Governance: Das Ende der Illusionen oder ein neues Ideal internationaler Frauenpolitik?', in Holland-Cunz, B. and U. Ruppert (eds), *Frauenpolitische*, pp. 44–66.

— (2002) 'Globale Frauen(bewegungs)politik – Inbild der turbulenten Welt?', in *Sammelband zur HSFK Jahrestagung 2000*, Frankfurt/M.: Peace Research Institute Frankfurt (forthcoming).

Stienstra, D. (1999) 'Of Roots, Leaves, and Trees: Gender, Social Movements and Global Governance', in Meyer, M. K. and E. Prügl (eds), *Gender Politics*, pp. 260–72.

Wichterich, C. (1999) 'Frauenrechtspolitik im Menschenrechtsdiskurs', in Braig, M. and U. Gerhard (eds), *Dokumentation des Workshops*, pp. 57–64.

— (2000) *The Globalized Woman. Reports from a Future of Inequality*, London: Zed Books.

CHAPTER 12

Economic and Social Rights of Women: A West African Perspective

Akua Kuenyehia

In recent times, the term 'human rights' has become a concept for the articulation of the concerns of women, and at the same time a movement for the realization of the ideals that have come about through the articulation of these concerns. Some of the ways through which women have sought to articulate their claims have been the various international treaties, as well as the United Nations World Conferences. Indeed, the Vienna Declaration, which was the outcome of the United Nations World Conference on Human Rights in 1993, provides a major milestone for the women's human rights movement. It affirms in part that: 'The human rights of women and of the girl-child are an inalienable, integral and indivisible part of universal human rights.'[1] By this affirmation, the women's movements succeeded in placing women's rights at the centre of the debate on human rights and challenged the traditional mainstream understanding of human rights.

Subsequently, the Fourth United Nations World Conference on Women held in Beijing in 1995 took further the process of consolidating women's rights as human rights. The Platform for Action, which resulted from this meeting, seeks to provide a framework for understanding the human rights of women. The platform confirmed women's rights as human rights, and the human rights of women and the girl-child as an inalienable, integral and indivisible part of all human rights and fundamental freedoms.[2]

The need to frame women's rights as human rights and to challenge the mainstream understanding of human rights arose out of the dichotomy between civil/political rights and economic/social/cultural rights which is prevalent in the concept of human rights, and which has not served the cause of women. There has always been a clear distinction between civil and political rights on the one hand, and economic, social and cultural rights on the other. Very often national constitutions, especially in West Africa, provide for the justiciability of civil and political rights. In contrast to this, economic, social and cultural rights are often, for example in Ghana, provided for under the rubric of so-called Directive Principles of State Policy – ideals that the state should aim at achieving.[3] This remains the case, in spite of fact that the Vienna Declaration states very clearly that: 'All human rights are universal, indivisible and interdependent and interrelated. The international community must treat human rights globally in a fair and equal manner, on the same footing, and with the same emphasis.'[4]

The hierarchies between those two groups of rights continue both at the national and the international level, and the mechanisms for enforcing civil and political rights continue to be better articulated than those for enforcing economic and social rights. Yet women's concerns mostly centre on economic and social rights. In this chapter, I will focus on the impact of the global women's rights discourse on the social and economic rights of women in the West African sub-region, and ask what opportunities this global discourse offers women of the South, especially women in West Africa. In particular, I will examine how the women's movements in this sub-region have used the global gains to further their cause, the challenges they face and the strategies that they have used to meet some of these challenges.

Impact of the global discourse

Even though international human rights are framed as being available without discrimination on the basis of sex, they have largely failed to advance the status of women. Additionally, many issues of central concern to women, such as underdevelopment, illiteracy, the adverse effects of structural adjustment programmes and systematic violence against women have not been defined as human rights issues by the mainstream.

The Universal Declaration of Human Rights adopted by the General Assembly by resolution 277A(iii) on 10 December 1948, states: 'All human beings are born free and equal in dignity and rights. They are endowed with reason and conscience and should act towards each other in a spirit of brotherhood.'[5]

The International Covenant on Civil and Political Rights (ICCPR) states:

All persons are equal before the law and are entitled without any discrimination to the equal protection of the law. In this respect, the law shall prohibit any discrimination and guarantee to all persons equal and effective protection against discrimination on any ground such as race, colour, sex, language, religion, political or other opinion, national or social origin, property, birth or status.[6]

This declaration clearly seeks to reinforce the provision of the Universal Declaration of Human Rights. The International Covenant on Economic, Social and Cultural Rights (ICESCR) states among other things that:

The States Parties to the present Covenant recognize the right of every one to an adequate standard of living for himself and his family, including adequate food, clothing and housing, and to the continuous improvement of living conditions. The States Parties will take appropriate steps to ensure the realization of this right, recognizing to this effect the essential importance of international co-operation based on free consent.[7]

There are also provisions on the right to work and the right to the enjoyment of the highest attainable standard of physical and mental health. This was the United Nations scenario of human rights that was available for the promotion of women's rights before the Convention on the Elimination of All Forms of Discrimination Against Women (CEDAW) was adopted in 1995.

The human rights framework used up until that point by the women's movements to articulate their concerns was fraught with inadequacies. The International Covenant on Economic Social and Cultural Rights, and the International Covenant on Civil and Political Rights, epitomize the dichotomy that exists between civil and political rights on the one hand and economic, social and cultural rights on the other hand. The civil and political rights are justiciable by virtue of the Optional Protocols, but economic, social and cultural rights are not.

It was against this background that the Convention on the Elimination of All Forms of Discrimination Against Women came into being. This convention has been hailed as the most comprehensive instrument dealing with the rights of women. CEDAW addresses discrimination against women, rather than discrimination on the basis of sex. It deals with the public as well as the private lives of women. The convention, however, has not really succeeded in addressing the fundamental problem of women's marginalization. This is partly due to the large number of reservations entered by some of the state parties, as well as a lack of political will on the part of governments to incorporate the provisions of the convention into domestic legislation.

In spite of these problems, the women's movements have succeeded

in using a combination of treaties and United Nations World Conferences to challenge mainstream human rights thinking and to make
significant gains. Through regional human rights systems like the
European and Inter-American Systems, significant gains have been made
in addressing some of the issues of concern to women. Between the
Forward-Looking Strategies of the Third World Women's Conference
in Nairobi (1985) and the Beijing Platform for Action of the Fourth
World Women's Conference (1995), significant advances were made.
Admittedly, the pace is slow and sometimes discouraging, but change is
nevertheless coming about.

How have West African women fared in all this, one may ask. How
have they utilized the debates on human rights? It has been observed
by Hilary Charlesworth that:

> From conception to old age, womanhood is full of risks; of abortion and
> infanticide because of the economic and social pressure to have sons in
> some cultures; of malnutrition because of social practices of giving men
> and boys priority with respect to food; of less access to health care than
> men; of endemic violence against women in all states.[8]

Part, if not all, of the above can be said to be true of the majority
of women in the West African sub-region. Structural adjustment programmes have compounded the economic and social problems faced
by women in the sub-region. These programmes were institutionalized
as part of the efforts of governments to save the economies of these
countries. They have succeeded in eroding the social and economic
rights of women by the removal of government subsidies, or reduction
of government expenditure on services such as health, education and
other social services.

These structural adjustment programmes have limited the ability of
governments to provide infrastructure, and they have limited the expansion of facilities in spite of population expansion. The removal of
subsidies on various products such as drugs, textbooks and agricultural
products, in an effort to reduce government expenditure, has resulted
in an increase in their costs to the consumer.[9] The net result is a serious
erosion of the economic and social rights of the populace, especially of
women. Traditional practices that are harmful to women are another
area of concern to women in the sub-region. A lot of these practices,
such as widowhood rites and food taboos, which deprive women and
girls of nutrition, lead to a number of health problems for girls and
women.

All these factors taken together have led to the feminization of
poverty, the prevalence of diseases and chronic ill health, illiteracy and

the myriad other woes of women. Governments have failed to make effective commitments towards ensuring that there is an adequate balance in the distribution of economic resources between men and women.

The women's movements in West Africa have taken part in the global discourse on women's human rights and participated very actively in the process of using the human rights framework to advance their rights. They were active in all the United Nations World Conferences on women and succeeded in having their concerns included in the final outcomes of these conferences. They have used the gains made at the various conferences to intensify their legal and political demands at the national level, pressuring governments and other institutions to address issues of concern to women.

The women within the sub-region have been empowered through networking with women from other parts of the world to use the standards developed by the women's movements to press home their demands for equality and equity. Usually governments ratify international conventions, but do not take the next step to translate the terms of the convention into national legislation, so as to benefit the society. Thus, the use of the human rights framework has made it possible for women in the sub-region to demand from their governments concrete actions towards implementing the contents of such conventions. The pressure of the women's movements throughout the world provides them with the necessary support.

In 1986, the government of Ghana ratified the Convention on the Elimination of All Forms of Discrimination Against Women. By doing so it undertook to adapt its legislation, as well as to introduce new laws where necessary, in order to translate the rights contained in the convention into rectification of some of the anomalies in the law, and thus to improve the status of Ghanaian women. Among the policy measures that needed to be taken upon the ratification of the convention as embodied in Article 2 of the convention are:

• The abolition of all existing laws, customs and regulations that discriminate against women.
• The establishment of institutions to protect women against discrimination.

The women's movement in Ghana, working together with other institutions, has used the human rights framework to challenge the government to live up to its obligations and to work towards the elimination of discrimination against women in a number of areas. Three examples of this are discussed below.

Education

The Constitution of Ghana guarantees the right to education to all persons, and also provides that basic education shall be free, compulsory and available to all.[10] Real steps have been taken to ensure that the country is well on its way to making this a reality. Within the context and framework of providing free compulsory basic education, there are special programmes to make certain that girls are given particular attention. Various policy decisions have been taken to ensure that the percentage of females in all levels of the educational process increases progressively.

As part of the effort to help girls receive education, the Forum for African Women Educationalists (FAWE), an Africa-wide NGO, has on-going programmes aimed at encouraging more girls to go to school and stay in school. Through networking with their counterparts in other parts of Africa, and utilizing resources that they are able to lay their hands on, they are ensuring that the education of girls in the country increases by providing scholarships and other incentives for girls.

Much progress is therefore being made towards increasing the number of girls who receive education. It must be noted that education, or lack of it, is one of the ways in which the subordination of women is perpetuated. With falling household income levels, it is the girl-child who is likely to be withdrawn from school in order to help her mother with whatever economic activity is needed for the survival of the family. This is the background against which one must consider the efforts of the women's movement, which works with government and other institutions to ensure that more girls continue to go to school and stay in school to reach higher levels of the educational ladder.

In any society, the benefits of education, especially to women, cannot be overemphasized. It is also an accepted fact that ensuring a high level of literacy for women is one of the ways in which equality between men and women can best be achieved, not only in Ghana but also in other parts of Africa.

Violence against women

The second example to demonstrate the connection between the national and the international level of activity is the area of violence against women, a central focus of the women's movement in Ghana. The movement conceptualized this issue within the framework of economic and social rights, and thereby linked it to the international women's human rights discourse and politics. It is a fact that international human rights law excludes many forms of violence pursued by non-state actors as well as those that take place in the private sphere, in particular the family. Thus, numerous violations which are committed against women in their communities, their workplaces and their own families are excluded from the purview of international human rights.

In December 1993, the United Nations General Assembly adopted the Declaration on the Elimination of Violence Against Women. This Declaration categorizes gender-based violence against women as a human rights issue in general, and one of sex discrimination and inequality in particular. The declaration thus situates violence against women firmly within the human rights discourse. It affirms that women are entitled to the equal enjoyment and protection of all human rights and fundamental freedoms, including the liberty and security of the person and freedom from torture and from other forms of cruel, inhumane or degrading treatment or punishment.

In March 1994, the United Nations Commission on Human Rights appointed the Special Rapporteur on Violence Against Women, its Causes and Consequences. Part of the mandate of the Special Rapporteur is to 'recommend measures, ways and means at the national, regional and international levels, to eliminate violence against women and its causes, and to remedy its consequences'.[11] She makes these recommendations in her annual reports to the Commission on Human Rights. The appointment of the Special Rapporteur was a boost for the women's movements. All over the world, women's movements are still grappling with the most effective ways of collaborating with the Rapporteur and making maximum use of this opportunity.

Violence against women in all its forms is very prevalent in Ghana. In the past, the failure to deal with the problem was attributed to a lack of basic data on the form, nature, extent and prevalence of the problem. Thus, the women's movement in Ghana has taken steps to mobilize resources to undertake a nationwide research study in order to document the phenomenon of violence within the country and provide data and statistics on the nature, extent and prevalence of violence.[12] Armed with this information, it is now possible to work on asking for a comprehensive legislative framework to tackle the problem of violence against women in Ghana. These actions are firmly situated within the context of the actions of women's movements throughout the world in the issue-area of violence against women. The international women's human rights approach has strengthened the argument of the Ghanaian movement that the problem of violence against women is inadequately dealt with under the rubric of the general criminal law, as has been done up to now. Instead, the movement demands that it needs to be dealt with as a human rights violation.

Similar work has been done in Nigeria and Sierra Leone. Through networking with other groups within the sub-region, as well as outside it, the women's movement is able to keep up with developments and to utilize strategies that have worked for others.

Health

The final example to show how the Ghanaian women's movement links its efforts to the international women's human rights discourse is that of health. As we are all aware, CEDAW provides in Article 12 that: 'States Parties shall take all appropriate measures to eliminate discrimination against women in the field of health care in order to ensure, on a basis of equality of men and women, access to health care services, including those related to family planning.'

In September 1994, the international community underscored the importance of the right to health, including reproductive choice for all, at the International Conference on Population and Development in Cairo (ICPD). The African Charter on Human and Peoples' Rights also gives every individual the right to enjoy the best attainable state of physical and mental health.[13] Since the introduction of structural adjustment programmes, governments in West Africa and other African countries are unable to allocate enough budgetary resources to the health sector. This is manifest in a number of ways, one of which is the removal of subsidies in the health sector, thus curtailing the provision of free medical services to low income and vulnerable groups in which women predominate.

The activities of the women's movements in the area of health and reproductive rights, especially in the wake of the ICPD in Cairo and the Plan of Action adopted thereafter, have provided the impetus for national action. Various NGOs, using the ICPD Plan of Action, have worked successfully to initiate activities to put pressure on governments for the provision of a comprehensive legislative framework within which to deal with women's rights to health. In Nigeria, a number of NGOs, including civil liberties organizations, have conducted extensive research on women's reproductive health rights using the ICPD Plan of Action as a reference point.[14] In Ghana, a comprehensive review of all laws affecting the reproductive and allied health rights of women in the context of the ICPD Plan of Action is under way. Since our governments in West Africa are normally part of the international community that makes various commitments to the various plans of action resulting from global conferences, these plans become easy reference points and are used as a basis for lobbying and advocacy for action.

What are the interlinkages?

If development is about the improvement of human well-being, the removal of hunger, disease and ignorance, and the productive employment of all, then its link with women's enjoyment of economic and social rights cannot be over-emphasized. At the same time, the conditions and actions that lead to development, such as trade liberalization and globalization, have resulted in the serious erosion of these same rights which women need to enjoy if they are to be a realistic part of the development process.

The challenges facing the women's movements in West Africa, as in other parts of Africa, are immense. There is the question of how to strike a balance between the move towards development on the one hand, using economic policies that are not necessarily women-friendly, and measures that would allow women to enjoy their economic and social rights on the other hand. Women can be fully integrated in the process of development only if they are able to enjoy their economic and social rights.

Using the human rights framework in the quest for gender equality and equity, through promoting women's economic and social rights, has been the strategy utilized by the women's movement to advocate and lobby at the national level. This has been done, because even though the framework has its limitations, it has been helpful in promoting the rights of women. The opportunities offered by this process have been fully utilized by the women's movements in the sub-region to advance the cause of women, especially in the promotion of their economic and social rights. Gender-based violence offers the best example of the focus of public attention on an issue in a way that has enabled the women's movement in Ghana to fully utilize that opportunity to move forward. It must be noted, however, that the human rights framework is more responsive to 'public' rather than 'private' violations of rights.

Conclusion

The struggle of African women for human dignity and well-being is firmly located in the context of political, economic and cultural domination. This is within an international system of allocation of resources that is neither just nor equitable. For the large majority of these women, the struggle for dignity is a struggle for basic needs and subsistence. It is therefore imperative that problems such as poverty and disease are addressed in the context of the discourse on human rights. Economic policies such as structural adjustment programmes, to name the most important ones, tend to be a major source of violation of the economic and social rights of women.

The language of rights and the associated strategies is most appropriate for challenging these violations and demanding redress. The strategic alliances with groups from other parts of the world through the global women's movement have been most beneficial for the efforts to challenge these violations. In forging alliances and using the human rights framework, the women's movements in Ghana and West Africa have been mindful of the social and cultural context within which they operate, and have therefore sought to form alliances on the national level that will help to promote rather than suppress their aspirations. The limitations of the human rights framework were starkly demonstrated at the Beijing + 5 Conference in New York. Nevertheless, this is not necessarily a cause for despair, but rather a further challenge for women the world over.

Notes

1. Article 18, Vienna Declaration and Programme of Action, 1993.

2. Articles 9 and 14, Beijing Declaration, 1995.

3. See chapter 6, 1992 Constitution of Ghana; chapter 2, 1999 Constitution of the Federal Republic of Nigeria.

4. Article 5, Vienna Declaration, 1993.

5. Article 1, Universal Declaration of Human Rights.

6. Article 26, International Covenant on Civil and Political Rights.

7. Article 11, International Covenant on Economic, Social and Cultural Rights.

8. Charlesworth, H. (1993) 'What are "Women's International Human Rights"?', in Cook, R. (ed.), *Human Rights of Women, National and International Perspectives*, Philadelphia: University of Pennsylvania Press, pp. 71–2.

9. For a discussion of structural adjustment programmes and women's rights in Ghana, see Akua, K. (1993) 'The Impact of Structural Adjustment Programmes on Women's International Human Rights: The Example of Ghana', in Cook, R. (ed.), *Human Rights of Women*, pp. 422–36.

10. Article 25, 1992 Constitution of Ghana.

11. See United Nations Commission on Human Rights Resolution L.8/Rev.1, 1995, for the full text adopted by the commission.

12. See Appiah, D. C. and K. Cusack (eds) (1999) *Breaking the Silence and Challenging the Myths of Violence Against Women and Children in Ghana. Report of*

a National Study on Violence, Accra: Gender Studies and Human Rights Documentation Centre.

13. Article16, African Charter on Human and Peoples' Rights.

14. See Akamadu, T. (1998) *Beasts of Burden. A Study of Women's Legal Status and Reproductive Health Rights in Nigeria*, Lagos: Civil Liberties Organization.

CHAPTER 13

Claiming Rights and Contesting Spaces: Women's Movements and the International Women's Human Rights Discourse in Africa

Sonja Wölte

Women in Africa can look back on a long and rich tradition of women's movements and women's organizing dating back to pre-colonial times. Women's practices of resistance and organizing against patriarchal, class, colonial and other forms of oppression and injustice have been as diverse as the many different societies and states across the continent (see for example, Mikell 1997; Parpart and Staudt 1989). One common root of the more recent African women's movements is their involvement in the fight against colonialism, during which women pursued many self-organized and autonomous forms of resistance. The colonial system profoundly reconstructed gender roles and gender relationships to serve the colonial aim of exploiting African labour, land and natural resources. This resulted, for example, in new forms of gendered division of labour and a new institutionalization of a gendered public–private divide. These interacted with the existing gender orders and created new structures of women's subordination and exclusion. Women's struggles against colonialism and for independence were often interwoven with demands for the renegotiation of women's roles and spaces and for women's rights. These included political and civil rights, land rights and rights regarding personal status law. In this sense, African women have long been affected by international politics and their movements have been situated in these politics, trying to claim their spaces within and in relation to them.

Today, as national and international politics are even more interdependent than in the 1950s and 1960s, African women's movements and organizations are active at the local, national, regional and international levels on a variety of issues. These issues include economic justice and globalization, racism, health and women's political participation. Since the UN Women's Decade (1976–85), women's organizations have increasingly formed political coalitions and networks at the regional and international levels. After the Women's Decade, which was dominated by the development paradigm, women's organizations in Africa, as well as in other continents, began to focus on the women's rights discourse and the law as a resource for women (see for example, Schuler 1986). As women's movements around the globe shifted from the development paradigm to the human rights paradigm at the beginning of the 1990s, they formed a strong international movement claiming the protection and demanding the implementation of women's universal human rights (see Peters and Wolper 1995; and Chapter 11 in this book). In recent years, African women's rights organizations have been at the forefront of setting the international agenda on women's human rights.

Feminist interpretation and appropriation of the international human rights discourse and instruments has become a key normative and political strategy in the domestic activities of African women's movements (see for example, Chapter 12). This chapter explores the significance of this discourse for the politics of women's movements and the improvement of women's status, with the focus on East Africa and, in particular, Kenya. It discusses the opportunities and challenges for women's movements that arise as a result of the engagement with the international women's human rights framework, in political contexts characterized by political transformation processes.

Between the state and the culture: charting the terrains of women's activism

The post-colonial constitution of the 'modern' state in Africa, which was in many countries modelled on European liberal concepts of the nation state, is profoundly gendered. It is characterized by the construction of a gendered dichotomy, whereby the sphere of modern state structures and institutions is male-dominated and few women have access to it. Women have generally been excluded from the public spheres of decision-making and state governance from the national to the local level (see Parpart and Staudt 1989; MacFadden 2002; Nzomo 1997).[1] Women's location is constructed as being – and in reality overwhelmingly is – at the social basis. Active in the organization of economic and social processes mostly at the community level, women have formed the social heart, the political basis and the economic backbone of an economically and socially increasingly weak and decaying nation state (Ruppert 1998). Yet, the status, roles and functions of women in this social context are often regulated by traditional cultural norms and institutions. These have been and continue to be to different degrees patriarchal, in that they structurally subordinate women.[2] In the majority of East African cultures, for example, women traditionally do not hold leadership or decision-making positions (see, for example, Nzomo 1997). Although economic survival today often requires women to work outside the home compound, most cultures and societies consider women's space to be in and around the family, the house and the farm, relegating them to the 'private' sphere.

This gendering of spaces is reinforced by the situation of legal pluralism in most African societies, where traditional institutions, norms and practices co-exist with modern state law (Merry 1988). Legal pluralism dates back to colonial rule, which institutionalized a legal system that combined colonial law with what was termed 'customary law'. Customary law was the attempt to cast cultural norms, conventions and practices into a polity system that was designed to serve the purposes of colonial rule. In today's post-colonial African states, cultural norms, practices and institutions which have changed over time are often more significant than statutory law for regulating communal life, particularly in matters of family, marriage and property relations (see, for example, Gopal and Salim 1998). In rural areas, this is often accompanied by a lack of access to many modern state institutions, bureaucracies and resources, which have therefore no, or very little, relevance to the lives of many people. In Kenya, this contrasts with semi-authoritarian structures through which the government exercises political control, even at the village level.

In the context of these structures of the post-colonial state, the gendered patterns of exclusion along the public–private divide effectively reinforce and complement one another to the disadvantage of women:

> The so-called traditional chiefs and their systems of 'culture and tradition' pose a major constraint to the democratization of women's relationships with the African state as individuals and as members of a political movement. The retention of social status laws – which are basically conventions and common practices – translates into the exclusion of women from the protections and entitlements of modern civic law. (MacFadden 2002)

In some countries, for example Kenya and Zimbabwe, constitutions allow for the limitation of women's rights in family relationships or matters of succession and inheritance, on the grounds that in such matters traditional rules and practices overrule modern state law (Gopal and Salim 1998).

Women's traditional roles and status have been constructed to represent and uphold the notion of African traditions and cultures, which are central to the identity of African nations: 'African tradition, institutionalized in customary law, is revered as the foundation for social cohesion and national identity' (VeneKlasen 1992: 251) in the African nation state. Women's behaviour, according to traditional norms and values, symbolically stands for and *de facto* functions to ensure the continuation of cultural traditions in a world of advancing modernization that brings insecurities and risks for many traditionally organized societies. Hence women's roles, rights and status are highly contested sites central to the complex relationship between modernity and tradition in African states.[3]

As a consequence of these patterns of exclusion and subordination, women's activism for more justice and equality in Africa has taken place both at the local level, which translates into the more 'traditional' sphere of activities, and the site of the modern nation state. In particular at the community level, Kenyan women draw on a long history of different forms of women's autonomous social, economic and political organizing and resistance to structures of oppression (Oduol and Kabira 1995; Khasiani and Njiro 1993). These are often based on informal and formal support networks and organizations, which offer women spaces to give voice to their disagreements with and resistance against oppressive traditions and norms (Kabira and Nzioki 1993). During the post-colonial era of authoritarian and single-party rule, African governments have generally tried to control women's organizations and activities, adapting them to their own political agendas and socio-economic needs. The Kenyan government institutionalized women's activities as a women's group movement consisting of local self-help groups, which are formally registered with the government administration. These groups have been situated within the country's development discourse and functionalized for its goals. In addition, from the local to the national level, women's political activities have been channelled into and directed by a dominant countrywide women's membership organization (Maendelo Ya Wanawake Organization) linked to the ruling party. Within these structures of control, women have tried to find their own autonomous spaces and forms of economic, social and political activities, which have been predominantly at the local level.

In the context of the Kenyan transition from an authoritarian political system to a democratic system since the beginning of the 1990s, new civil society actors such as human rights groups, new political parties, and societies for the promotion of democracy have emerged at the national level. At the same time, the Kenyan women's movement has begun to insert itself into the new political spaces opened up by these processes (Nzomo 1997, 1994; Oduol and Kabira 1995; Khasiani and

Njiro 1993). Women founded new and independent non-governmental organizations (NGOs) with the aim of engaging from an autonomous position with the state and its institutions, in particular on the issues of women's rights and women's political participation. These organizations critically challenge the patterns of women's exclusion from the modern state sphere as well as the cultural construction of women's roles and rights, which in their interaction serve to restrain women from becoming citizens and actors in shaping the state democratization process. Some of the newly founded organizations are membership organizations which link the national level with the local level of women's activities and politics. Other organizations are predominantly lobbying and advocacy NGOs operating at the national level. They seek to gain access to the spheres and processes around the setting of the national political agenda, and to integrate women's issues and rights into that agenda.

The current landscape of the Kenyan women's movement is therefore characterized by a plurality of new and old women's organizations. New NGOs on the national level, that is, in mostly urban settings, coexist with some older countrywide women's membership organizations and with the self-help groups and their networks in rural areas. Consequently, the women's movement faces the challenge of bringing together a variety of different modes and structures of women's organizing, women's issues and ways of women's communication. From a movement perspective, this raises the problem of forming sustainable relationships and links between these different forms of women's organizing in each of their contexts. Such relationships, in turn, are crucial for the formation of a political base that allows the Kenyan women's movement to establish itself as a political force expanding into all areas of domestic politics, be it at the national or at the rural level, and in the modern as well as in the 'traditional' spheres. The relationship between these various forms of women's organizations is an important factor in influencing the degree to which the women's human rights discourse is able to develop as a significant common political concept and strategy within the women's movement as a whole.

The entitlement notions of the international women's human rights discourse

The international women's human rights discourse offers a normative framework that translates into a source of political and normative legitimacy for the activism of women's movements in a number of ways. This is due to two interdependent entitlement notions inscribed in the international human rights discourse. This dual character of entitlements is based on the distinction between the universal rights of human beings and the internationally codified rights of citizens, both of which are enshrined in the international human rights documents.[4]

The Universal Declaration of Human Rights (UDHR), for example, as the core international agreement on the normative standard for human rights, recognizes the basic and fundamental rights of all human beings, who are 'born free and equal in dignity and rights' (Article 1). According to this document every human being enjoys political, civil, economic and social human rights. This principle of universality, which is repeated in other international treaties, entitles anyone to apply the text of the declaration to himself or herself and to claim the rights enshrined in the text. It therefore serves as a continuous measure of all types of oppression and exclusion experienced by human beings, and allows them to be reconceptualized as human rights violations. These may include structures of oppression or practices of rights violations in diverse political, legal, social and cultural spheres. Most importantly, they may also be human rights violations outside what is defined as the sphere of the nation state, as the feminist application of the human rights discourse to violence against women in the private sphere has demonstrated (see for example Copelon 1994).

The second entitlement character of the international human rights discourse refers more specifically to the rights of citizens *vis-à-vis* the nation state. Based on the UDHR, international human rights treaties such as the International Covenants on Civil and Political and on Economic, Social and Cultural Rights, and in particular the international women's rights treaty CEDAW,[5] spell out concrete legal and political obligations requiring states to implement human rights. The international human rights discourse is premised on states as key actors in the protection and realization of human rights. It thus entitles women as citizens to specific rights, to be protected and granted by the nation state they live in. According to more recent interpretations, the protection of women's human rights by the state also extends to the social, the cultural and partly even the economic sphere (Cook 1994). Within the international human rights system, a variety of mechanisms are in place to hold states accountable in respect of the implementation of their legal obligations. This logic of accountability entitles women and women's organizations to demand the protection by the state of their internationally codified rights. The mechanism of entitlement and accountability serves as a legitimizing basis for women's political or legal claims *vis-à-vis* the state.

International human rights treaties form the legal framework for the international agreements reached at UN world conferences, such as the 1993 Vienna World Conference on Human Rights or the 1995 Beijing Fourth World Conference on Women. These policy documents, although formally less binding, are translations of international treaty law into international political standards and measures. They are therefore political and normative guidelines to which governments have agreed and committed themselves. The Beijing Platform of Action is dominated by women's human rights language and the international community's commitments to the implementation of women's human rights. It is therefore part of the international source of entitlements for women's rights as human beings and as citizens.

Legitimizing the political space for women's organizations

How, then, do the international women's human rights discourse and these entitlement notions develop their effects for the women's movement and its forms of activism, and what significance do they have? In Kenya, as in many other countries around the world, national women's organizations are key actors in shaping the women's human rights discourse. In their plurality, as described above, they are the crucial actors in advancing the women's rights agenda by engaging on the local, national and international levels of women's activities.[6]

The majority of Kenyan women's rights and women's political organizations consider themselves to be part of a global women's human rights movement. In fact, this movement, and the various UN world conferences with which it has interacted, provided an important political context in the formation of many Kenyan women's NGOs in the early 1990s. In particular, the international, regional and national preparatory processes for the 1995 Beijing Conference on Women helped Kenyan women's organizations gain new political ground in a number of ways. First, it legitimized the existence of strong women's civil society organizations as key actors in the international Beijing process. Because the government wanted to present itself to the outside world favourably, it gave up its previous resistance to the registration of some women's NGOs. Second, the process provided the political opportunity for women's organizations to define or sharpen their political agendas, strategies and mandates. Third, it forged alliances and networks between women's organizations based on a common analysis of Kenyan women's main concerns and common goals. Fourth, and as a result of this, women's rights issues gained wider publicity and heightened visibility in the Kenyan public around the Beijing process. Thus the Beijing process strengthened the Kenyan women's movement as a collective political actor, which was able to expand its activities into the newly emerging space of Kenya's civil society and the country's political landscape.

However, the Kenyan government and the majority of male political leaders contested this political intrusion by delegitimizing the Beijing Conference and its outcome document, the Beijing Platform for Action. In an effort to defend the exclusionary gendered division of spaces in the Kenyan nation state against the challenges of the women's movement, government representatives deliberately discredited the conference, misinforming the public about its purpose and goals. Drawing on the discourse of traditional women's roles in connection with the preservation of Kenyan culture, the conference's aim was portrayed as the destruction of the Kenyan family and traditions and as harmful to Kenyan society as a whole.

Despite these efforts, the Beijing Platform for Action and the CEDAW convention have become the two most important international reference points for Kenyan women's organizations. They provide the normative framework and inform the mandate of the majority of these NGOs. Comments by the former director of Kenya's leading women's rights organization, the Federation of Women Lawyers Kenya (FIDA-K), capture the significance of these international women's human rights norms and policies: 'The international level is the only space where the government obliges itself to such far reaching standards on women's rights. They don't make such far reaching commitments on the national level.'[7] As a consequence, the majority of Kenyan women's organizations relate their analysis of the different forms of Kenyan women's discrimination closely to the standards entailed in these documents. FIDA-K's annual reports on the legal status of women, for example, are guided by the CEDAW framework, which thus serves as a basis for reinterpreting discrimination against women as human rights violations.[8] For many other women's organizations and issue-oriented coalitions, such as those working on the issue of violence against women, the Beijing Platform of Action provides the major normative and political frame of reference.

As in many other countries, Kenyan national women's NGOs function as transmission belts between the local, national and international political levels. They are active in international networks and in setting the international non-governmental and governmental women's human rights agenda so that both take account of the concerns of Kenyan and African women. Second, they translate international agreements and women's rights into the national and local settings. This process can be called 'contextualizing', 'localizing', or, as some Kenyan NGO representatives put it, 'domesticating' international women's human rights norms and policies. The 'domestication' of the international women's human rights discourse has several important aspects. First, it refers to the adaptation of these norms and policies to women's experiences of political, legal, and social injustices and the needs of women situated in their concrete political, socio-economic and cultural contexts. The second aspect of the 'domestication' of international women's human rights norms and policies refers to their implementation by the state through legal, policy and institutional measures. The third aspect refers to the strategies of women's organizations in working for the *de facto* realization of women's rights in women's lives. In order for these strategies to be effective, they need to be localized and contextualized within the concrete political and socio-cultural settings in which women's organizations operate.

Working the international women's human rights framework at the national level

The international legal and policy documents on women's rights provide women's organizations with the political and legal legitimacy that enables them to critically scrutinize the government's domestic policies and laws affecting women. The 'monitoring' carried out by women's organizations is strengthened by the regional and international follow-up processes around the Beijing Conference and the UN's monitoring mechanisms for the human rights conventions, because its results feed into these processes. In their domestic monitoring, however, women's organizations in Kenya cannot legally challenge the government to implement its obligations under international law, because the Kenyan parliament has not passed the formal domestication acts for CEDAW or, indeed, for any of the international human rights conventions and policy documents (Kibwana 1996). This creates a paradoxical situation in which, although the government has ratified these documents, they do not have the legal power in the domestic context that would force the government to adapt Kenyan laws and legal codes to accord with them. Yet, as women's organizations keep pressing for such an act of domestication, and as they continue to critically engage with the government on the implementation of international documents, the international structures and processes have a political significance, because they secure women's organizations' domestic political spaces and their positions as civil society actors.

As a consequence of these developments, individual women's organizations as well as issue-centred coalitions between them, for example under the roof of the Kenyan Women's Political Caucus,[9] have in the recent years regularly drawn on the CEDAW convention and the Beijing

Platform for Action in their various political initiatives and lobbying efforts on women's rights and women-friendly policies. For example, drafting proposals for women's legislation, such as the Equality Bill or the Affirmative Action Bill, draw on international documents as well as on similar laws in other African countries. The proposals for a Domestic Violence (Family Protection) Bill, for instance, took language from the International Declaration on the Elimination of All Forms of Violence Against Women from 1993.[10] References to the universal human rights discourse and to Kenya's international obligations also play an important role in the lobbying efforts for and during the parliamentary discussion of these bills. In their lobbying efforts, women's organizations work closely with the few female members of the Kenyan parliament.[11] The woman MP who presented the motion on the Equality Bill in December 1999, for instance, justified the intention and contents of the bill not only by referring to the situation of Kenyan women, but also by situating the bill in the context both of CEDAW and of the universal human rights standards in general.[12]

The discussions of these bills (none of which has yet been adopted by the Kenyan parliament) have taken place in the larger political context of a constitutional reform process that has been going on since the end of one-party rule. Again, as women's organizations claim their spaces in this process and try to integrate a women's rights agenda into it – demanding, for instance, the abolition of the constitutional protection of 'customary laws' or constitutional provisions for affirmative action – they also continually draw on the international women's rights discourse to legitimize their demands.

Connecting the national with the local

Many of the newly founded women's rights and political organizations which initially concentrated on working at the national political level have more recently begun to engage with the community level. In Kenya, the most common rights violations in women's everyday lives are connected with matters of succession, property and marriage rights, violence against women, land disputes, exclusion from local decision-making and harassment by local government representatives. Consequently, one major goal, and at the same time challenge, for women's organizations is to improve women's human rights within their concrete everyday existence. This is a difficult undertaking, because the root causes of women's rights violations are generally – and not only in Africa – part of a complex and intricate system of gendered structures, norms, and mechanisms of exclusion and inclusion on an individual and collective basis. The second goal and challenge is to build a politically strong women's movement by strengthening the relationship between the national and the community level of women's activities and forms of organizing. While the political mobilization of women at the local level is crucial for the women's movement, it has in the past been prevented by the Kenyan government, and continues to face a lot of resistance by national and local government authorities today.

Within this context, the domestication of the international women's human rights discourse at the local level faces various challenges. In order for the women's human rights framework to be applied to women's specific experiences of injustice, it needs to be situated within local forms of women's organizing and interaction, which are often confronted with a number of social, political and economic constraints. The women's human rights approach can only become an effective instrument for change and transformation at the local level if it is accepted and owned as a legitimate discourse and instrument among women actors and as part of their activities for change.

Kenyan women's organizations pursue a number of strategies in their attempt to tackle these challenges. The following discussion deals with selected examples, referring to training programmes set up by women's organizations for community-based paralegal workers and civic educators.[13] Through these programmes, women who are based in their communities and often have local functions as teachers or presidents of women's groups, are supposed to become 'agents for transformation'.[14] They are trained by national women's organizations in women's human rights, civic issues and rights, and in strategies for mobilizing women and acquiring resources. Backed by the institutional support and assistance of the respective women's organization, the paralegals or civic educators share and apply their knowledge to the specific situations in their own communities. This may take place in meetings such as women's or church group meetings, via individual counselling, or through organizing women around issues that affect them.

In the paralegal and the civic education programmes, the universal (women's) human rights discourse and documents serve as sources of political legitimacy and women's mobilization. During the training sessions, women's experiences of injustice in their very specific socio-cultural contexts are reframed by the trainers and the trainees themselves as human rights violations, or as violations of their birthrights, by drawing on the UDHR, CEDAW, the Beijing Platform for Action, or the African Charter on Human and Peoples' Rights. By making the connection between internationally acknowledged women's universal rights and women's lived experiences of injustice at the local level, women's feelings of violation are legitimized and validated. Furthermore, women's often diffuse awareness of injustice and discrimination can be turned into a consciousness of their entitlement to certain rights, and consequently about their entitlement to an end to their violations. In this way, the international women's human rights discourse offers an instrument enabling women to speak about injustices as rights violations, in a context where rights are absent or silenced (Braig 1999).

In their own communities, paralegals and civic educators apply their knowledge to their specific socio-cultural setting. Interviews conducted with some of them show that they do not usually explain international women's human rights documents, which are difficult to grasp, to local women. However, depending on the situation and the context, they do mention the idea of women's human rights – often also explained as God-given rights – and the existence of international agreements about them. Depending in particular on the political circumstances, they carefully introduce a rights language which draws its legitimacy from a notion of universality located outside and above the nation state. Based on this legitimacy, the rights language offers women at the community level the opportunity to rename the injustice they experience as rights violations. In doing so, women reconstruct their own identity as bearers of natural rights, with entitlements to certain rights based on their being human. This in turn allows women to think and speak critically about forms of discrimination and subordination which they were taught to endure on the grounds that they were supposedly part of their role and status as women.

Via the act of constituting themselves as subjects with entitlements to certain rights, women empower themselves to challenge structures, norms and practices of exclusion, subordination and the denial of rights. As a consequence, women are mobilized to devise individual as well as collective strategies for claiming their rights and new spaces in the family and communal context. This includes the renegotiation of their status and roles and of gender relationships, the distribution of social and economic resources, and access to decision-making processes and fora. The community-based paralegals serve as resource persons assisting such personal and collective transformation processes. They help women on an individual basis in finding suitable strategies for claiming their rights and improving their situations.[15] This is framed by collective activities which include men and women and which discuss gender roles in relation to specific local problems, such as in the areas of health, agriculture or infrastructure. The services and activities offered by paralegals at community level are in great demand and very popular.

Many paralegals report that the rights discourse enjoys a high level of acceptance among women when it is linked to their concrete needs in their everyday lives.

As women are constructed as subjects of internationally agreed upon human rights, their entitlement to protection and implementation of these rights by governments comes into focus. Paralegals and civic educators inform women at the community level about their civic rights, about the government's responsibilities for the implementation of women's human rights, and about the restraints on the government. As this knowledge gains ground, a new status and identity of women as citizens, based on rights and entitlements, begins to be constituted. Depending on the context, spreading awareness of the gap between the Kenyan government's rhetorical commitments to women's human rights in the international sphere, and the lack of their domestic implementation, is also employed as a mobilizing strategy. It adds a source of legitimacy to women's demands and underlines women's entitlement to citizenship status, which is characterized by a rights relationship to the state.

Women's organizations report that women have, based on this identity and status as citizens, begun to resist harassment by local government officials. They have begun to demand access to legal assistance by the government authorities and the police, for instance in cases of violence or disinheritance. Finally, they have begun to claim and exercise representation in local civic bodies and local committees, for example on development or HIV/Aids. In sum, women at the local level – as well as at the national level – have begun to engage with the state and its institutions from a position of entitlement to rights. In doing this, they are beginning to challenge not only their exclusion from these institutions but also the exclusiveness of the rights discourse as a mode of interaction, between men and in the male-dominated modern state and its institutions (MacFadden 2002).

Women's human rights – new political spaces for women's movements?

The example of Kenya shows that the international women's human rights discourse may open up new, albeit contested, spaces for women's political and rights activism in the domestic setting. This can enhance the political power of women's movements, which strengthens their political efforts to advance a women's political agenda and to improve the rights status of women. The discussion has also shown that the opening up of these spaces for the women's movement depends on several factors, which from different perspectives raise important issues for further study and political practice. One is the interconnectedness of all political levels of women's movements' activities – the international, national and local levels (see Chapter 11). Only if women's movements act on all these levels simultaneously are they able to defend those spaces against continuous resistance and contestation, at least in the case of Kenya. This in turn strengthens the claim of women and their movements to influence the current democratization processes, and their ability to insert their own agendas into them at the various political levels.

Second, the international women's human rights discourse provides women and their movements with a framework for the renegotiation of the relationship between women and culture/tradition as well as of that between women and the state. The impact of this discourse as an instrument of political change depends on its legitimacy in the different socio-political contexts. Thus, as women's organizations connect the various levels of their political activities, they draw some of their legitimacy to claim new political spaces from the international women's rights discourse and politics. This legitimacy from 'above' needs to be complemented by a legitimacy stemming from women and their organizations at the local level, that is, a legitimacy from 'below'. In order to understand the significance of international women's human rights norms in the domestic sphere, the interaction and dynamics between women's agency and the sources of legitimacy for the rights framework at the various political levels are key aspects requiring closer study.

The Kenyan example also reflects central issues for the study of political transition processes, which are often neglected by the mainstream discourses. The women's human rights discourse may strengthen women's movements in their challenge to the interacting patterns of discrimination and exclusion in what is constructed as the traditional and the modern sphere. The reconstruction of these spheres, and the redefinition of the relationship between them, are key elements in the current political modernization and democratization process, both in Kenya and in many African nation states. Hence the study of women's movements activities in this process, and the challenges they face, are central for understanding democratization processes in Africa.

The final aspect is related to the level of international (women's) human rights politics. The practice of women's human rights by many women's organizations, not only in Kenya but across the African continent and the globe, proves the applicability and relevance of the women's human rights frame in varying contexts. Seen from an international political and normative perspective, this shows that this frame offers a common ground for very diverse issues of women's struggles at very diverse sites of struggle. Therefore, the notion of universality lives through its application by women around the world. Domestic women's human rights practice demonstrates that the indivisibility of all human rights, be they personal, political, social, cultural or economic, is a key premise for the political power of the women's human rights framework in these diverse sites of struggle. This shows how important it is that feminist debates and practice on human rights continue to defend the indivisibility of all human rights. It also shows the necessity of engaging in continuous discussions about the political and theoretical implications of this indivisibility, and the universality of human rights discourse and practice, from a feminist perspective.

Notes

1. Inclusion in modern African state institutions and access to political power are also mediated by the construction of class and ethnicity which interact with gender, but which cannot, for reasons of space, be discussed here.

2. This is not to say that all traditional cultural norms are *per se* bad for women. Also, where traditional norms and institutions were originally intended to have positive payoffs for women, in that, for example, women would benefit from collective social and economic safety networks or be granted freedoms to engage in certain activities under male guardianship, these benefits have often been lost in the processes of economic and social modernization that have permeated most African rural areas and disrupted the socio-economic order on which many traditional rural societies have been premised.

3. One very clear example was the ruling of the Supreme Court in Zimbabwe in April 1999, which denied a woman the right to inherit her father's property by giving precedence to customary law over the constitution. This took place in the political context of a comprehensive overhauling of the Zimbabwean Constitution, which at that time still allowed for exceptions to the prohibition of discrimination against women in issues relating to (a) adoption, marriage, divorce, burial, devolution of property on death or other matters of personal law; (b) the application of African customary law. The constitution has not yet been changed to abolish this section, as the constitutional reform process has stalled (see MacFadden 2002).

4. This concept builds on Cornelia Visman's (1998) analysis of the French *Déclaration des droits de l'homme et du citoyen*, and Marianne Braig's interpretation (1999) of it. Visman argues that the declaration entails two texts, one protecting the rights of the human being and the other the rights of the French citizen. While the latter authorizes (at that time still only male) French citizens to speak about their rights, the former, as a text of universal and suprahistorical validity, authorizes any human being to speak about rights.

5. Convention on the Elimination of All Forms of Discrimination Against Women.

6. The following sections are based on several months of field research in Kenya in 2000, during which I interviewed representatives of 21 women's organizations and participated in a number of NGO activities and seminars. These were mostly NGOs working in the areas of women's political participation, women's rights and violence against women. Therefore, the following discussion generally refers to these types of organizations. I want to gratefully acknowledge that the research was made possible by funding from the German Academic Exchange Service (DAAD), the University of Frankfurt, the Cornelia Goethe Centre and the State of Hesse. For their support and friendship I particularly thank Kamau Mubuu and the staff of Women and Law in East Africa; Jael Mbogo, Patrick Onyango and Pamela Tuiyott of the Education Centre for Women and Democracy; Beatrice Konya of the League of Kenya Women Voters; Hilda Mawanda of the Coalition on Violence Against Women; and Ann Nyabera at the Federation of Women Lawyers, Kenya.

7. Interview with Jean Kamau, 21 August 2000.

8. See for example, the Annual Report 1997: *'Bado Mapambano'* – *Kenyan Women Demand their Rights*, Kenya August 1998; and the Annual Report 1998: *Institutional Gains, Private Losses*, Kenya September 1999, both published by the Women's Rights Monitoring and Report Writing Project, FIDA-Kenya.

9. The caucus is an alliance of about 70 Kenyan women's organizations.

10. *The Family Protection Act*, Draft by FIDA-K and the Attorney General, February 2000.

11. Currently, nine out of 222 MPs are women.

12. *Parliamentary Debates*, 1 December 1999.

13. Paralegals are trained to offer legal assistance and contribute to human rights awareness in their communities, while civic educators concentrate on spreading awareness of civic rights. A number of Kenyan women's and other human rights organizations run paralegal and/or civic education programmes. The following section is based on interviews and participation in the activities of the Education Centre for Women and Democracy (ECWD), which runs paralegal programmes, and the League of Kenya Women Voters (LKWV), which trains civic educators. In both training programmes, however, the human rights framework does play a significant role. Therefore, most of what is said below applies to both cases, although some aspects might be derived from ECWD's paralegal programme and others from League of Kenya Women Voters' civic educators programme.

14. Interview with Patrick Onyango of ECWD, 27 September 2000.

15. This may be in terms of socio-psychological advice or mediation in family disputes, or in the form of filing cases with the police or courts. The realization of women's rights claims through the legal justice system is limited for a number of reasons which cannot be discussed here. What is of importance here is that through the human rights discourse women, as individual and

collective actors, feel entitled to challenge injustices ingrained in the existing gender order and relationships.

Bibliography

Braig, M. (1999) 'Menschenpflichten versus Frauenrechte?', in Braig, M. and U. Gerhard (eds) (1999) *Dokumentation des Workshops: 'Frauenrechte sind Menschenrechte'*, Frankfurt: Zentrum für Frauenstudien und die Erforschung der Geschlechterverhältnisse an der Johann Wolfgang Goethe-Universität., pp. 79–96.

Cook, R. (ed.) (1994) *Human Rights of Women. National and International Perspectives*, Philadelphia: University of Pennsylvania Press.

Copelon, R. (1994) 'Understanding Domestic Violence as Torture', in Cook, R. (ed.), *Human Rights of Women. National and International Perspectives*, Philadelphia: University of Pennsylvania Press, pp. 116–52.

Gopal, Gita and M. Salim (eds) (1998) *Gender and Law. Eastern Africa Speaks*. Conference organized by the World Bank and the Economic Commission for Africa, Washington: World Bank.

Kabira, W. M. and E. A. Nzioki (1993) *Celebrating Women's Resistance. A Case Study of Women's Groups Movement in Kenya*, Nairobi: New Earth Publications.

Khasiani, S. A. and E. I. Njiro (eds) (1993) *The Women's Movement in Kenya*, Nairobi: AAWORD-Kenya.

Kibwana, K. (1996) *Law and the Status of Women in Kenya*, Nairobi: Claripress.

MacFadden, P. (2002) 'Women's Movements, Democracy and the State: Gendered Relationships of Power', in Braig, M. and S. Wölte (eds), *Demokratisierung, Bürgerinnenrechte und Frauenbewegungen*, Cornelia-Goethe-Centrum für Frauenstudien und die Erforschung der Geschlechteverhältnisse, Frankfurt/M.: Johann Wolfgang Goethe-Universität (forthcoming).

Merry, S. E. (1988) 'Legal Pluralism', *Law and Society Review*, Vol. 22, No. 5, pp. 869–96.

Mikell, G. (ed.) (1997) *African Feminisms. The Politics of Survival in Sub-Saharan Africa*, Philadelphia: University of Pennsylvania Press.

Nzomo, M. (1994) 'Empowering Women for Democratic Change in Kenya. Which Way Forward?', in Friedrich Ebert Stiftung: *Empowerment of Women in the Process of Democratization. Experiences of Kenya, Uganda and Tanzania*, Dar es Salaam: Amref.

— (1997) 'Kenyan Women in Politics and Public Decision-Making', in Mikell, G. (ed.), *African Feminisms. The Politics of Survival in Sub-Saharan Africa*, Philadelphia: University of Pennsylvania Press, pp. 232–54.

Oduol, W. and W. M. Kabira (1995) 'The Mother of Warriors and her Daughters: The Women's Movement in Kenya', in Basu, A. (ed.), *The Challenge of Local Feminisms. Women's Movements in Global Perspective*, Boulder, CO: Westview Press, pp. 187–208.

Parpart, J. L. and K. Staudt (eds) (1989) *Women and the State in Africa*, London: Lynne Rienner.

Peters, J. and A. Wolper (eds) (1995) *Women's Rights – Human Rights. International Feminist Perspectives*, New York/London: Routledge.

Ruppert, U. (1998) 'Demokratisierung oder Modernisierung von Machtlosigkeit? Geschlechterverhältnisse in Prozessen gesellschaftlicher Transition in Afrika', in Kreisky, E. and B. Sauer (eds) *Geschlechterverhältnisse im Kontext politischer Transformation*, Opladen: Westdeutscher Verlag, pp. 491–511.

Schuler, M. (ed.) (1986) *Empowerment and the Law. Strategies of Third World Women*, New York: OEF International.

VeneKlasen, L. (1992) 'Women's Legal Rights Organizing and Political Participation in Africa', in Schuler, M. and S. Kadirgamar-Rajasingham (eds), *Legal Literacy. A Tool for Women's Empowerment*, New York: OEF International.

Visman, C. (1998) 'Menschenrechte: Instanz des Sprechens – Instrument der Politik', in Brunkhorst, H. (ed.), *Demokratischer Experimentalismus. Politik in der komplexen Gesellschaft*, Frankfurt/M.: Suhrkamp, pp. 279–304.

PART V

*Feminist Intrusions into the Discipline
of International Relations? Perspectives
from the Mainstream*

CHAPTER 14

. . . .

Difference and Dialogue in Development

Lothar Brock[1]

There is hardly any other field of politics in which gender issues have come to play such a prominent role as that of development co-operation. In this field, gender has achieved considerable status as a focus for defining problems, determining agendas and designing strategies. Nevertheless, as Marianne Braig has pointed out,[2] new attempts at theory building in development studies largely ignore women's studies or those on gender. In other words, while development co-operation has reached the stage of mainstreaming gender, academic writing on development itself appears to be characterized by the absence of it. How can this discrepancy be accounted for?

Development discourses

Over a period of almost three years beginning in late 1995, the journal *Development and Co-operation*, which is published by the German Foundation for International Development, ran a series of articles on new approaches to theory building in development studies. There were 35 contributors and 32 contributions. Only two of the contributors were women. Of all contributions, only one (the article by Braig mentioned above) dealt with 'women's interests in the theory and politics of development'. If I am not mistaken, none of the other contributions, including that of the second female author and my own, made more than a passing reference to feminist literature. So the very publication in which the article by Braig appeared[3] seems to confirm her observation.

However, there is a growing body of feminist publications on development which challenges any claim of the gender-ignoring literature to represent today's theory building in the field of development. The crux of the matter is that feminist literature is also, to a large extent, self-referential in the sense that it ignores non-feminist writings. As a matter of fact, the more women have written on development issues, the more elaborate the intra-feminist debate has become. Thus, feminist literature has developed its own cosmos of thought on development.[4] This is to say that the issue, of course, is not the absence of feminist positions from academic writing on development. Rather, in recent years, such writing has proceeded, and continues to proceed, on two tracks: a feminist and a non-feminist one. These two tracks run at some distance from each other. With a few notable exceptions, the rule seems to be that feminist and non-feminist scholars refer to each other, if at all, for the purpose of staking out epistemic territory or claiming additional legitimacy for their respective work. In this sense, there prevails a mutually reinforcing pattern of relative isolation between feminist and non-feminist scholars.

It would be difficult to merge the two tracks and follow an integrated approach. A merger would not only call for a revision of certain findings of current research, it would also challenge the very epistemic foundations on which the work of the feminist and the non-feminist scholars is built. These epistemic foundations are rooted in the different experiences of men and women in their mutual relations. After all, the struggle over gender issues still proceeds as a battle of the sexes (albeit an unequal one), no matter how much one may stress the need to go beyond dualistic conceptions of *gender* by differentiating between the socially constructed roles of 'male' and 'female' which the term gender is used to signify. For the time being, what is at stake is the relationship between the sexes, though changes in this relationship do not concern biological givens, but rather socially constructed images and the political order that they represent.[5] Apart from such reasoning, the attempt to merge feminist and non-feminist approaches could lead to the same problems which seem to accompany efforts to mainstream gender in development *politics*. According to Claudia von Braunmühl (see Chapter 5), the rift between verbal references and actual accommodation of gender concerns in development politics seems to be growing. The same could happen as a result of attempts to engender general academic writing on development. Here, too, there would be the danger of mere tokenism or of clouding the issues. For this very reason, apart from being difficult in practice, it may not even be advisable to work towards the integration of feminist and non-feminist approaches.

Yet, in view of the perplexities of unequal development, there is an urgent need for a dialogue among all of those who feel that they have something meaningful to say on this subject. Therefore, we should be careful not to turn the recognition of difference in the social experience of men and women into a mutual disqualification as partners in a dialogue on developmental issues. A lot could be gained from a continuous and systematic inter-paradigm debate between feminist and non-feminist approaches to development. Before pointing out some of the issues which, in my view, would be of relevance in this respect, I would like to give a brief summary of the story of gender in the study of development as I see it. It is from this perspective that I derive my understanding of important objects of an inter-paradigm (gender to non-gender) dialogue.

Gender in the study of development

As is now commonly accepted, the story of gender in the study of development made considerable headway with Ester Boserup's contribution to making *women* visible as agents of development. Boserup's observation found relatively easy entry into the world of development co-operation because it was well suited to the task of doing something for the basic needs of the poor (instead of waiting for economic growth to do the job – a proposition which could not be upheld any longer after the Pearson Report). As women seemed to be crucial in securing basic needs, a gender dimension was included in the relevant pro- grammes. However, Boserup's study showed not only how women were overlooked, but also how they were discriminated against, and that such discrimination could actually be spurred by development co-operation. Thus she added a new aspect to the critique of unintended results of development co-operation, which in those days was also voiced with a view to the support of authoritarian regimes (in the context of the East–West conflict), or the intensification of dependency in the name of overcoming it (in the context of the new international division of labour).

In the wake of this critique, which was soon extended to include the mere instrumentalization of women for externally determined ends, and in view of the many setbacks of development co-operation, a lot of soul-searching took place among the proponents of modernization. What they came up with as a cure was the idea of *regional development*, which would integrate urban and non-urban, industrial and agricultural economic activities. This was to be pursued by addressing the special need of women to gain access to the basic means of production (con- sidered first of all to imply access to small loans). With the help of those who were willing to make the best of the new situation in a pragmatic way, this resulted in the institutionalization of women's issues as part of overall development co-operation (Women in Development).

This 'solution' fell far short of what the more radical feminist critique of the underlying economic mechanisms had in mind – it identified women's unpaid labour as one of the central features of the international division of labour. The focus of critical theory, which had previously been shifted from 'the proletariat' to 'the Third World' and the 'periphery' (traditional or informal sectors) of the 'periphery' (Third World countries), was thus shifted once more. But just like the previous 'keys' to understanding unequal development, the new key also turned out to be just one of many. On the one hand, the new division of labour (that is, the internationalization of production) seemed to depend more on *under*paid than on *un*paid labour. On the other hand, the notion of both unpaid and underpaid women's labour did not suffice to turn women into a global social class. Instead, during the second half of the 1970s and during the 1980s, it became quite clear that the category of difference, which had served the purpose of establishing feminist thinking so well, also applied to women themselves. This insight was quite in line with the post-modern critique of Western universalism which contested the claim, supposedly derived from the Enlightenment, that Western civilization represented a model the entire world would (have to) follow. The debate on these issues corresponded with bringing *identity* (back) in as a determining factor, not only of who we consider ourselves to be but of how we shape the world by *identifying* ourselves and others, because identification determines practices of inclusion and exclusion.[6]

One of the consequences of the self-assertion of women from non-industrialized countries, in combination with the critique of Western universalism, was the call for the empowerment of women. Empowerment referred to developing the ability of women to articulate their interests and to increase their impact on politics. Thus it stood for emancipating the interests and policies of women in development from externally determined ends.[7] At the same time, the concept of *women in development* was superseded by *gender and development*. Under this label, a debate evolved on how to move from women's projects to mainstreaming gender. As Chapters 5 and 7 demonstrate, considerable headway was made with regard to the mainstreaming agenda. Mainstreaming was even included in the 1996 Maastricht Treaty of the European Union. However, as already mentioned, mainstreaming *in practice* appears to many observers as a strategy to cover up problems instead of spelling them out. The reason for this seems to be that development agencies translated empowerment to mean that women were enabled to work more effectively than before towards the very ends that these agencies set up (for example, establishing small enterprises in the context of structural adjustment).[8] Does this mean that there has been no progress in development co-operation?

Points of reference for an inter-paradigm debate

First, conceptual thinking on development issues is in constant flux. An important part of the change of concepts has been the incorporation of feminist arguments. As Renate Rott argues in Chapter 7, the rhetorical codes used by development agencies in Latin American countries display a rather high degree of political correctness in respect of gender. This probably holds true for most of the agencies elsewhere and may be seen as the manifestation of a learning process. But what kind of a learning process? Are development agencies just learning to sell their products in new wrappings, or does their learning pertain to the 'product' itself? This is a question which needs to be dealt with, not only with a view to gender issues, but to development co-operation in general. I suspect that both kinds of learning are involved – improving salesmanship and the product to be sold. This could explain why so few groups (be it in the gender, human rights or environmental areas) are ready to withdraw from co-operation with official development agencies. The fear of being instrumentalized and taken for a ride is outweighed by the confidence that participation opens up, and helps to defend spaces for the advancement of one's own cause.

Carolyn Medel-Añonuevo argues very convincingly that empowerment, despite the incorporation of the term into the language of development agencies, still signifies a site of contest and resistance. Similarly, Claudia von Braunmühl holds that gender mainstreaming should be seen as negotiating space between different social actors. This seems plausible, and it points to the need to consider the possibility of finding new modes of combining empowerment and mainstreaming, in order to turn the latter into a tool for overcoming cultural hierarchization. On the other hand, non-governmental groups and organizations in the field of development, including feminist groups, develop strategic interests of their own which pertain to sustaining the existence of the group, retaining access to financial resources and opening up new ones, for instance by qualifying as consultancy organizations. These groups, therefore, may be tempted to join conceptual debates for purely strategic reasons, depending on whether or not this fits into the constellation of interests in which they operate. Therefore it may be worthwhile clarifying the very *meaning of the political* as understood by non-governmental organizations, self-help groups and social movements in the field of development. In such an endeavour, one should not try to hide the (strategic) self-interests of the actors in social struggle. Rather, they should be taken into consideration as an aspect of empowering, which, however, is in need of constant self-observation, because empowerment, of necessity, includes self-serving activities on the part of social actors.

Second, there also seems to be a need felt on both sides to strike a new balance between conceptual innovation and empirical research. In this respect, if I read her correctly, Gudrun Lachenmann points out two corresponding directions in which an inter-paradigm debate could move.[9] One refers to a reconsideration, on the basis of thorough empirical research, of the role of women in the world economy under the present conditions of world market-oriented structural adjustment. The other direction refers to a serious effort to base the fight against poverty on a sound analysis of the social and cultural embeddedness of poverty and the role of women in it, in order to enhance the prospects of reducing the unintended consequences of development co-operation in general, and of gender politics in particular. Both fields should offer a rich source of new insights. Thus, with a view to world market integration, it has been shown how women who need to feed their families act in and between war zones ('between the lines'). As traders of machine guns or penicillin they connect the remotest corners of these war zones, which for an outsider seem to be completely isolated from the rest of the world, to the world market.

With regard to the social and cultural embeddedness of poverty, there are innumerable challenges not only to the meanings attributed to poverty by official development agencies, but also in respect of non-governmental organizations trying to fight poverty. The NGOs have the advantage, simply because they are non-governmental, of having a better understanding of poverty and better access to the poor than the official agencies. The competency of NGOs, however, may easily be overrated. Even if they acquire an adequate understanding of the context in which they operate, they may still do more to weaken the social competency of their clientele than to empower them. Thus Mary Anderson summarized her findings on humanitarian work in crises and conflicts under the title 'do no harm'.[10] Part of the problem concerns the issue of building and strengthening state structures versus circumventing them. Doing the latter is not always the right answer to the failure or perversion of the state. Rather, general considerations of these issues have to be related to the specific conditions prevailing in each of the arenas of action. This sounds like a platitude. But it is extremely difficult to establish a constructive interchange between macropolitical and macroeconomic analysis on the one hand, and microsocial (or cultural) studies on the other. It seems to me that Gudrun Lachenmann is pointing to a way in which such an interchange could work with the help of a gender focus.

Third, as already mentioned, gender studies contributed to, or formed part of, the post-modern critique of universalism. In my view, after the critique of cultural hierarchization as an inherent feature of Western human rights thinking, there remains the need to find a balance between this critique and the positive potential of human rights as a political and legal concept. Cultural hierarchization (which was supported by the invention of the *state of nature*, as Beate Jahn has demonstrated[11]), is only one side of the coin. The other is political emancipation. Therefore, the idea of human rights, just like any other idea of progress in human affairs, may be ambivalent, but it is certainly not altogether paradoxical, in the sense that it could contribute as much to oppression as to the realization of human rights. Gender studies have gone a long way to deal with this ambivalence in a constructive way. One example of this is the reinterpretation of the French Declaration of Human Rights as pertaining to the concrete revolutionary struggle in France and as a common asset of humankind. Gender studies have brought the tension between culture and universal rights into focus, by demonstrating how reference to universal rights can open up spaces for talking about injustice in specific cultural contexts (see Chapters 12 and 13).[12]

Another example is the discussion of women's rights in the context of human rights. The struggle for women's rights has led to the questioning of liberal notions of equality, or of the private sphere. In liberal reading, political rights are to shield the private sphere against state oppression. Feminist studies focusing on these issues have shown how human rights have served to buy public liberty at the expense of 'private' oppression.[13] But the redefinition of the public/private sphere which resulted from the critique of 'private' oppression, while challenging the liberal reading of human rights, offers no reason to discard the concept of human rights altogether, because it demonstrates the emancipatory potential of human rights. It seems to me that Karen Offen's distinction between 'individualist feminism' (Anglo-American tradition) and 'relational feminism' (Continental tradition) actually mirrors this observation.[14]

In my view, a dialogue between the proponents of a general and a gender-specific understanding of human rights is more important than ever in order to cope with the ambivalence of human rights, if not with the ambivalence of law as such. Law has always served particular interests, but can be upheld in this function only by bringing its universalistic foundations to bear (that is, its character as a force transcending particularistic interests). With the growing emphasis on democracy and good governance in development co-operation, and in view of the increased virulence of 'humanitarian interventions', it seems essential to open up the human rights debate beyond its present confines, in order to get to grips with the universalistic need to build and protect spaces for addressing injustice in specific cultural contexts. Feminism as such is a universalistic concept, which, however, has learned to face the specificity of the problems it deals with. It thus has a lot to offer to the project of unfolding a reflexive universalism that lives up to its own claims, without using these claims as yet another device for fostering particularistic ends.

Summary

In answering the introductory question, it can be stated that theory building in development studies is proceeding on two tracks which run at some distance from each other. In view of the epistemic differences between feminist and non-feminist studies it would be difficult to merge the two tracks. Furthermore, with regard to the lessons to be learned from mainstreaming gender in development co-operation it may, for the time being, not be advisable to work towards a merger. However, what is needed is a dialogue between those travelling along the two tracks (with their many branch lines, some of which already meet). The possibility of such a dialogue should not be ruled out from the start by each side disputing the other's competence. While the differences in social experience are real, they do not constitute an insurmountable obstacle to communication. In contrast, such communication will mirror the differences in experience as long as these persist. With this background it would be especially urgent, in my view, to deal with the symbolic and the material aspects of conceptual learning in development co-operation; with the difficulties of bridging the gap between micro-social and macropolitical, as well as economic levels of analysis; and with the need to work towards a reflexive universalism, in the face of the observation that due to its very nature reflexive universalism can never be achieved, and yet is essential for working towards any improvement of human affairs.

Notes

1. I would like to thank Martina Blank, Sabine Fischer, Claudia Neusüß, Heike Brabandt and Sonja Wölte for comments on an earlier version of this text.

2. Braig, M. (1999) 'Fraueninteressen in Entwicklungstheorie und -politik. Von *Women zu Development* to *Mainstreaming Gender*', in Thiel, R. E. (ed.), *Neue Ansätze zur Entwicklungstheorie*, Bonn: Zentrale Dokumentation der Deutschen Stiftung für Internationale Entwicklung, pp. 110–20.

3. Thiel, R. E., *Neue Ansätze*.

4. If I have counted correctly, in the contribution of Claudia von Braunmühl

to the present volume, out of 41 references, three pertain to male authors, and in the paper by Renate Rott the female-to-male ratio is 18 to two.

5. Thus, in the relevant literature, the terms *gender* and *women* are more often than not used interchangeably. To give an example:

> In the 1980s, feminist scholarship in international relations, international political economy and the related field of development studies demonstrated the importance of understanding the gender-specific impact of development politics and of examining the impact on gender relations of the activities of international organizations and multinational corporations. What is the position in the 1990s? Is the 'New World Order', as some commentators claim, characterized by 'gender apartheid'? While there are differences between women across the world, there are also many commonalties and while the pattern of gender inequality varies between regions, it is nevertheless a global phenomenon ... As the least unionized and poorest-paid of all workers, women are particularly vulnerable.

Krause, J. (1998) 'Gender Inequalities and Feminist Politics in a Global Perspective', in Kofman, E. and G. Youngs (eds), *Globalization. Theory and Practice*, London: Pinter, p. 226.

6. Zaleweski, M. and C. Enloe (1995) 'Questions About Identity in International Relations', in Booth, K. and S. Smith (eds), *International Relations Theory Today*, Oxford: Polity Press, pp. 279–305, see p. 288.

7. See the contribution of Carolyn Medel-Añonuevo, Chapter 6.

8. See the contributions of Claudia von Braunmühl and Renate Rott, Chapters 5 and 7.

9. Lachenmann, G. (1999) 'Engendering Embeddedness of Economy in Society and Culture', *Reihe: Frauen in Entwicklungsländern*, Working Paper No. 23, Bielefeld: University of Bielefeld, Sociology of Development Research Centre.

10. Anderson, M. (1999) *Do No Harm: How Aid Can Support Peace – or War*, Boulder, CO: Lynne Rienner.

11. Jahn, B. (2000) *The Cultural Construction of International Relations. The Invention of the State of Nature*, Houndmills, Basingstoke: Palgrave.

12. See also Braig, M. (1999) 'Menschenrechte versus Frauenrechte?', in Braig, M. and U. Gerhard (eds), *Frauenrechte sind Menschenrechte*. Frankfurt: Zentrum für Frauenforschung an der Johann Wolfgang Goethe Universität, Frankfurt/M., pp. 79–86; Wölte, S. and G. Krell (1995) *Gewalt gegen Frauen und die Menschenrechte*, Report 2/1995, Frankfurt/M: Peace Research Institute Frankfurt.

13. Gerhard, U. (1998) 'Including Women – The Problematic Relationship Between the Women's Movement and the Law', in Braig, M. and U. Gerhard (eds), *Frauenrechte*, pp. 65–77.

14. Offen, K. (1988) 'Defining Feminism', *Signs*, Vol. 14, No. 1, pp. 119–57, cited in Gerhard, U., 'Including Women', p. 67.

CHAPTER 15

Feminism and Mainstream International Relations Theory

Harald Müller

•

My task is to assess the compatibility of academic feminism with the current mainstream theories of International Relations (IR). It is not to discuss the various applications of feminist theory to International Relations. Of course, the limited space available makes it impossible to do the job comprehensively. In order to present some meaningful results, I therefore summarize very briefly my understanding of the core common features of academic feminism. Next, I characterize the main characteristics of IR theories, with emphasis on the sources of conflict and the possibility of conflict management, and check whether and to what degree they could accommodate these features of feminism. In the second part of my comments, I focus on a few points concerning conflict management proper that have been emphasized by the contributors in the chapters on peace and conflict. Finally, I propose some precautionary considerations designed to counter a bias that feminist theory could suffer from and that could potentially distort inquiries into the field.

How do I define academic feminism?

Again, space is too limited to permit a comprehensive answer. In a nutshell, I see academic feminism as characterized by three distinctive features:

- It emphasizes a *problematique* that has been neglected in IR and defines a related empirical field.
- It contains a theory of rule, patterned as hegemony/subordination. This makes academic feminism clearly part of political sociology, in its structuralist, constructivist and post-modernist versions.

- It aims at a praxeology destined to foster and complete female emancipation worldwide, and as such pursues a normative orientation.

Feminism and mainstream IR theories

How do these features fit mainstream theories and International Relations – and vice versa?

For realism, interstate conflict is endemic in the international system, as the structure of anarchy does not permit the emergence of co-operative rules. Structural insecurity forces states into the security dilemma, in which both alternatives, arming and offering cooperation, could lead to disaster, without any way of knowing in advance what reactions either strategy would provoke. Violent conflict emerges from growing imbalances; creating and maintaining balances of power, including in particular the formation of alliances, is thus the only sensible method of conflict management.

Realism is a systemic theory orientated towards a quasi-natural science model. It is thus not interested in rule and has no way of integrating considerations of substate sociology. For these reasons, it appears fundamentally incompatible with the feminist project: women appear in realism only in their capacity as states*men*.

Rational choice institutionalism starts from differences in actors' interests and, therefore, also regards conflict as endemic. Violent conflict emerges from particularly adversarial constellations of contradictory preferences, or, in milder conflict situations, from the lack of adequate institutions for conflict management. However, in contrast to realism, this theory regards the design of effective institutions for conflict management as possible. Such institutions help to enhance mutual information and to assure a distribution of values along Pareto-optimum lines, thereby reducing both uncertainty and interest differentials. At its core, rational choice institutionalism is a theory of interdependent decision-making machines. It lacks any instruments for theorizing about the societal roots of preferences. Apart from the possibility that it might be used as a tool for modelling the consequences of the contest between male and female preferences – a very modest utility indeed – it also appears fundamentally incompatible with academic feminism.

For political economy, societal and international conflict is endemically rooted in the competition for scarce resources. Violent conflict may occur either through particular resource bottlenecks that intensify competition, or through particularly blatant unequal distribution of resources based on structural inequalities. Conflict management or solution can be achieved through regimes setting rules for competition or even for resource distribution, or – for marxist-informed political economy – through fundamental changes towards a more equitable socio-economic structure.

Since political economy privileges as its basis a set of variables quite different from feminism, namely economic and/or class structure, I see no fundamental compatibility between the theories. The sympathy for feminism expressed by political economists like Immanuel Wallerstein grows out of political opportunism, not theoretical coherence. However, the economic distribution analysis is a useful tool, if combined with a gender perspective, to account for inequalities in domestic and international structure.

Neoliberalism, in particular democratic peace theory, views conflict as a natural outgrowth of society, but whether such conflict will turn violent or not depends on the institutional context. Violent conflict is caused by non-democratic institutions. Conflict management thus requires democratization and/or international organization led by democracies. This theory is largely institutionally, not sociologically, grounded, and so it is not evidently compatible with feminism. But it would be worthwhile asking how a gender-enriched understanding of democracy could affect the neoliberal argument on the peacefulness of democracies.

For constructivism, conflicts grow out of specific cultures consisting of incompatibly constructed identities, normative frameworks and ensuing interests. Violence may obtain when high salience is ascribed to what is at stake. Since all important elements of conflicts are socially constructed, change is possible. Conflict management may entail constructing new institutions that help compromise between competing interests (like the institutionalist project), adapting normative frameworks, or, at the deepest level, reshaping identities. As basically politico-sociological theory, constructivism is fully compatible with the feminist project; the term gender is indeed a constructivist one.

Post-modernism looks for conflict not in social reality, since only verbal representations are observable and prone to be analysed; conflict is seen among competing discourses, usually in an double inclusion/exclusion, hegemony/oppression scheme. Violence occurs if discourses contain the order to use force to suppress certain types of tabooed challenges. Post-modernism has not proposed an elaborate conflict management approach; most accounts suggest that things will improve if the dissenting voices become more prominent. However, deconstruction could be read as a sort of conflict management therapy, as the sources of domination and violence-requesting norms are uncovered and revealed and thus become possible objects of criticism. As post-modernism is a language-based political sociology, compatibility is given; indeed, quite a few feminist writings follow the line of the post-modernist argument.

Conflict management: some comments

I agree with Cordula Reimann and Donna Pankhurst that conflict management approaches are both largely atheoretical and largely un-gendered. This seems to be astonishing at first glance, since they are interventions in the societal fabric and thus should pay due attention to the role of gender inequalities and ensuing role-playing in causing and sustaining domestic violent conflict. But there are understandable reasons for this shortcoming.

Conflict management approaches are by and large praxeologies, built on successful and failed attempts to stop, contain and resolve conflicts. The method of construction of the approaches is not deductive or theory-orientated (with the possible exception of basic needs theory), but inductive-empirical. Conflicts are largely articulated, organized and fought by men. Conflict parties are overwhelmingly led by men, and established 'Western' as well as established traditional, local conflict management procedures are largely male-dominated. Since the over-whelming objective of intervening in a conflict is to stop violence, deeper-rooted structural features that may well be connected with underlying causes of conflict are ignored – here I agree completely with Pankhurst – including, in particular, discrimination against women.

But maybe there are some ways in which the gender aspect can be given greater prominence. First, with the growing amalgamation of development policy and conflict management policy, new opportunities are opening up for the transfer of the gender perspective from the former – where, as emphasized by Reimann and Pankhurst, it is now increasingly accepted – to the latter. One should be ready to take advantage of this opportunity. Emphasizing the – well-documented – importance of women for the concept of sustainability may offer the best prospects.

Second, in conflict intervention, one has to walk a tightrope between an unacceptable culturalist relativism (for example, condoning circum-cision as culturally legitimate) on the one hand, and cultural imperialism (that is, transferring the Western ideal of female emancipation) on the other hand. A pragmatic approach may be best: propose, but do not impose, a dialogue about women's rights and alternative societal struc-tures empowering women; and support all groups of active women in the conflict regions.

Risks of bias

Theoretical perspectives are always in danger of succumbing to perceptual bias: since one expects to see certain things but not others, one sees exactly these things even when they may not be there, and overlooks others that are in fact there.

Realism looks for conflicts among states defending their autonomy and interdependence. It tends to overlook secular changes in the understanding of sovereignty in many parts of the world; far-reaching co-operative endeavours even in the sensitive field of security policy; and the growing and significant impact that non-governmental actors have on world order. Post-modernism expects, in deconstructing existing discourses, to discover self/other, inclusion/exclusion dichotomies, and hegemony/subordination structures. It is ill-equipped to look for, and find, polarities containing more than two poles, overlapping identities, partial compatibilities, symmetrical but competing discourses, discourses of harmony, and compromises, though all these are theoretical possibilities and can be found in practice.

In the same vein, the feminist approach looks for gendered issues. As Fatima Ahmed Ibrahim has reminded us, inequalities and oppression have more than just the gender aspect, and men are necessarily part of the solution of conflict, as they are part – frequently the major part – of its causes. While it is not necessarily endemic to the theory, the gender perspective runs the risk of engendering non-gendered social relationships and overlooking compatibilities and possible areas of conflict solution as a result of this bias. Regular self-deconstruction and intensive dialogue with other theories might be the best, though difficult, antidote as a way of avoiding flawed analysis and prescription as a result of theoretical bias.

Final remarks

The only point where I sense some fundamental disagreement with Reimann is in respect of her reinterpretation of violent conflict as a possible process of female emancipation. In (very) *extremis*, that may be so; Eritrea may present an example, though we will have to wait and see what the societal consequences of the most recent, interstate, war might be for gender relations. Normally, violent conflicts do not have this effect. Normally, women are – statistically – the main victims of such conflicts. War brings the sharpest realization of the macho societal order, with men taking the beloved hegemonic role of warrior, while women are relegated to the role of either object of protection or object of rape. That some women are privileged to participate happily in the slaughter is as little reason, in itself, to participate as the take-over of the role of corrupt state leader by Benazir Bhutto or of the role of atomic bomb enthusiast by Indira Gandhi. That war is a heroic moment, shattering societal structure and turning society upside down, thus promoting social revolution and emancipation, has been part and parcel of revolutionary ideology from ancient times to fascism. In most cases it has proved an illusion: after war the old order was thoroughly restored, sometimes directly, sometimes as a travesty (as in the Soviet Union). Feminism should not fall for this illusion. To put it in a nutshell: 'Give war a chance' is not, in my view, a promising slogan for the feminist project.

CHAPTER 16

Feminism, Human Rights and International Relations

Gert Krell

I was asked by the editors to think about and comment on three rather general questions with regard to the policy field of human rights: the entry points of the feminist human rights notion in (1) mainstream politics and in (2) International Relations (IR) as a field of study; and the influence of the women's movement on mainstream IR overall. Because of limitations of space as well as competence, my response will be impressionistic rather than comprehensive. I will first discuss the relationship between men and feminism.

On the relationship between men and feminism

I do not think men should call themselves feminists. The feminist movement has been launched, guided and developed by women, politically as well as intellectually, and however positively men may relate to it, they should respect it as that and avoid even the semblance of appropriation. They should not try to run away from their maleness, their responsibility for and their reflection about being male, or from their emotional and psychological grounding in their own sex and gender. So I prefer the term 'pro-feminist' for men who are sympathetic to the feminist movement. Actually, pro-feminist men stand in a long tradition. When Michael Kimmel and Thomas Mosmiller began research for a documentary history of such men in the USA, some of their feminist friends were very sceptical. One of them suggested that it would surely be a very short book. In the end they compiled a weighty volume containing only a fraction of over 1,000 documents indicating the support of at least some men for women's rights throughout US history.[1]

Men can have a number of motivations for being or becoming pro-feminist, some more ingenuous, some less. One motive may be the search for advantage in the competition among males, another the old patriarchal notion of the lost, sinful or contaminated male world, which can be saved – individually or collectively – only by woman/women. While I, for one, have not always remained completely free of such sentiments, at least subconsciously (both have a certain charm in our still patriarchal culture), the two more obvious and more important motives are first, intellectual and political consistency, and second, curiosity. I believe it is impossible to uphold progressive intentions, or even very generally to hold on to the Enlightenment project, without accepting and welcoming the feminist movement as a legitimate part or a necessary outgrowth of it (and of its inconsistencies). Peace, development and human emancipation cannot be conceived truly and successfully without gender equality. Feminism and the women's movements are one of the greatest political and intellectual challenges, not just of our time but of modernity, and of the social sciences in particular. Women and men can learn a lot about the world, about themselves, and about how to improve both, from these traditions. Michael Kimmel once discussed the question of whether men could, should, or must support feminism. He suggested another reason why: to tear away the veil of complicity shielding male violence against women. Violence between the sexes, in particular sexual violence, is highly asymmetrical – although both men and women can be violent and peaceful, just and unjust, perpetrators and victims. If this is not a challenge for women *and* men, politically and intellectually, what is?[2]

On the status of women's rights

In May 1776, two months before the signing of the Declaration of Independence, Abigail Adams pointed out in a letter to her husband John – later the first vice-president and the second president of the United States – that she was concerned about the new laws of the nation:

> I cannot say that I think you are very generous to the ladies, for whilst you are proclaiming peace and good will to men, emancipating all nations, you insist upon retaining an absolute power over wives ... if particular care and attention is not paid to the ladies, we are determined to foment a rebellion and will not hold ourselves bound by any laws in which we have no voice, or representation.[3]

John Adams jokingly and casually dismissed this intervention, but history has been on Abigail Adams's side, although the changes she requested and predicted took much longer than she had probably imagined.

One hundred and eighty years later, when the Parliamentary Council of the West German states (Bundesländer) debated the new 'Basic Law' (a kind of constitution) of the country and also the basic rights of men and women, the majority wanted to incorporate the relevant paragraph from the constitution of the first German Republic of 1918. This stated that men and women had the same rights and obligations as citizens. For Elisabeth Selbert, one of the 'mothers' of West Germany's Basic Law (usually we talk about the 'fathers' of our constitution, but we also have four 'mothers'), that was not enough. Although she did not consider herself a feminist, she thought women should be equal to men not just as citizens who could vote and be elected, but in all dimensions of the law. She suggested the following: 'Women and men have equal rights'. This version was voted down twice, and the conservatives presented their alternative: 'The law must treat what is equal equally, and what is different according to its specific characteristics'. To be sure, they did not have in mind the feminist debate about difference and equality, but they knew very well what they meant. In this situation, Elisabeth Selbert started a mobilization campaign, giving lectures throughout the country and asking women to speak up. Tons of letters of protest were sent to Bonn. On 18 January 1949, the council finally accepted that women and men have equal rights. Afterwards, none of the male representatives was prepared to admit that he had objected, considering the burdens that had fallen upon women during and after the war. The whole affair had been nothing but a misunderstanding, they said.[4]

Of course it had been more than that, and it took the Federal Republic of Germany at least another 30 years to legally guarantee women equal rights in all areas of political, social and personal life, the formula which the German Democratic Republic had chosen for its constitution of 1949. As late as 1966, the highest court below the German Constitutional Court, the Bundesgerichtshof, ruled that women had to grant sexual intercourse to their husbands 'in marital affection and self-sacrificing'. They were (legally!) forbidden to show indifference or aversion, even if they did not enjoy it, be it 'from disposition or for other reasons'.[5] Today, women and men do have equal rights in Germany, which – according to the interpretation of the Joint Constitutional Commission of 1993 and the addition to the constitution of 27 October 1994 – also means their factual assertion. The government is required to actively work towards equality and towards the removal of existing disadvantages.[6] Many of these still exist, particularly in political representation, in employment and pay, in the division of labour in the family, and in the exploitation of female sexuality.

One of the consequences of the activities of the international women's movements and of the United Nations Women's Conferences is an increased awareness of the gender dimension in the development of human rights, and more reports on it.[7] Worldwide, women and girls have made great progress in the last generation, in life expectancy, health and education, as measured by the United Nations Development Programme's (UNDP) Gender-related Development Index (GDI). Unfortunately, this progress does not translate to the same extent into the economic and political domains, as measured by the UNDP's Gender Empowerment Measure (GEM). Major areas of violations of women's rights are still (1) discrimination in economic, political, and social opportunities, (2) inequality in family life, including in marriage and reproductive decision-making, and (3) gender-based violence, violence at home and in the community, of the state and during armed conflict.[8]

The most recent UN statistics on 'The World's Women' provide a good overview of the advances made and the gaps remaining in six specific fields of concern: population, women and men in families, health, education and communication, work, human rights, and political decision-making.[9] Thus, the gender gap in enrolment in primary and secondary levels of schooling is closing, and in higher education women have made significant gains in most regions of the world. However, nearly two-thirds of the illiterates worldwide are still women, and the literacy gap will persist because the populations for which the gender gaps in enrolment and literacy are the widest – Southern Asia and sub-Saharan Africa – are also among the fastest growing. Recent declines in early marriage and early childbearing have improved the quality of women's lives in most regions, again with the exception of Southern Asia and sub-Saharan Africa. Despite lower fertility rates, many women still lack access to reproductive health services. A woman's lifetime risk of dying from maternal causes is 1 in 16 in Africa compared to 1 in 1,400 in Europe. More than a quarter of all adult women in developing countries have pregnancy-related health problems.

In spite of all the activities of women, individually and as members of non-governmental organizations, women's participation in the top levels of government and business remains low. In early 2000, only nine women were heads of state or government, and in 1998 8 per cent of the world's cabinet ministers were women. Sweden is the only country with a majority of female ministers. In 1999, 11 per cent of parliamentarians were women, as compared to 9 in 1987. The gender gap in rates of economic activity is narrowing, but the kind of participation in the labour force continues to vary between men and women. Home-based work and work in the informal sector are an important and expanding source of employment for women, with many disadvantages in security and working conditions. Women continue to spend substantially more time on unpaid work than men, mainly in the household: 'It is difficult to tell from the data at hand if there has been any movement in recent years toward gender equality in unpaid work.'[10] However, paid work or independent sources of income are a basic requirement for women's emancipation from male domination, exploitation, and violence.[11]

The feminist notion of human rights and the study of International Relations

Feminist thinking on women's rights and human rights has been very influential in enlarging or revising traditional concepts in International Relations. One of the most fundamental challenges concerns the social contract, a foundational concept of modern political thought. We have been reminded by feminists – although we could or ought to have known this all along – that liberal civil society was originally based on a contractual relationship, real or imagined, between equal men as heads of households (at the beginning it wasn't even all men) who had full command over their wives and children. The blatant contradiction between the promise of equality and the reality of gender domination was built into the very structure of our early modern societies. While the reservation of a private domain, protected against intervention by the state, has been an important achievement, it was an achievement heavily biased against women. Thus women (and some men) fought (and are still fighting) for a renegotiation of the boundary between the public and the private sphere in two ways: they demand(ed) equality for women in the public domain and the dissolution of male privilege and domination in the private realm. Since the division between the public and the private is in itself socially constructed and heavily politicized, in political science we can no longer pretend that politics are only concerned with the public sphere and public affairs.

Feminist analysis and the activities of international women's movements have also helped to weaken or bring about re-conceptualization of another demarcation in International Relations, the division between different levels of analysis, in particular states versus societies on the one hand and the international system on the other. Order versus anarchy is an important dichotomy in 'realist' thought, one of the major traditions in IR theory. Other traditions argue that this distinction, while not completely invalid, needs serious revision. Feminist thinking and feminist activities in the area of human rights support redefinitions of agency (transnational non-governmental organizations have become important global actors), and structure (dimensions of 'disorder' – violence against women, for example – in societies, and elements of 'order' in international relations must be reintegrated into theory).

A third dimension concerns the debate about objective versus subjective notions of rights. This is not a new debate, rather an enlarged one. It is obvious that many women in the world do not support feminist agendas, or only parts of them. Many women have internalized traditions of male domination, and some are even involved in or practise violence against their own sex, as in the case of female genital mutilation. One feminist thinker has suggested applying the concept of 'internal colonization' to this problem.[12] While this may be useful, and obvious in the case mentioned, great care and responsibility is required to define a general standard of a 'non-colonized mind', and especially to propagate and enforce it. The discourse, or rather the non-discourse, between the few feminist and the many non-feminist women in Algeria shows that human rights and women's rights must be discussed and worked on in specific social and cultural contexts.[13]

This leads us to the debate about universalism versus cultural relativism. Feminist theory and analysis shows that *both* concepts have an ideological dimension. Universalism has *de facto* always been particularistic in several ways: by excluding large groups of human beings by definition, or by tolerating circumstances in which the realization of their human rights has remained largely illusory. The advantage of universalism is that it also provides a basis for challenging its relativist practice. This is more difficult with regard to explicit cultural relativism, which can be more obviously turned into an instrument of ideological camouflage for subordination and discrimination. Here, women are often granted gratification in the symbolic sphere of cultural independence or resurgence, as compensation for cementing their legally, politically and economically inferior status.

The feminist discussions about human rights and women's rights also touch on important dimensions of the analysis of violence. Apart from the fact that both politics and political science, including IR, have for a long time ignored violence and discrimination against women, a number of old theoretical questions need to be rediscussed. When does discrimination turn into violence? When should we speak of cultural discrimination or sexism, when of injustice, when of cultural or structural violence? Can or should we use the same term for systematic discrimination and for physical violence? How do cultural discrimination, structural violence, and personal violence interact, how do they relate to each other? Can they be disconnected, or do they have to be addressed together? What does male violence against women tell us about males and male-dominated political spheres? How is political violence influenced by gender divisions and asymmetries? Does the gendered order of the military and of war only represent the general gendered division of labour, or are gendered divisions of labour in themselves a cause of conflict and war? What would foreign policies and IR look like if they were not affected by, or structured along, gendered divisions and asymmetries?

Some of these considerations can be brought together in a more general debate about the process of civilization. 'Civilization' is a heavily biased concept, in political theory and in practice. Historically, it has been used to legitimate oppression, violence, 'ethnic cleansing' and outright annihilation on a large scale by those 'civilizations' which considered themselves more developed than the ones which they colonized.[14] Even today, the idea of a process of civilization is also an androcentric concept, with its focus on the legitimate state monopoly of violence and the rule of law on the one hand, and international law and the institutionalization of international relations on the other. While all this is undeniably very important, it again neglects the asymmetrical relationship between men and women, in particular with regard to male violence against women. The relationship between the developmental levels of different cultural communities, and their levels of discrimination or violence against women, is not deterministic, and it is not even consistently correlational. Some very rich countries/communities display a high level of violence against women, and some very poor countries/communities have good gender-specific human rights records. We thus have to rethink our concept of civilization and the dichotomy of the civilized and the non-civilized. We must do this by taking account of the conquered or displaced peoples in the so-called civilization process, of the roles of men and women (and of masculinity and femininity) in this process, and of the subjection of the natural environment in it. In doing so, we may even find that the concept of 'civilization' is based on a connection between those three dimensions: an androcentric feminization of nature (and 'wilderness') which 'man' can, will, and needs to control and exploit.

On the influence of the women's movement on mainstream IR

My remarks on the influence of the women's movement on mainstream IR will be even more impressionistic than what I have said so far. A more comprehensive answer would first have to operationalize 'influence' and then measure it in various ways. Does influence refer to the numbers of women in advanced positions in political science or its sub-discipline of International Relations? Would these women have to be feminists? My impression is that the male-dominated field of IR has become more open towards women in recent years. Even a cursory glance through books and articles in major IR journals reveals an increasing number of women among the authors, quite independent of the subject matter or the schools of thought, including 'realism', which many feminists regard as 'masculinist'. Feminist books and articles have become a broad tradition in their own right, even in IR. In 1994, a bibliography by Kenneth Boutin on 'Gender and International Relations', which listed only the literature in English, already had 145 pages.[15] There also exist a few articles by pro-feminist men on gender and IR.[16] This cursory survey does not, however, answer the question of how the feminist school of thought has influenced *mainstream* IR.

From my limited experience in two institutions of research and learning, the Peace Research Institute Frankfurt and the Social Sciences Faculty at the Goethe University in Frankfurt/Main, I can say that both experienced a strong challenge from feminists in the 1980s. Both challenges led to changes in norms of hiring and teaching. The Goethe University obliges members of all faculties to include feminist points of view and feminist research results in their teaching. If you look at the list of courses and lectures offered in our Social Sciences Faculty, you will find many that address, or at least include, feminist concerns.

Let me conclude with a rough and ready empirical test, which will give you at least some idea of the balance of integration and exclusion. I checked my personal library for recent German and English-language books on human rights and on International Relations theory. I deliberately excluded the feminist literature on both topics. Among the four new German books on human rights recently acquired, not counting – as I said – books on women's rights, the three edited volumes have at least one chapter on women's rights and/or violence against women.[17] The fourth book is a very good monograph on the question of universalism versus cultural relativism. While it does not explicitly discuss women's rights or the feminist challenge to the human rights discourse, the author does, however, mention the 'sexist curtailment' of republican self-determination in the French Revolution and Olympe de Gouges's protest against it.[18] He adds that for a hundred years, Condorcet remained the major (pro-feminist) exception in the male-dominated and reductionist Enlightenment discourse on human rights.

Among eight recent non-feminist books on IR theory and global politics in my library, the five in English all include at least one chapter on feminism or gender and IR; two reprint J. Ann Tickner's critique of

Morgenthau's realist principles.[19] From reading two very recent German books on IR theory, however, one written by a man and one by a woman, you would not know that feminism existed at all.[20] But there is a new revised edition of another introduction to IR written by a male colleague, which integrates feminist approaches.[21] And, good news, my own introduction to the major grand theories in International Relations has a full chapter on feminism.[22] I know that my test is impressionistic rather than statistical. Nevertheless, you would not have seen such a result ten years ago. Let's wait and look again in another ten years.

Notes

1. Kimmel, M. S. and T. E. Mosmiller (eds) (1992) *Against the Tide. Pro-Feminist Men in the United States 1776–1990. A Documentary History*, Boston, MA: Beacon Press, p. XIX.

2. See Krell, G. and S. Wölte (1995) *Gewalt gegen Frauen und die Menschenrechte*, Report 2/1995, Frankfurt/M.: Peace Research Institute Frankfurt (PRIF).

3. Quoted in Kimmel, M. S. and T. E. Mosmiller (eds) (1992), *Against the Tide*, p. 1.

4. This information is from Rodrian-Pfennig, M. (1998) 'Frauen und Männer sind gleichberechtigt', in Helbig, L. (ed.), *TatSache Politik*, Vol. 3, Frankfurt: Diesterweg, pp. 38–65, p. 56.

5. Quoted in Friebel, H. (1991) *Die Gewalt, die Männer macht. Lese- und Handbuch zur Geschlechterfrage*, Reinbek: Rowohlt, p. 70. The thinking behind this ruling goes back to the social contract theory of the sixteenth to eighteenth centuries and to nineteenth-century romanticism. The German philosopher J. G. Fichte was particularly influential in combining female subordination with the romantic ideal of love. Since woman was by nature inferior to man, her only chance to achieve equal status was to become a loving instrument of his satisfaction. See Gerhard, U., 'Menschenrechte – Frauenrechte – Unrechtserfahrungen von Frauen', in Reuter, H.-R. (ed.), (1999) *Ethik der Menschenrechte. Zum Streit um die Universalität einer Idee I*, Tübingen: Mohr Siebeck, pp. 201–35, p. 205.

6. See Rodrian-Pfennig, M. 'Frauen und Männer sind gleichberechtigt', p. 57 and Gerhard, U. 'Menschenrechte', p. 216.

7. For a recent overview of global gender politics and feminist strategies, see Meyer, M. K. and E. Prügl (eds) (1999) *Gender Politics in Global Governance*, Lanham, MD, Boulder, CO, New York: Rowman & Littlefield. For data on gender and human development, see United Nations Development Programme (ed.), (2000) *Human Development Report 2000*, New York, Oxford: Oxford University Press, in particular pp. 147–55 (What Do the Human Development Indices Reveal?); pp. 161–8 (GDI and GEM); pp. 174–7 (Comparison of Human Development Indices); pp. 255–76 (Gender and Education, Gender and Economic Activity, Women's Political Participation).

8. UNDP, *Human Development Report 2000*, p. 117.

9. United Nations (ed.) (2000) *The World's Women 2000. Trends and Statistics*, New York: United Nations, pp. XIII–XX (Main Findings and Future Directions).

10. United Nations, *The World's Women 2000*, p. XVII.

11. See Sen, A. (1990) 'More Than 100 Million Women are Missing', *New York Review of Books*, Vol. 37, No. 20, 20 December 20, pp. 61–6.

12. Albrecht-Heide, A. (1986) 'Männliche Helden – weibliche Tränen', in Büttner, C. and A. Ende (eds), *Die Rebellion der Mädchen, Jahrbuch der Kindheit*, Vol. 3, Weinheim: Beltz, pp. 51–64.

13. Class and education are important factors influencing different human rights concerns of women; see Gessner-Lazar, E. (2000) *Frauen im Islamdiskurs in Algerien*, unpublished thesis for the teachers' exam, Social Sciences Faculty, Goethe University, Frankfurt/M.

14. The Indians, for example, knew neither the term 'civilization' nor 'wilderness'. While they were defeated, displaced and murdered by our 'civilized' European ancestors, their way of living in an undifferentiated civilization/ wilderness may in the end turn out to be superior to ours. See Ortiz, A. (1998) 'Indian/White Relations. A View from the Other Side of the "Frontier"', in Hoxie, F. E. and P. Iverson (eds), *Indians in American History. An Introduction*, Wheeling, IL: Harlan Davidson, pp. 1–14. (To avoid romanticization, let me add that Amerindians in general were by no means free of supremacist thinking and practice in their own affairs.)

15. Kenneth Boutin, J. D. (1994) *Gender and International Relations. A Selected Historical Bibliography*, York: Centre for International and Security Studies.

16. See for example, Steve Smith on 'Masculinity, Gender, and International Relations', and Craig N. Murphy on 'Masculine Roles in International Relations', both in Zalewski, M. and J. Parpart (eds) (1998) *The 'Man' Question in International Relations*, Boulder, CO: Westview Press.

17. Moller Okin, S. (1998) 'Konflikte zwischen Grundrechten. Frauenrechte und die Probleme religiöser und kultureller Unterschiede', in Gosepath, S. and G. Lohmann (eds), *Philosophie der Menschenrechte*, Frankfurt/M.: Suhrkamp, pp. 310–42; Schöpp-Schilling, H.-B. (1998) 'Das Frauenrechtsübereinkommen – ein wirksames Instrument für die weltweite Gleichberechtigung und Gleichstellung von Frauen?', pp. 155–65; Flor, P. (1998) '"Gender Mainstreaming" – Damit die Gleichberechtigung der Geschlechter Wirklichkeit wird', pp. 167–77, both in Baum, G., E. Riedel and M. Schaefer (eds), *Menschenrechtsschutz in der Praxis der Vereinten Nationen*, Baden-Baden: Nomos; and Chinkin, C. (1998) 'Gewalt gegen Frauen ist keine Privatsache mehr. Frauenrechte sind heute anerkannter Teil des Menschenrechtskatalogs', in Köhne, G. (ed.), *Die Zukunft der Menschenrechte. 50 Jahre UN-Erklärung: Bilanz eines Aufbruchs*, Reinbek: Rowohlt, pp. 104–23.

18. Bielefeldt, H. (1998) *Philosophie der Menschenrechte. Grundlagen eines weltweiten Freiheitsethos*, Darmstadt: Primus-Verlag, p. 84.

19. DerDerian, J. (ed.) (1995) *International Theory. Critical Investigations*, Basingstoke, London: Macmillan, has J. Ann Tickner's article on Morgenthau,

and also one by Jean Bethke Elshtain on 'Feminist Themes and International Relations'. Booth, K. and S. Smith (eds) (1995) *International Relations Theory Today*, University Park, PA: Pennsylvania State University Press, has one chapter by Bethke Elshtain on 'International Politics and Political Theory', one by Marysia Zalewski and Cynthia Enloe on 'Questions About Identity in International Relations', and one by J. Ann Tickner on 'Re-Visioning Security' – a summary of her book on *Gender in International Relations*. Art, R. J. and R. Jervis (eds) (2000) *International Politics. Enduring Concepts and Contemporary Issues*, 5th edn, New York, Reading, MA, Menlo Park, CA: Longman, has J. Ann Tickner's critique of Morgenthau's principles. Baylis, J. and S. Smith (eds) (1997) *The Globalization of World Politics. An Introduction to International Relations*, Oxford, New York, Athens: Oxford University Press, has a chapter by Jan Jindy Pettman on 'Gender Issues', and MacMillan, J. and A. Linklater (eds) (1995) *Boundaries in Question. New Directions in International Relations*, London, New York: Pinter, has one by Jill Krause on 'The International Dimension of Gender Inequality and Feminist Politics'.

20. Lehmkuhl, U. (ed.) (1999) *Theorien internationaler Politik*, 2nd edn, München, Wien: Oldenbourg; Gu, X. (2000) *Theorien der Internationalen Beziehungen. Einführung*, Munich, Vienna: Oldenbourg.

21. Albrecht, U. (1998) *Internationale Politik. Einführung in das System internationaler Herrschaft*, 5th edn, Munich, Vienna: Oldenbourg.

22. Krell, G. (2000) *Weltbilder und Weltordnung. Einführung in die Theorie der internationalen Beziehungen*, Baden-Baden: Nomos, pp. 213–37 (feminism).

Selected Further Readings

Women/Gender, Women's Movements and International Relations

Afshar, H. (ed.) (1998) *Women and Empowerment. Illustrations from the Third World*, London: Routledge.

Basu, A. (ed.) (1995) *The Challenge of Local Feminisms. Women's Movements in Global Perspective*, Boulder, CO, San Francisco, CA, Oxford: Westview Press.

Beckman, P. R. and F. D'Amico (eds) (1994) *Women, Gender, and World Politics. Perspectives, Policies and Prospects*, Westport, CT, London: Bergin and Garvey.

Einhorn, B. (1993) *Cinderella Goes to Market*, London: Verso.

Enloe, C. (1989) *Bananas, Beaches and Bases: Making Feminist Sense of International Politics*, London: Pandora Press.

Grant, R. and K. Newland (eds) (1991) *Gender in International Relations*, Bloomington, IN: Indiana University Press.

Meyer, M. and E. Prügl (eds) (1999) *Gender Politics in Global Governance*, Lanham, MD, Oxford: Rowman & Littlefield.

Mohanty, C. T., A. Russo and L. Torres (eds) (1991) *Third World Women and the Politics of Feminism*, Bloomington: Indiana University Press.

Nelson, B. and N. Chowdhury (eds) (1994) *Women and Politics Worldwide*, New Haven, CT: Yale University Press.

Peterson, S. V. and A. S. Runyan (1993) *Global Gender Issues*, Boulder, CO: Westview Press.

Pettman, J. J. (1996) *Worlding Women: A Feminist International Politics*, London: Routledge.

Rupp, L. (1997) *Worlds of Women. The Making of an International Women's Movement*, Princeton, NJ: Princeton University Press.

Spivak, G. (1985) 'Can the Subaltern Speak? Speculations of Widow Sacrifice', *Wedge*, Vol. 7, No. 8, pp. 120–30.

Steans, J. (1997) *Gender and International Relations*, Cambridge: Polity Press.

Stienstra, D. (1994) *Women's Movements and International Organizations*, Basingstoke: Macmillan.

Sylvester, C. (1994) *Feminist Theory and International Relations in a Postmodern Era*, Cambridge: Cambridge University Press.

Tickner, A. J. (1992) *Gender in International Relations*, Oxford: Columbia University Press.

Wichterich, C. (2000) *The Globalized Woman. Reports from a Future of Inequality*, London: Zed Books.

Zalewski, M. and J. Parpart (1998) *The 'Man' Question in International Relations*, Boulder, CO: Westview Press.

Selected resources and data on women by UN agencies

UN Department for Public Information (2000) *The World's Women 2000: Trends and Statistics*, New York: UNDPI.

UNDP (1995) *Human Development Report 1995*, New York: UNDP.

— (2000) *Human Development Report 2000*, New York: UNDP.

UNIFEM (2000) *Progress of the World's Women 2000. UNIFEM Biennial Report*, New York: UNIFEM (see http://www.unifem.undp.org/).

Women/gender and development

Boserup, E. (1970) *Women's Role in Economic Development*, London: George Allen & Unwin.

Development and Cooperation (D+C) (2000). *Third World Women Speak Out*, 3, May/June.

Elson, D. (ed.) (1995) *Male Bias in the Development Process*, Manchester: Manchester University Press.

Goetz, A. M. (ed.) (1997) *Getting Institutions Right for Women in Development*, London: Zed Books.

Jackson, C. and R. Pearson (eds) (1998) *Feminist Visions of Development. Gender, Analysis and Policy*, London: Routledge.

Lesser Blumberg, R., C. A. Rakowski, I. Tinker and M. Monteón (eds) (1995) *EnGENDERing Wealth and Well-Being*, Boulder, CO, San Francisco, CA, Oxford: Westview Press.

Marchand, M. and J. Parpart (eds) (1995) *Feminism/Postmodernism/Development*, London: Routledge.

Molyneux, M. (1985) 'Mobilisation without Emancipation? Women's Interests, the State and Revolution in Nicaragua', *Feminist Studies*, Vol. 11, Summer, pp. 227–54.

Moser, C. (1993) *Gender Planning in Development. Theory, Practice and Training*, London: Routledge.

Nussbaum, M. and J. Glover (eds) (1995) *Women, Culture and Development*, Oxford: Clarendon Press.

Scott, C. V. (1995) *Gender and Development. Rethinking Modernization and Dependency Theory*, London: Lynne Rienner.

Sen, G. and C. Grown (for DAWN – Development Alternatives with Women for a New Era) (1985) *Development, Crisis and Alternative Visions. Third World Women's Perspectives*, London: Earthscan Publications.

Women/gender and conflict

Anderson, M. B. (1999) *Do No Harm: How Aid Can Support Peace – or War*, Boulder, CO: Lynne Rienner.

Breines, I., D. Gierycz and B. Reardon (eds) (1999) *Towards a Women's Agenda for a Culture of Peace*, Paris: UNESCO.

Dyan, E. M. and S. R. McKay (1999) *Women and Peace Building*, Essays on Human Rights and Democratic Development No. 8, Montreal: International Centre for Human Rights and Democratic Development (see http://www. ichrdd.ca/111/english/commdoc/publications/womPeace.html).

Elshtain, J. B. (1987) *Women and War*, Brighton: Harvester Press.

Enloe, C. (2000) *Manœuvres. The International Politics of Militarizing Women's Lives*, Berkeley, Los Angeles, London: University of California Press.

— (1993) *The Morning After. Sexual Politics at the End of the Cold War*, Berkeley, Los Angeles, London: University of California Press.

Jacobs, S., R. Jacobson and J. Marchbank (eds) (2000) *States of Conflict. Gender, Violence and Resistance*, London: Zed Books.

Lorentzen, L. A. and J. Turpin (eds) (1998) *The Women and War Reader*, New York, London: New York University Press.

Moser, C. and F. Clark (eds) (2001) *Victims, Perpetrators or Actors? Gender, Armed Conflict and Political Violence*, London, New York: Zed Books.

Skjelsback, I. and D. Smith (eds) (2001) *Gender, Peace & Conflict*, London, Thousand Oaks, New Delhi: SAGE Publications.

Sørensen, B. (1998) 'Women and Post-Conflict Reconstruction. Issues and Sources'. WSP Occasional Paper No. 3, June, (http://www.unrisd.org/wsp/op3/toc.htm).

Women and human rights

Bunch, C. and N. Reilly (1994) *Demanding Accountability: The Global Campaign and Vienna Tribunal for Women's Human Rights*, New Jersey, New York: Centre for Women's Global Leadership.

Charlesworth, H., C. Chinkin and S. Wright (1991) 'Feminist Approaches to International Law', *American Journal of International Law*, Vol. 85, No. 4, pp. 613–45.

Cook, R. (ed.) (1994) *Human Rights of Women. National and International Perspectives*, Philadelphia: University of Pennsylvania Press.

Hildon, A. M., M. Macintyre, V. Mackie and M. Stivens (eds) (2000) *Human Rights and Gender Politics. Asia-Pacific Perspectives*, London, New York: Routledge.

Kerr, J. (ed.) (1993) *Ours by Right. Women and Human Rights*, London: Zed Books.

Landsberg, I. L. (ed.) (1998) *Bringing Equality Home. Implementing the Convention on the Elimination of All Forms of Discrimination Against Women*, New York: UNIFEM.

Oloka-Onyango, J. and S. Tamale (1995) '"The Personal is Political" or: Why Women's Human Rights are Indeed Human Rights. An African Perspective on International Feminism', *Human Rights Quarterly*, Vol. 17, pp. 691–713.

Peters, J. and A. Wolper (eds) (1995) *Women's Rights – Human Rights*, New York, London: Routledge.

Schuler, M. A. (ed.) (1995) *From Basic Needs to Basic Rights: Women's Claim to Human Rights*, Washington, DC: Women, Law & Development International.

Women, Law & Development International/Human Rights Watch. Women's Rights Project (1997), *Women's Human Rights Step by Step, a Practical Guide to Using International Human Rights Law and Mechanisms to Defend Women's Human Rights*, Washington, DC: Women, Law & Development International.

Index